Foundations of an Open Economy

Foundations of an Open Economy

Trade Laws and Institutions for Eastern Europe

Edited by L. Alan Winters

Centre for Economic Policy Research

The Centre for Economic Policy Research is a network of over 250 Research Fellows, based primarily in European universities. The Centre coordinates its Fellows' research activities and communicates their results to the public and private sectors. CEPR is an entrepreneur, developing research initiatives with the producers, consumers and sponsors of research. Established in 1983, CEPR is a European economics research organization with uniquely wide-ranging scope and activities.

CEPR is a registered educational charity. Institutional (core) finance for the Centre is provided by major grants from the Economic and Social Research Council, under which an ESRC Resource Centre operates within CEPR; the Esmée Fairbairn Charitable Trust; the Bank of England; 15 other central banks and 33 companies. None of these organizations gives prior review to the Centre's publications, nor do they necessarily endorse the views expressed therein.

The Centre is pluralist and non-partisan, bringing economic research to bear on the analysis of medium- and long-run policy questions. CEPR research may include views on policy, but the Executive Committee of the Centre does not give prior review to its publications, and the Centre takes no institutional policy positions. The opinions expressed here are those of the authors and not those of the Centre for Economic Policy Research.

Published by Centre for Economic Policy Research
25–28 Old Burlington Street, London W1X 1LB

British Library Cataloguing in Publication Data
A Catalogue record for this book is available from the British Library

ISBN: 1 898128 16 2

Contents

Part 2 Complementary Policies and Institutions

Preface

In autumn 1993 the PHARE Programme of the European Union commissioned from the Centre for Economic Policy Research a study of the institutions, laws and policies for the international trade of the Central and East European countries (CEECs) participating in the PHARE Programme. This was to be done explicitly from the viewpoint of the Union, but directed towards informing analyses and decisions to be made both by the EU and by the CEECs themselves. The papers were planned and discussed at two workshops in Brussels organized by DG II (Economic and Financial Affairs) of the European Commission and then revised extensively. The authors are grateful for comments from the Commission's services and other discussants.

The project has benefited from the active involvement of the Commission's services, in particular, Alan Mayhew, Director of the PHARE Programme, and Joan Pearce, Head of Unit for Central and Eastern Europe in DG II. CEPR is pleased to cooperate with the Commission in producing economic policy research that we believe should be valuable to all decision-makers and analysts concerned with the economies of the CEECs and their full integration into the international economy.

We should like to thank Linda Machin for her work on this volume and CEPR staff, in particular our Publications Manager, Kate Millward.

The views expressed in this volume are those of the authors, writing in their personal capacities. Neither the European Commission nor CEPR takes any responsibility for these views; and CEPR takes no institutional policy positions.

Richard Portes
15 November 1994

Foreword

The Centre for Economic Policy Research has brought together a strong team of economists from across the European Community, as well as from Hungary, to address some key trade issues for Central and Eastern Europe. Two timely studies have resulted. The study on trade laws and institutions for Eastern Europe is published in this volume, while the study on trade between the European Union and Eastern Europe is published in a companion volume.

The Community realized early on in the development of its relations with the post-central planning countries of Central and Eastern Europe that, though the immediate need might be for policy advice, the anchoring of these countries as market economies required the construction of sound institutions. For this reason, institution-building has been an important concern of the Community's assistance programmes, both PHARE and macro-financial assistance, and of the pre-accession strategy announced at the European Council in Essen in December 1994.

Robust institutions are of particular importance in former command economies, where pressures to revert to the ingrained practices of the previous regime may sometimes be hard to resist. When the countries of Central and Eastern Europe embarked on transition they rapidly opened their economies. Their bold stance on free trade was well rewarded: without it they could not have achieved swift adjustment to world relative prices, the creation of competitive conditions and integration into the world economy, all of which helped reinforce the transition at an early stage.

Yet, in the face of a very steep fall in output, recession in the Community, which by 1992 was their major market, and the resurgence of forces that had been subdued in the immediate aftermath of the regime changes, governments came under pressure to resort to protectionist solutions. Sound institutions will help to ensure that the liberalism that served the countries of Central and Eastern

Europe well in the early phase of transition is preserved and reinforced.

The countries of Central and Eastern Europe have a clear advantage in that they are starting out with a clean slate. They can benefit from the experience of Community member states and other market economies, and avoid the complicated accretion of laws and regulations that has occurred as these countries have developed trade institutions over several decades. Their new institutions will have the advantage of being more streamlined, but to become effective they will need time to accumulate experience and to acquire the ability to adapt to changing circumstances. This volume offers valuable guidance both in the design of trade institutions and in their development.

Leon Brittan
Henning Christophersen
Brussels, December 1994

List of Contributors

David B. Audretsch *Wissenschaftszentrum Berlin für Sozialforschung and CEPR*
László Csaba *Institute for Economic Market Research and Informatics, Budapest*
Bernard Hoekman *The World Bank and CEPR*
Petros Mavroidis *GATT Secretariat*
Patrick A. Messerlin *Service d'Etude de l'Activité Économique, Paris*
Michael Rauscher *Universität Kiel and CEPR*
André Sapir *ECARE, Université Libre de Bruxelles and CEPR*
L. Alan Winters *The World Bank, University of Birmingham and CEPR*

1

Trade Policy Institutions in Central and Eastern Europe: Objectives and Outcomes*

L. Alan Winters

1.1 Introduction

Mao Tse-Tung said 'Give a man a fish and you feed him for a day, but give him a fishing line and you feed him for a week.' Similarly with international trade policy: give a country a sound policy and you have affected behaviour for a year, but give it the institutions to make sound policy and you affect it for a decade. More than any other countries, the new emerging economies have scope to heed this advice, and this book is designed to help a subset of them – Bulgaria, the Czech Republic, Hungary, Poland, Romania and the Slovak Republic – to do so. As these Central and East European countries (the CEECs) struggle with the myriad problems of transition it is important to ask not only what international trade policy is now, but what it will be in the future. Given the desirability of open trade policies for small countries, how can the market instincts and internationalism that characterized the first flush of post-revolutionary enthusiasm be locked in and preserved through the long haul of transition? More concretely, how should the CEEC governments design the institutions of trade policy in order to maximize the chances of preserving and extending their initial degrees of liberalism?

One way of locking in policy – and a vital one in the context of trade law and trade institutions – is international agreements. Thus the CEECs have all sought to join the GATT or to renegotiate their old protocols of accession with it. Full membership of the WTO, which will replace the GATT, will impose some policy disciplines – for example, on the use of subsidies, voluntary export restraints

* The views expressed in this Chapter are the author's and should not be attributed in any way to the CEPR or the World Bank. I am grateful to Richard Portes and the contributors to this book for comments.

and variable levies in agriculture – and will introduce or reinforce existing caps (bindings) on the levels of tariffs that may be charged without renegotiation with trading partners. These are important restraints, but they are not sufficiently tight to ensure a sensible and liberal import regime. For example, tariff bindings commit members not to charge above declared maximum tariffs and are useful for the security that they give potential and actual traders, but the levels of these bindings agreed in the Uruguay Round are very high in some cases; for example, Romania has generally bound industrial tariffs at 35% and has agricultural tariffs ranging up to 333%. Similarly, the restraints on applying anti-dumping duties are far too weak to prevent serious abuse of that instrument. Thus within the confines of the GATT/WTO there is still room for significant discretion about trade policy.

The Europe Agreements (EAs) between each of the CEECs and the European Union (EU) also impose a policy-making discipline – in fact, a rather tighter one in some respects than that from the GATT. The EAs will eventually impose a regime of more-or-less free trade in manufactures between the EU and the CEECs. Moreover, because this will be in the context of much wider cooperation in areas such as infrastructural links, aid flows, legal harmonization and political cooperation, it will be more secure; serious defection on trade policy can be made much more costly by withdrawing cooperation in areas other than trade.

In an optimistic scenario one might think that the free trade elements of the EAs would spread to the CEECs' most favoured nation (i.e. general) trade policy. If CEEC producers are open to fierce competition from the EU about which they can do nothing, they may not resist the opening of their markets to non-EU suppliers in addition. If one is forced to change jobs because of imports, it does not matter much whether they are German or Japanese, so one might at least have the consumer benefits of allowing both in freely.

Unfortunately, there are several places where this chain of reasoning can break down. First, the EAs allow both parties several derogations from free trade, especially for sensitive products. For example, special safeguards may be invoked up to three years after a trade flow is freed from restriction, state aids may be used for infant industry and restructuring purposes, and anti-dumping duties may be invoked. Second, pressure from one trading partner can translate into greater pressure for protection from another, especially if the two partners produce different varieties: as, say, Czech producers of tools lose one market to Germany they may push even harder for protection from Japanese imports in another. Third, agriculture is excluded from the EA-driven liberalization. The quantities traded will be allowed to increase somewhat and some tariff and levy revenues will be transferred from the EU to CEEC exporters, but, not surprisingly given the nature of the Common Agricultural Policy, there will be little role for prices and markets.

The less-than-perfectly-liberal nature of the EAs gives rise to the first of the principal issues addressed in this book: how, in fact, have the EAs affected trade policy and related policies? Have they constrained the excesses of protectionism, or have they, by cloaking everything in a false respectability and diverting attention to other issues, allowed managed trade to take root? Similarly, have the EAs allowed or obliged the CEECs to establish appropriate laws and institutions in trade-related policy areas, such as those pertaining to competition, industry and the environment, or have they distorted the growth of these nascent institutions? The assessments by our different authors vary somewhat on these issues, but all agree that, while the EAs bring significant benefits to the CEECs, there is certainly nothing to be complacent about.

The second principal issue that the book addresses arises because, even with the EAs, there is plenty of scope for trade policy discretion. Hence the question of policy-making institutions remains on the agenda. Here the chapters are more normative than positive, discussing, in the light of experience elsewhere, how the CEECs might best prepare for the difficulties of making rational trade policy in the face of strident and powerful sectional interests within their economies. This introduces the matter of the design of domestic trade policy-making institutions.

Getting the institutions right is another way of trying to lock in liberal policies. Experience from the West shows that, while liberal trade policies are perfectly feasible, they are not universal in their coverage and they come under constant challenge from particular import-competing interests. One cannot – indeed, in a democracy, must not – legislate such forces out of existence, nor can (or should) one legislate that they will always be ignored. One can, however, try to design institutions that redress the natural asymmetry that exists between the proponents and opponents of liberalism. The advantages of free trade are generally diffuse and abstract (new jobs *some*where doing *some*thing), while the costs are concentrated and concrete. Thus, even when the ruling philosophy and rhetoric of a society are intensely market oriented, there is a continuous flow of special cases in which the costs of adjustment can be made to look unreasonable and for which a little temporary protection looks humane and efficient. Sound institutional design is required to prevent this flow from overwhelming the basic principle of liberalism, and it does so by ensuring that the diffuse, but almost always larger, losses from protection get equal weight with the gains.

This book is divided into two parts. Part I, Trade Policy Institutions, looks directly at the way international trade policy in the CEECs has evolved under the EAs and at how institutions may be designed to defend and reinforce the liberal thrust of the early post-revolutionary days. Part II, Complementary Policies and Institutions, looks at three areas of policy which should be complementary to, and certainly not substitutable for, trade policy: competition policy, industrial policy and environmental policy. In each case there are dangers not only that these policies could counteract the effects of sound trade policy, but that they could be established in such a way as to render them open to capture by the very forces which trade policy institutions have been designed to control. The chapters in Part II cover both positive and normative aspects of these questions, and consider them both from the point of view of experience (theoretical and practical) elsewhere and in the context of the CEECs and the EAs.

The book focuses closely on the European experience both in terms of the EAs, which are unique to the CEECs, and in terms of the discussions of the actual institutions that have emerged so far. Its relevance is not restricted to the CEECs, however, for the other emerging market economies face the same challenges and sometimes the same environment. For example, Slovenia and the Baltic states (Estonia, Latvia and Lithuania) are already courting the EU and EFTA actively, and the other former Soviet Republics in Europe are likely to advance along a similar track. Even the Asian Republics and the more isolated emerging economies, such as Mongolia, Vietnam and Tanzania face the same issues of making general trade policy.

1.2 Trade Policy Institutions

Part I looks directly at trade policy institutions in Central and Eastern Europe. It asks, first, how institutions might be designed for these countries in such a way as to maximize the chances of obtaining and preserving a liberal trading regime, and, second, how the EAs have affected, and might best affect, that process.

The Part opens with a broad-ranging normative chapter by myself. It seeks to distil the experiences of trade policy-making in the western world, mainly the United States and the EU, into a series of 'dos' and 'don'ts'. It is concerned with trade policy in the large rather than with the detailed application of trade law: issues such as how fast should the CEECs liberalize their tariffs under the GATT (or otherwise), and should they use the safeguards clauses in the EAs? I argue that the correct set of institutions is necessary for them to be able to put their liberal intentions into practice. Signing international agreements alone is not sufficient.

Ultimate responsibility for trade policy in a democracy lies with the legislature. As US experience in the late 1920s shows, however, legislatures cannot handle all the details without the process degenerating into a protectionist free-for-all. Legislators will always come under some protectionist pressure, because their constituencies will depend disproportionately on a subset of production activities, and there will be strong incentives for coalitions of legislators to emerge supporting protection for 'each others' industries'. Strong committee structure and sound parliamentary procedures are important in ameliorating these problems, but they cannot prevent them entirely.

The detail of trade policy is typically – and correctly – delegated to the executive. The executive will normally be more liberal than individual legislators, because its constituency (the whole country) is less concentrated than a single region. This effect can be offset, however, if the executive can evade responsibility for some trade policy outcomes. For example, administered protection, whereby protection is granted according to a predetermined set of criteria, looks essentially apolitical and hence executives can at least partly avoid the blame for the higher consumer prices that it induces. Similarly, the confusion in the public mind about whether the Commission, the Council or national governments are responsible for EU trade restrictions relaxes the political constraints. Finally, if different branches of government struggle for control of trade policy the outcome is usually more protectionist. The conclusion is, then, that responsibility for trade policy must be unitary, clear and cover all dimensions of the consequences.

Executives require bureaucracies to administer trade policy. Here I argue, as does László Csaba in Chapter 4, that there should be a separate and senior Ministry of Trade with access to the Ministries of Finance and Foreign Affairs. Sectoral Ministries, for example Agriculture, Energy, Industry, will not generally be either willing or able to run liberal trade policies. Bureaucratic secrecy is another problem. Complex (and even secret) protectionist instruments suffer less opposition because their costs are less well known and understood. Hence a vital ingredient of sound trade policy is publishing the policy and the evidence on which it is based in an accessible way. Bureaucrats should be required to do this themselves and should, in addition, be supplemented by a Review Body which can argue cases against protection within the bureaucracy, analyse cases publicly outside it, and offer general comment on official policy from an objectively national point of view. Trade institutions should ensure that opponents of protection – user industries, exporters and consumers – are heard in administrative and political processes, and this Review Body can play an important role in focusing their input.

Information is very important. Ultimate power resides with the electorate, who need information and analysis with which to understand the issues on which they have to decide. The biases in trade policy formation also afflict information about policy and so it requires positive action to establish an institution – the Review Body – to represent the public interest. This should be a high priority for the CEECs, and one for which World Bank or EU assistance might be appropriate.

Chapter 2 concludes by reviewing trade institutions in the CEECs, finding them weak in the area of consumer and user-industry inputs into policy-making, and by listing a number of concrete rules for establishing trade policy institutions.

In Chapter 3 Patrick Messerlin asks: why did it take only a couple of years for the CEECs' ostensibly liberal trade regimes to be significantly undermined by piecemeal protectionism? He argues that the essential obstacle to stability in the trade regime is the failure of CEEC trade laws to take 'substitutability' properly into account.

First, CEEC trade policies were based on the belief that regional disciplines were a good substitute for nondiscriminatory worldwide disciplines. But relying on the EAs and neglecting GATT disciplines has led the CEECs to grant ever expanding privileges – preferential tariffs, then privileged investment deals, then preferential non-border measures – to an ever narrower set of partners: first to all EU-based firms, then to only a few of them. The benefits of GATT disciplines are shown by the striking contrast between those CEECs without bound tariffs under GATT and the former Czechoslovakia which enjoyed GATT-bound tariffs. Between 1991 and 1992, the former increased their tariffs from 5.5% to 18.4% (Poland) or from 12.4% to 18% (Romania), while the former Czechoslovakia maintained relatively stable protection in the manufacturing sector, its import surcharges imposed in 1991 and 1992 being eliminated in 1993 in accordance with her GATT obligations.

A related problem is the low legal status of most existing import rules in the CEECs. This leaves ample room for discretionary decisions from many parts of the executive, including from low levels of the bureaucracy. It fosters an impenetrable web of relations and coalitions, including between some CEEC public authorities and foreign firms. Indeed, recent tariff increases are highly correlated with the presence of foreign direct investments, which suggests that the CEECs are using trade policies as a way of attracting foreign direct investment. This tends to make domestic markets noncompetitive and leads to an unfortunate confusion between privatization and monopolization.

Concerning the second aspect of substitutability, CEEC trade laws have not taken into account sufficiently the potential substitutability between instruments of protection. Firms looking for protection always seek the least-cost alternative. This is particularly relevant in considering the instruments of contingent protection – anti-dumping, safeguard and anti-subsidy – which recent experience in OECD countries has shown may be tailored to deliver the exact dose and form of protection wanted by domestic lobbies.

There are already cases of contingent protection in at least three of the CEECs: a few anti-dumping and safeguard cases in Poland and Romania, and many safeguard measures (about a hundred) in Hungary. In considering these Messerlin notes that CEEC laws are currently laxer than the GATT requires, but that 'GATT consistency' is the wrong criterion. This is because GATT Articles VI and XIX look *only* at the interests of the import-competing producers, rather than at the national interest as a whole. As he remarks, the logic of GATT Article VI is equivalent to allowing only landlords to vote on urban zoning or only millionaires to vote on income taxes.

If a government feels it must adopt contingent protection laws (and there is no obligation under the GATT to do so), national laws should do *more* than the GATT provisions require. Messerlin insists on the need for involving institutions *supportive* of the cost–benefit approach of protection – that is, institutions able to argue the costs of protection for the national economy. He also stresses that all the contingent protection instruments should receive *common* legal treatment, particularly in their capacity to balance the interests of the protectionist import-competing industries against those of other producers and consumers, in order to develop the same degree of resistance to manipulation by lobbies.

Messerlin also suggests that the contingent protection (Articles 91–93 and 115) provisions of the Treaty of Rome should be substituted for the EAs' provisions. By signing these parts of the Treaty of Rome, the CEECs will become immediate yet partial members of the Union – an important political step towards complete accession. More importantly, however, the Treaty is economically sounder than the EAs. For instance, it allows countries to treat 'dumping' by re-exporting the allegedly dumped goods to the country of origin, creating powerful forces towards effective market unification.

Chapter 4 by László Csaba argues that both the opening of the CEEC economies in 1988–90 and its partial reversal in 1991–4 have been reflections of the domestic balance of forces. The EAs are too limited to provide an effective bulwark against the tide of special interests: local politicians, Csaba states, have been claiming credit for resisting or delaying market opening – protecting local interests, as they say; the EAs contain many derogations from free trade; the EAs offered little improvement in the CEECs' access to EU markets relative to the 1991 position in which the EU had already offered GSP (General System of Preferences) facilities, abolished some quantitative restrictions (QRs) and expanded textiles and clothing quotas; the EAs contained no financial commitments; and, finally, they made no concrete offer of EU membership.

Internally the forces of protection have been well organized and vocal in the CEECs. Although import penetration has increased by only two to three percentage points, critics claim to have identified very large damages from liberalization in Central Europe and, after a brief period of disorganization, the old lobbies have re-emerged, such as those in agriculture and industry, supplemented and reinforced by new ones, such as small private business and the political clientele of the new elites which have taken over many of the crucial sectors of the economy. Particularly noteworthy is the resurgence of the bureaucracy, especially the sectoral ministries. Shorn of one set of functions these have sought out another, looking actively for casualties which they can nurse. Csaba argues that such nursing frequently entails ostensibly non-trade policies, for example regulation and standards, that happen to restrict international trade. Having observed Western democracies' behaviour in this respect, the CEECs find it hard not to emulate them.

Csaba therefore proposes retaining or creating a special governmental agency for free trade which would not be part of any other governmental department. He lists some of the issues that might threaten liberal trade and shows why various departments of government are likely to prove inadequate guardians of openness. Protectionism, he says, does not need an agency to administer its many intricacies, and can in fact flourish among the many departments. Free trade, on the other hand, and the job of managing the congruence between domestic and EU legislation, do require cross-sectoral overview and organization.

Csaba maintains that EU cooperation could aid this process in a number of ways. For example, technical assistance could focus on helping to avoid the premature standardization of norms, or the creation of new structural rigidities, especially in legislation on farming and on labour markets. Indeed, offering such broad perspectives in a convincing way may be a much more important contribution than the actual sums to be transferred to 'Eastern partners'. On the other hand, the limited generosity of the EAs in terms of market access and of membership commitments, or getting the wrong sequencing in the standardization of legal norms, may also breed short-sighted and counterproductive outcomes on the part of the CEECs. Short of the prospect of full EU membership, Csaba states, such limited and technical measures will probably prove insufficient to roll back the mounting and multidimensional pressure for procedural and other non-tariff protection. This may result in a non-transparent and internationally uncontrollable trend towards protectionism in the CEECs for quite some time to come.

André Sapir takes a more positive view of progress in the CEECs in Chapter 5, comparing the depth and speed of their liberalizations favourably with those in the developing world. He nevertheless recognizes that, after a flying start, the 'honeymoon' of trade liberalization is over, and that since 1991 there have been serious pressures for retreat. These arguably stem from the speed of the previous opening, the lobbying by foreign investors for protection as the *quid pro quo* for investment, and the collapse of CMEA trade. Sapir notes that the CEECs' situation fits well with political economy analyses that suggest that protectionist pressures are likely to dominate trade opening during the transition from socialism, unless trade policy is credibly non-discretionary. These analyses typically argue that institutional arrangements such as the EAs can play a major role in limiting the discretion of governments and thus in bolstering liberalism.

Sapir examines the impact of the EAs on the process of trade policy formulation in the CEECs and then investigates their role in constraining the actual outcome of trade policy. The central questions are whether the EAs are successful in tying the hands of governments in favour of liberal trade policies, and whether they have simply led CEEC governments to shift protection from the EU to other trade partners. Sapir argues that one should not measure the EAs against a yardstick of free trade, which they were never designed to achieve, but against a notion of politically realistic liberalism.

To answer these questions Sapir examines in detail one country: Hungary. The EAs impose a number of bilateral obligations on Hungary's trade relations with the EU. These are in addition to multilateral obligations contracted under the GATT and serve further to constrain Hungarian trade policy with the EU. The degree of constraint, however, differs markedly between industrial and agricultural products. For industrial products, Hungary now has very little room for unilateral manoeuvre. All tariffs and QRs on imports from the EU will be eliminated at the latest by 1 January 2001 and in the meantime are, at the very least, bound at their levels of 1 March 1992. Para-tariffs are also bound and are to be progressively abolished. In agriculture, on the other hand, the EA leaves existing tariffs and quotas largely untouched. Moreover, it does not bind them at their 1992 levels, nor does it prevent Hungary from introducing variable levies.

Sapir notes that derogations from EA obligations in the form of increased tariffs are possible, but only for a limited time and in exceptional circumstances. Moreover, although the EA safeguard clauses allow discrimination, since they may be applied on a selective bilateral basis rather than multilaterally, selectivity, was already permitted under Hungary's special Protocol of Accession to the GATT.

Perhaps the main additional constraint imposed on Hungary's trade policy lies in the process of consultation with trade partners. As a GATT member, Hungary is subject to regular consultation and review, but this is essentially *ex post* and GATT's record on enforcement is patchy. Consultation under the EA, on the other hand, tends to take place during the process of formulating trade policy and consequently, Sapir argues, coupled with the EU's status as Hungary's premier trade partner, the EA has acquired almost instantly a significance that surpasses that of the GATT. In any trade matter, Hungarian authorities probably consider their EA obligations prior to their GATT obligations.

In the second part of his chapter, Sapir analyses the trade policy outcome in Hungary and the role of the EA. Since 1991, the demand for protection has risen substantially and by 1992 it was in full swing, fuelled by the falls in output and employment, the surge of imports and the resurgence of special interest groups. Among the latter, large foreign investors were the first to campaign successfully for protection, but domestic producers soon followed using their substantial political weight, especially the agrarian lobby and large state enterprises.

The government's resolve to resist protectionist pressures and sustain import liberalization was strengthened by two complementary decisions. The first was the adoption in March 1991 of the liberal-minded four-year 'Programme of conversion and development for the Hungarian economy'. The second decision was the signature in December 1991 of the EA.

Sapir argues that, in spite of strong protectionist pressures, Hungary was able to maintain its liberal course and continue with trade liberalization, and this was at least partly due to the EA. The exception proves this rule: the EA imposes little discipline regarding the protection of agricultural products, and as a result much of Hungary's recent protection has taken place in this area. Sapir also argues that, despite the EAs' limited coverage, there is little evidence that protectionist pressures were diverted to other suppliers.

Sapir concludes by wondering whether the EA provides a sufficiently solid environment to enable Hungary to continue with trade liberalization in the face of two major developments. First, the deterioration of the trade balance has produced liberalization fatigue. In December 1993 the government presented an economic programme aimed at reducing the deficit through a combination of export promotion and import-curtailing measures. The latter included the reintroduction of licences and the increase of import duties for certain agricultural products as well as the freezing for 1994 of the global quota for consumer goods at the 1993 level. The second development is the May 1994 election, which produced a new majority whose commitment to resist protectionist demands remains untested.

1.3 Complementary Policies and Institutions

One of the themes of Part I of this book is the degree of substitutability between trade policies and trade institutions. In Part II this issue is considered on an even broader front, by asking whether ostensibly quite different policies might deputize for trade policy if the latter is too tightly constrained. Recent discussions in the GATT have raised the interactions between environmental policy and competition policies on the one hand and trade policy on the other, and the pattern of policy-making in the pre-revolutionary CEECs makes it necessary also to consider industrial policy. These areas of policy can be used either to reinforce or to undermine trade policy and, although they cannot be wholly subordinated to the latter, it is essential that they be at least consistent with it. In particular there is little virtue in defending trade policy-making from predatory special interest groups if one leaves these other areas completely vulnerable. Thus particularly in the cases of industrial and environmental policy we ask quite explicitly what is necessary to eliminate or reduce the possibility of their capture by protectionist interests.

Part II starts with Chapter 6 by Bernard Hoekman and Petros Mavroidis on competition policy. They focus on the competition policy aspects of the EAs and do so from the perspective of the trade policy stance of the CEECs. They explore possible institutional mechanisms that could be implemented by CEEC governments with a view to increasing the sensitivity of competition law enforcement to trade and investment policy.

The objective of competition policy in most jurisdictions is efficient resource allocation and thereby the maximization of national welfare. Governments pursue trade policies for a variety of reasons, of which efficiency is not usually one. An active trade policy redistributes income between segments of the population by protecting specific industries and the factors of production employed there, and usually does so in an inefficient manner. Competition law aims at protecting competition (and thus economic efficiency), while trade policy aims at protecting competitors (or factors of production). Governments should try to attain a balance between the two objectives, which requires the design of institutional mechanisms that allow them to consider explicitly the competition implications of particular trade or investment policies.

The EAs require that the CEECs adopt the basic competition rules of the EU for practices that affect their trade with the EU. These rules relate to agreements between firms restricting competition, the abuse of a dominant position, the behaviour of public undertakings (state-owned firms) and competition-distorting state aids. Almost all the CEECs have now passed competition legislation and allocated the responsibility for enforcing their competition rules. There are several inconsistencies in these laws with EU language and implementation criteria/guidelines, some of them substantial, but the thrust of existing provisions is certainly pro-competitive.

CEEC competition authorities have been given relatively broad mandates to identify the costs of government policies and actions that restrict competition. Trade policy is an obvious priority area in this connection. Competition offices have two ways of 'internalizing' trade policy. The first is to oppose trade policies that harm competition unduly on the domestic market; the second is to countervail the anti-competitive effect of trade policy on an *ex post* basis. The first, 'direct' approach has been actively pursued by a number of the CEEC competition offices. In this they compare favourably to competition offices in OECD countries. By commenting on or opposing suggested or existing trade policies, the competition offices ensure that the economy-wide implications of sectoral policies/lobbying are recognized and discussed. The main power of competition offices is, however, of an *ex post* nature. Active enforcement, with guidelines that clearly specify that trade policy will be an important consideration in implementing competition laws, will help bolster the effectiveness of *ex ante* opposition to policy proposals that restrict access to markets.

Hoekman and Mavroidis identify a number of actions through which competition law enforcement might be strengthened and be made even more sensitive to trade policy. First, the scope for antitrust agencies in the CEECs to act on their own initiative does not yet appear to have been exploited fully. Second, detailed guidelines would help to reduce uncertainty regarding the priorities given by the competition authorities to different types of competition-reducing practices. CEEC legislation offers competition agencies wide discretion. While allowing them to treat cases on their merits this can also complicate their function because it means that various specific and presumptively harmful practices cannot be automatically prohibited. Third, the trade policy stance pertaining to an industry should explicitly be taken into account when defining the relevant market in the enforcement of antitrust. Whenever market shares are used to define dominant positions they should be linked to considerations of market contestability. Fourth, agencies should publish the reasoning underlying their decisions.

Despite their agreement to adopt EU-compatible competition disciplines, and despite the fact that free trade and freedom of investment will be achieved within ten years, there is no provision in the EAs specifying that anti-dumping duties will be abolished on EU–CEEC trade. Continued threats of contingent protection on the part of the EU imply that CEEC firms will face different standards from their EU competitors. EU firms will be permitted to engage in price discrimination or sell below cost on the EU market, whereas CEEC firms will be constrained from pursuing such a strategy by the existence of EU anti-dumping procedures.

Hoekman and Mavroidis argue that during the transition phase towards full implementation of the EAs a link be established between anti-dumping and antitrust in instances where CEECs are facing anti-dumping threats or actions in the EU. The European Commission could be asked to apply competition policy criteria in anti-dumping investigations against products originating in the CEECs, in order to verify that there is a threat to EU competition, not just a threat to an EU competitor. Clearly, the best strategy is to seek the elimination of anti-dumping but, if this proves to be impossible, a second-best policy could be to formalize the link between competition law enforcement and anti-dumping investigations. Since the CEECs have adopted legislation comparable to that of the EU in the competition field, one can assume that, if they enforce their competition laws vigorously, EU-consistent minimum standards will be respected. This may effectively raise the threshold for EU import-competing industries seeking anti-dumping relief. Vigorous enforcement of competition disciplines in service industries, especially distribution-related industries, may further help reduce the potential for EU firms to seek contingent protection.

In Chapter 7 David Audretsch considers the design of institutions to devise and implement industrial policy in the CEECs. One of the main issues confronting industrial policy institutions worldwide is how to avoid regulatory capture, whereby policy-makers with a mandate to manage an industrial policy become spokespersons and champions for particular interest groups. In the context of this book, he asks in particular how to make industrial policy consistent with international trade policy, if the latter can be kept fairly liberal.

Audretsch develops an analytical framework for thinking about industrial policies, their interaction with trade policies, and the institutions charged with policy formulation and implementation. At the heart of this framework is a clear distinction between sectoral policies, which essentially target specific industries and even firms, and horizontal policies, which essentially focus upon improving the quality of inputs to the production process. There are a number of reasons why industrial policy institutions of this second type are less prone to regulatory capture than those of the first type. The main one is that capture is more likely to result when the benefits of industrial policy are concentrated upon relatively few firms, as in the case of industrial targeting, than when the recipients are more widely dispersed, as is the case of horizontal industrial policies.

There are two lenses through which to view the interaction between trade and industrial policies. The first focuses on the impact of trade policies on the domestic industrial structure and ultimately on the performance of domestic firms. The second focuses on industrial policy as an instrument to strengthen the international competitiveness of domestic firms. A tension emerges when the interests of the domestic industry demanding protection from foreign rivals and domestic entrants pre-empt the broader and more dispersed social interest in an efficient and competitive domestic industry. Trade policy is particularly likely to be captured by the constituents for targeted industrial policy – namely, concentrated and capital-intensive industries that are confronted by a competitive disadvantage and have strong tendencies towards and experience of vigorous rent-seeking activities. Unfortunately, this is the prevalent industry structure in the CEECs.

Audretsch next turns to designing institutions of industrial policy and international trade in order to avoid regulatory capture. A problem particular to the CEECs is that the centralized power and interest groups that have been established through inherited coalition structures can influence the political process and restrict, or at least impede, the entry of new domestic firms and foreign competitors which would undermine their power. Administrative procedures to diminish the influence of such political rent-seeking activities generally need to provide for accountability, independence and transparency. The principle of accountability suggests that a greater degree of political scrutiny is required to help compensate for the inevitable imbalance between the concentration of producer interests on the one hand, and the relatively dispersed interests of the general public on the other. Somewhat in conflict with accountability, the principle of independence suggests weakening the control of administrative agencies by elected representatives in order to reduce the likelihood and extent of regulatory capture since the representatives are often the agents of capture. The principle of transparency requires that institutions implementing industrial and trade policies should be charged with revealing to the public the maximum amount of information and reasoning upon which policies are based.

The privatization process poses a special problem involving both industrial and trade policies. Should restructuring occur prior to or subsequent to privatization? And whose interests should prevail in the privatization process? The German approach to privatizing the former East German *Kombinate* provides a useful model to the CEECs. Regulatory capture has been avoided to a great extent because the inevitably bureaucratic nature of the privatization process has been moderated by the *Treuhandanstalt*. In particular, four essential functions are provided, which could easily be adapted in neighbouring countries: (1) the creation of supervisory boards and the monitoring of management; (2) the evaluation of the potential viability of enterprises and the adjustment of balance sheets in terms of writing off the old debt; (3) the reorganization of enterprises, including closure in appropriate cases; and (4) the search for and evaluation of potential purchasers, along with the imposition of ancillary conditions. These functions are implemented by a relatively independent (from the government) institution, which has contributed significantly to the avoidance of regulatory capture.

The final chapter of the book is by Michael Rauscher who examines the link between environmental and trade policies. He starts from the position that, while both theoretical and empirical models tend to suggest that this link is not generally close, there are some sectors where environmental taxes and standards definitely affect foreign trade and where foreign trade affects the environment. For example, environmental policy may be captured by protectionist interests, with the result that among the available environmental policy instruments the most protectionist (instead of the most efficient) instruments are chosen; a (misconceived) drive for international competitiveness may lead governments to relax environmental regulation, leading to competition in laxity in the environmental field; unilateral policies for coping with global environmental problems may lead to the relocation of pollution-intensive production to less regulated countries, which reduces the effectiveness of such measures; and international environmental agreements like the Montreal Protocol provide for the possibility of trade restrictions in order to achieve environmental goals.

The CEECs start from a particularly disadvantageous position in environmental terms, but this should not be allowed to distort their long-run institutions for environmental policy. Cheap energy, the use of coal as the predominant primary energy source, the neglect of environmental issues, the use of inadequate environmental-policy instruments and poor enforcement have left their industrial production some ten times as pollution intensive as that of Western Europe. Adjustment towards international energy prices is shifting the CEECs' comparative advantage from pollution-intensive to 'cleaner' goods. This means that while they may find themselves accused of ecological dumping during the first years of transition, in the longer run they may themselves complain about pollution havens in other countries.

Rauscher argues that an important starting point in thinking about trade and environmental policy is that national trade law should respect the sovereignty of other countries in their environmental policies. Lax environmental standards abroad are not ecological dumping and not a reason to implement countervailing duties. The use of barriers to trade should be restricted to the case of severe transfrontier pollution problems and should be made conditional upon the joint decision of a group of countries in the framework of an international environmental agreement. The environmental targets of these measures should be well defined. Additionally, to reduce the impact of covert non-tariff barriers, trade laws should make explicit the application of the principle of the country of origin as opposed to the country of destination. That is, goods should be required to meet the (nondiscriminatory) environmental standards of their place of origin, not their place of sale.

As far as environmental policies are concerned, the design of laws and institutions should take account of regulatory capture. One way of doing this is to maximize the distance between environmental-policy institutions and protectionist interest groups. The responsibility for environmental policy should rest with the ministry of the environment and its affiliated institutions but not with, for example, the ministries of agriculture, energy, industry or development. Environmental policy should primarily address pollutants instead of polluters. Sector- or plant-specific process standards tend to be much more subject to interest group influence than more general policies that affect all sectors of the economy. In this context, emission taxes are desirable instruments. Moreover, in the CEECs they have another advantage over the command-and-control approach. Command-and-control solutions often generate rents to incumbent firms, which will accrue abroad when enterprises are owned by foreigners (despite the pollution being at home) and, anyway, set up incentives for rent-seeking activities to defend these rents. These problems can be avoided if firms have to pay for the right to pollute. Finally, monitoring plays an important role in the avoidance of regulatory capture. It makes sense to establish an independent institution that reports publicly on the appropriateness of environmental policy on a regular basis. It is essential to have consumers represented in this monitoring process and it may also be useful to involve foreigners, at least in an expert/advisory role.

International trade agreements like the GATT, the EAs and the NAFTA acknowledge the sovereignty of signatory parties in conducting their own environmental policies – under the restriction that these policies be designed in the least distortionary and discriminative way. Despite its emphasis on subsidiarity, however, the EU is not so clear on this issue. The Single European Act defines environmental policy as one of the areas where coordination on the EU level is desirable. For the CEECs the problem may arise that the EU demands the adjustment of environmental standards to the EU levels, even if no transboundary pollution problems are involved, for example in the case of drinking water standards. From the point of view of the CEECs (and of EU citizens) this is neither efficient nor desirable, and the CEECs should attempt to resist unnecessary harmonization requirements.

International trade agreements should also be more explicit on the admissibility of 'green' barriers to trade. The NAFTA, which gives precedence to international environmental agreements over its own provisions, shows how this can be achieved. The importance of this lies in defining precisely when green barriers may be used according to multilateral agreement, rather than leaving it open to domestic interpretation of essentially bilateral agreements. Since the latter usually occurs under the duress of a crisis, it is not likely to give the same weight to long-run cosmopolitan considerations as the former. Another issue deserving international coordination is the problem of jurisdictional competition towards too-low environmental taxes. Because of their political pressures and the necessity of a rapid improvement of income and living standards, the CEECs may be tempted to participate in such a competition. Self-binding mechanisms taking the shape of minimum environmental standards agreed upon in multilateral treaties are a way out of this dilemma. Multilateralism also has a role in dispute settlement over trade and environmental issues even if these conflicts are only bilateral. Independent referees, like the European Court of Justice, are helpful if other conflict resolution mechanisms fail. They do, however, tend to restrict the sovereignty of individual states, which can sow the seeds of potential future conflicts. Hence they should be used only as a last resort.

1.4 Conclusion

The chapters of this book examine many aspects of the design of trade policy institutions for the CEECs. They range widely over topics and thus offer different perspectives in detail for different problems. A number of nearly universal themes emerge, however, which bear repeating.

The danger in trade policy-making is not so much actively bad government as weak government: government that falls prey to special interest groups. No component of government is immune from the pressures, and all must be bolstered against them. One defence is explicit public scrutiny. Every author recommends that trade policy-making be as public as possible with the nature of the policy, its costs and benefits, and the reasons for adoption spelt out. Requiring such publicity – indeed, encouraging it – would be a major step forward for the CEECs.

A second and related prescription is to ensure that at each stage – legislation, execution, administration and review – the victims of protection have the same rights to be heard and the ability to prepare their cases as the proponents. This requires conscious governmental effort to level the (internal) playing-field.

A third common theme is the desirability of international agreements in binding governments to 'good behaviour'. The GATT represents a constructive and liberal element of this, while the EAs offer a deeper and probably more enforceable, but somewhat less liberal standard. While they clearly improve vastly on pre-revolutionary circumstances and compare favourably with what other industrial countries have offered the CEECs, they are only partially successful when measured against many economists' goals of free trade. Moreover, they do not promise much further progress towards such a goal. Thus, while recognizing the political constraints felt on both sides of the agreements and admitting that the situation could be a good deal less liberal, the majority of our authors suggest improvements that could be easily and virtually costlessly implemented.

PART 1

Trade Policy Institutions

2

Who Should Run Trade Policy in Eastern Europe and How?*

L. Alan Winters

> ... democracy is the worst form of Government except all those other forms which have been tried from time to time
>
> Winston Churchill

2.1 Introduction

This chapter is about who should run a country's international trade policy and how, and its tenor echoes Churchill's famous quip about government in general. As one surveys the possible location and modalities of trade policy-making within a modern democratic government, none seems ideal. Indeed, each seems to entail significant dangers. Not only can one not design institutions that guarantee a rational outcome in trade policy-making, but one should not. It is part of democratic government that electorates must ultimately be able to act as they wish, even if that seems unwise from the outside. Thus in one sense the most important element of sensible trade policy – by which I mean a liberal one – must be convincing a substantial body of electors that maintaining open borders represents the best general prescription. The role of institutional design is to try to ensure that this message does not get overturned lightly and that it is not unduly corrupted or captured, either by a grand vision that promotes autarchy (as communism did) or by an unholy alliance of special interests seeking tailor-made protection.

* Thanks, but no blame, are due to the members of the CEPR programme 'Trade Laws and Trade Institutions for the Central and East European Countries', in particular Bernard Hoekman, for comments, and to Minerva Pateña and Sue Williams for typing. The views expressed are solely those of the author. They should not be attributed to the World Bank or CEPR.

Of the two dangers, the former is the lesser. After four decades of inward-looking central planning, the electorates of the Central and Eastern European Countries (the CEECs) needed no persuasion of the virtues of either democracy or internationalism. Thus the basic thrust of CEEC trade policy since the revolutions of 1989 has been strongly internationalist: accession to or renegotiating membership of the GATT, trade agreements with Western countries and the reduction of barriers to imports and exports. It was exactly the same ideal of internationalism at the end of the Second World War that led to the creation of the liberal economic institutions – the GATT, the IMF and the World Bank – that have presided over the unprecedented period of Western economic growth since that time. Provided that the transition is not so painful (so badly handled) that populations forsake the market-economy model wholesale, I believe that we can be confident that the ruling rhetoric in the CEECs will be relatively liberal.

But good intentions and sound rhetoric are not sufficient. They need bolstering by institutions which protect and nurture them and which allow them to operate in a relatively uncompromising fashion. This is no easy task, because in trade policy-making the forces of protectionism are almost always more passionate, better organized and more vocal than those of liberalism. The few who lose from imports of a particular commodity (producers) face greater individual costs than do the many who benefit from them (consumers), even though aggregate benefits outweigh aggregate costs. Thus the losers have a greater incentive to lobby policy-makers and have fewer problems than their opponents in organizing such a lobby. Moreover, most lobbying for trade policy is by industries facing adjustment costs due to imports (expanding industries usually look elsewhere for support). Thus the returns to winning protection will generally be concentrated on the set of existing producers. This further increases the incentive to lobby, because there is less chance of the benefits being dissipated by new entrants, and it allows the lobby to identify personally the casualties of the trade flow, which is a great help in public relations. In addition, industries that suffer because the government has reduced their protection can argue that the government is penalizing them for responding positively to previous policy (i.e. expanding output behind the protective wall) and can also appeal to the public's natural conservatism. Finally, no single industry seeks to overthrow the general policy of liberal trade; rather it seeks to redress a particular (and undoubtedly unintentional!) anomaly which the policy throws up: protection is pragmatic not principled in this world. The problem is that if many industries behave in this way, and are successful in their objectives, the liberal trade policy is undermined.

This chapter considers how institutional design can help to keep these asymmetries in check whilst still recognizing that informed beneficent dictatorship is not possible and that elected governments must ultimately have the right to pursue their own trade policy. It comprises a set of cautionary tales rather than a constitutional manifesto. Moreover, while it is concerned with international trade policy and is conditioned on the details of that activity, its main messages apply to other areas of redistributive politics. By the same token, the practices adopted for dealing with other, similar, issues will largely determine the structures adopted for trade policy-making. Hence the chapter is a small contribution to the grand constitutional debate rather than a self-contained solution to one part of it. The chapter has five substantive parts dealing respectively with the legislature, the executive, the bureaucracy, the general public and anti-protectionist lobbies, and the current situation in three of the CEECs. Before commencing with these, however, I should mention the role of international agreements and the constitution.

In the context of designing a trade policy, international organizations and international agreements are the tactics not the strategy. No CEEC was obliged to join the GATT nor to sign a Europe Agreement with the EU. Having done so, however, it takes on a set of responsibilities and constraints and receives a set of broadly reciprocal concessions. Signing such agreements is a means whereby a government can, first, strengthen its bargaining hand against domestic special interests and, second, bind itself and future governments to particular policy sets. In these respects accession to the GATT and signing the Europe Agreements are critical elements for the credibility of policy reform in the CEECs. But there remains a wide range of discretion within the confines of these agreements. The CEECs have to determine the speed with which to liberalize within the GATT and even, to some extent, their initial levels of protection within it. In the Europe Agreements they must decide how to exercise the protective instruments they still have access to and whether to accelerate or decelerate implementation. Thus trade policy and trade policy-making is still a major issue for small potentially open economies such as these. Merely proclaiming that 'we have joined the GATT' or 'we have signed a Europe Agreement' is not sufficient. One needs to build on that base.[1]

One might make similar arguments about enshrining trade policy in the Constitution, which would give it greater force and stability than ordinary law. The difference, however, is that, while long-held conventions and the other parties to international agreements help to keep such agreements reasonable, there are fewer constraints on a newly written Constitution. Hence, unless one is confident that the trade policy clauses would be satisfactory, one should be extremely cautious in declaring *ex ante* that they should have constitutional force. Moreover, to my (limited) knowledge, no country does currently enshrine external trade policy in its Constitution in any operational form.

2.2 The Legislature

The most obvious locus for tax policy-making is the legislature – the ultimate source of power in a market democracy – and since trade policy is effectively taxation, this is where ultimate responsibility for trade policy must lie. The problem, however, is that trade policy is typically very complex and detailed and legislatures are not well suited to deal with it. The best illustration of the difficulties involved is the United States prior to 1931, in which Congress not only had the power to make trade policy, but exercised it. Schattschneider (1935) gives a marvellous account, as well as an acute analysis, of the process of making the Smoot–Hawley tariff of 1930.

Following President Hoover's campaign commitment in 1928 to revise the tariff for agriculture, the Congress initiated a general review and revision of the tariff. The House Ways and Means Committee issued notice in December 1928 of public hearings, which were intended to last 35 days and 5 evenings during the first 2 months of 1929. During the following 2 months they would attempt to draw up a tariff bill, and possibly seek additional written briefing from the public. The tariff was ostensibly to equalize foreign and US costs of production. This was economically a crazy objective which, in Schattschneider's view, granted industries an implicit right to protection and became a mere fig leaf for negotiating protection. Moreover, it hardly served to define and constrain the nature of the evidence collected, with the result that the Committee was overrun by petitioners: many were never heard, many were allowed just 5 minutes to give their evidence, and over 11 000 pages of evidence were collected. The Senate Finance Committee also held hearings and collected another 9 000 pages of evidence! No attempt was made to check evidence on either overseas or domestic costs, and many of the hearing sessions degenerated into implicit or even explicit bargaining over tariff rates.

The chaos surrounding the consultation and subsequent lawmaking increased the advantages of insiders over outsiders. The inadequate notice, the failure to publish proposals for debate and the need to fight for a hearing, all favoured experienced lobbying groups and members of Congress themselves. Congress made little effort to check the standing of petitioners nor their claims to speak for the majority of a particular interest. A further misfortune was the arrangement to hear evidence and consider the bill commodity by commodity. This virtually ruled out any consideration of the general principles involved because they did not ever meet the strict germaneness rules imposed by session Chairmen. Thus, say, the steel day was about steel, not about the wisdom of protection in general. The result was effectively to disenfranchise consumer interests. Even consuming industries had to decide whether to use their time to argue *against* tariffs on their inputs or *for* tariffs on their outputs. No contest!

There was an undoubted sympathy in Congress for the tariff, but not as a principle so much as a whole series of special cases. Industries tended to own members of Congress, possibly by explicit 'purchase', but more commonly because the latter recognized the industrial concentrations in their constituencies. Members of Congress in their turn essentially represented their clients in Congress, for example by fixing meetings, ensuring that they were heard in the evidential proceedings, and by managing their appearances before the

Committees (even if the sponsor was not a member of the relevant Committee). Apparently almost all members of Congress had clients and a culture of mutual non-interference grew up: members of Congress would not seriously challenge colleagues' commodities and expected the favour to be returned in kind. The 'costs rule' offered a smoke-screen for this, and tariffs for ostensibly similar products were set similarly with virtually no debate. Only the excessively greedy were challenged, and then only rarely.

Schattschneider observed the pressures on members of Congress to jump onto the bandwagon, noting that it was safer to get aboard than to try to stop it. He described the outcome as 'universal', as do Weingast (1979) and Shepsle and Weingast (1981a) in their formal analysis of the process. Essentially, the need to build a coalition of special interests led the initial tariff reformers implicitly to welcome new members with new interests. As the coalition grew and the probability of it winning increased, it became ever more important for further interests to accrete, because the cost to them of being one of the few sectors without protection increased with the size of the coalition and the tariffs it promised. Protection is relative, and Schattschneider argued that, by making the tariff politically strong, i.e. universal, advocates were making it economically weak, i.e. indiscriminate and hence non-protective. There is some truth in this, but a uniform tariff is still distortionary: it protects import-competing interests relative to exporters and non-traded sectors.

With parliaments in the CEECs jealous of, and anxious to exercise, their newly won powers, legislative trade policy is a distinct possibility over the next few years. Moreover, with no recent tradition of parliamentary procedure designed to take real decisions, there is scope for the CEECs to replicate many of the problems of the United States in 1929–30. This is perhaps most obvious in Romania which concluded the Uruguay Round with a bound tariff rate of 35% on most industrial goods and of up to 333% on agricultural goods.[2] These rates exceeded the actually applied tariff rates in nearly all cases, making it clear that the Romanian authorities were reserving the right to alter the tariff schedule subsequently. Since parliament is yet to discuss trade legislation for the post-revolutionary era, there are real dangers of universalism setting in.

What, then, are the lessons that can be drawn from the US interwar experience? With production relatively concentrated geographically and legislators dependent on particular geographical districts for re-election, one cannot avoid them coming under intense pressure to vote for protection at times. Moreover, since lobbying relies on various fundamental rights such as freedom of speech and freedom of association, one cannot avoid that pressure being skilfully focused and knowledgeably articulated. Rather, the system must be designed to cope with it.

One line of defence is to insist on good administrative procedures: adequate and widespread notice of hearings, clear publication of the issues to be debated, a commitment to warn explicitly interests on both sides of the debate that evidence will be heard, and a willingness to summon relevant witnesses where they do not put themselves forward. Petitioners should be required to prove their standing in the industry, so that biases become apparent, and to commit to the verity of their evidence; Schattschneider suggested accepting only sworn statements. Some rudimentary checking of evidence should be conducted, with threats of punishment if deliberate misinformation is discovered, and care should also be taken to prevent the leakage of privileged information to interested parties.

A second line of defence is to recognize the inevitable asymmetry of lobbying power in the race for protection and seek to redress it. A legislature could seek, or even establish the means to generate, anti-protectionist pressure from export and non-tradable producers and from consumers. For example, the negotiation of reciprocal trade arrangements automatically brings exporters (as well as foreigners) into the frame, while a commitment to calculate and publish economic assessments of trade policy highlights the consumer and competitiveness costs. When the heat is on, no legislator will willingly fund the opposition to their proposals, but between rounds or when procedures are first being designed many could probably be persuaded to see the wisdom of balancing up the scales. The establishment of a small independent unit with access to the relevant data could be charged with preparing the consumer case against the particular trade policies which it felt were most deleterious. Establishing such a body would amount to funding an official 'opposition', which is, after all, one of the major elements of many Western parliamentary systems.

An important feature identified by Schattschneider is the tendency for trade policy debate rapidly to degenerate into discussion of highly specific cases and thus to overwhelm any attempt to hear the case fairly.[3] Such circumstances favour the growth of unfair practices and the mutual legislator support associated with universalism. If this is to be avoided the legislature needs to deal only with general principles, leaving all commodity-specific details to another time. This does not prevent the pressure groups from pursuing their interests into general legislation, but it does at least make it more difficult for them to do so covertly under a tidal wave of paper.[4]

Schattschneider, and after him Destler (1992), noted that the US Constitution allows members of Congress great scope for individual expression without responsibility. The lack of party discipline and the famous checks and balances allow them to support specific interests freely, without seriously threatening their party's hold on power or the shape of legislation. This makes them particularly vulnerable to pressure groups: why refuse to support a group when accommodating it carries so few risks? But if all members of Congress behave like this, disasters like the Smoot–Hawley tariff can occur.

The lesson here is not so much the virtues of a party system – the rigid party discipline of the United Kingdom's House of Commons hardly encourages the review and constructive refinement of the executive's legislation – but the need for a means to ensure that freedom does not degenerate into irresponsibility. This might entail Committee review within the legislature or delegating some responsibilities to the executive. In 1934, recognizing the damage that the Smoot–Hawley tariff had done, the US Congress did the latter in the Reciprocal Trade Agreements Act (RTAA).

Before examining the RTAA, however, I consider briefly the role of committees in a legislature. Arrow's impossibility theorem suggests that bodies subject to pure majority rule will experience substantial instability and cycling in their decisions, but in fact this appears not to happen. One convincing explanation for the observed stability is Shepsle's (1979) structure-induced equilibrium. Shepsle argues that the existence of committees, their procedures and, even more, the legislature's procedures for receiving committee proposals, constrain majority rule sufficiently to eliminate much of the instability (see also Shepsle and Weingast (1981b) and Krehbiel (1987)).

Most legislation in the US Congress is written by committees and all is considered in detail by them. These committees are defined by topic and their Chairs are assigned by seniority. The former entails that particular issues always go to the same committees, while the latter means that committee membership, and even more so leadership, is fairly stable. Thus the effective legislative analysis of US trade policy is the prerogative of the 60 or 70 members of the House Ways and Means and the Senate Finance Committees.

The Ways and Means Committee, which reports to a House of 435 members, takes its responsibilities seriously and seeks to bring forward bills which are, first, viewed as responsible by the House as a whole and, second, very likely to pass the House. The former means, according to Baldwin (1985), that there is strong informal pressure against including sector-specific clauses in House bills because any such clause would be both disreputable and encourage debate within the full House. The latter means that the compromises necessary to achieve a majority have already been struck and have been weighed against the overall shape and content of the bill by a small group which, in some sense, owns the bill. This group can veto a bill – by failing to submit it to the House – if the compromises undermine the bill too far. Thus the unmanageable accretion of special interests characteristic of the Smoot–Hawley process becomes less likely.

The job of designing bills that will pass in the House is aided by the rules under which the House receives proposals from the Committee. A 'Rules Committee' assigns to a bill a rule for considering amendments from the floor of the House. If no rule is assigned, there is no debate and no passage, so the Rules Committee offers another opportunity for vetoing bad legislation. The available rules have three characteristic forms: relatively closed rules, whereby the House basically has only to accept or reject the bill as presented; a germaneness rule whereby only 'germane' amendments may be made; and an open rule, in which virtually anything goes. Bills proposed by the Ways and Means Committee traditionally receive relatively closed rules in which floor amendments are difficult. This grants to a sophisticated Committee, which can accurately assess the mood of the House, enormous power; it can select its preferred legislation from among the set of bills which will satisfy some majority of the House. (The conditions for getting a closed rule appear to include assuring the Rules Committee that there is a broad acceptance of the bill.)

Baldwin (1985) argues that the House of Representatives is relatively liberal and fairly rigorously non-product-specific in its trade legislation because of these rules. He explicitly contrasts it with the Senate in which the use of open rules for debate allows the Committee less power and opens up the way for accretions of special, commodity-specific interests. This is a powerful comment on the importance of procedure (structure in Shepsle's term), because, *ceteris paribus*, one would expect Representatives, with smaller constituencies and two-year terms, to be far more sensitive to pressure than Senators, with huge constituencies, six-year terms and an historic mission to stabilize lawmaking and to take the long view.

2.3 The Executive

The executive seems likely to be more liberal than the legislature in its trade policy because its constituency is broader. Industrial concentration means that, for virtually any industry, some legislators perceive a direct and individual benefit to providing protection for it, because the benefits to producers in their constituencies exceed the costs to consumers. The executive, on the other hand, is responsible to the whole electorate, so that, if aggregate costs exceed aggregate benefits, its constituency is the net loser. There remain the asymmetries between the two sides of the protection debate, in terms of their incentives and ability to organize, so the executive may still find it necessary to compromise for political reasons, but at least the substantive calculation favours liberalism. It is also arguable that the executive's responsibility for general foreign policy and its extensive international contacts will reduce its tendency towards isolationism and economic xenophobia. This too will foster a liberal outlook (Baldwin, 1985).

The hypothesis that the executive will be more liberal than the legislature has never really been subjected to searching test, however. In the US case, the Smoot–Hawley tariff was sufficiently high that the only realistic direction of change was down, and there was a widespread, if not universal, perception that the worldwide round of tariff increases that it precipitated was a disaster. Moreover, even though in the postwar era it appears that the Presidency has usually been more liberal than the Congress apparently wishes to be, this is in the context of a very particular set of institutions. Hence while Baldwin (1985) and Destler (1992) argue for the liberalism of the executive and, while it is a very plausible view, it is certainly not proven beyond question.[5]

Starting in 1934, Congress has periodically delegated trade policy to the executive, but never completely and never without safeguards. The periodic trade laws which empower the President to negotiate are time limited and restricted in the concessions that they permit. Among the safeguards which Congress has sought, and which have gradually been extended over the years, are the growing power of an 'executive broker' (Destler, 1992) and the relaxation of the rules for administered protection.

The RTAA effectively charged the State Department with US trade policy. Congress, however, soon began to doubt State's sensitivity to the claims of domestic industry and so started gradually to retract the delegated powers by constraining the executive's freedom of action. It was able to do this because the executive had repeatedly to return to Congress to renew its negotiating rights. Take, for example, the post of special trade advisor to the President, which grew up during the 1950s. In 1962, mistrusting the Departments of State (too liberal) and Commerce (too insensitive to agriculture) to reflect its interests in the multilateral negotiations, Congress gave the trade advisor explicit responsibilities and position in the executive as the Special Representative for Trade Negotiations (STR) as a *quid pro quo* for approving legislation to initiate the Kennedy Round. In 1972, in preparation for the Tokyo Round, the whole office was made formally part of the executive and the STR was given Cabinet Rank. Although located in the executive, the STR was partly Congress's man (or woman). His/her appointment was subject to Senate approval and reporting requirements ensured frequent meetings with Congress. Moreover, someone whose job is concerned solely with trade negotiations and attempting to pry open foreign markets is normally going to be more sympathetic to US trade restrictions than a Secretary of State with broader responsibilities.

The other crucial element of the delegation of trade policy powers to a more liberal executive was the growth of contingent and administered protection.[6] This allowed Congress to pre-specify conditions under which protection would be granted and to make the determination of the applicability of those conditions to a particular case a quasi-judicial procedure. These rules were a comfort and a safety valve, and as Finger (1981) and Finger *et al.* (1982) have argued, they took the politics out of protection. The existence of such rules, which offer a safety net if import pressure proves intolerable or competitors cheat, is probably the *sine qua non* of liberalization in a modern democracy and is thus probably unavoidable in the CEECs. Moreover, on the large canvas with which this chapter is concerned it is probably constructive. On the other hand, experience in the United States, let alone the EU, suggests that the rules have been subject to abuse and that the safety valve has become little more than a bypass allowing determined and powerful industries to obtain protection essentially by political means. An important aspect of trade policy institutions is to try to avoid this evolution.

The constructive view of administered protection is quite simple. Its existence makes liberalism the norm and protection the exception, the case for which has to be argued and proven. It allows trade policy pressures to be diverted away from legislators and the executive into a formal procedure in which, ostensibly, every interest can be fairly examined. At most the politicians are only brought back at the end to give final approval and at that stage they have, formally speaking, the right only to accept or reject a recommendation, not to negotiate or amend it.[7]

An apparently attractive component of the United State's administered protection armoury was trade adjustment assistance: a commitment that if trade liberalization hit particular sectors or factors in the economy, they would be compensated and helped to retrain, retool etc. This is economically rational – winners compensating losers – but, apart from its practical difficulties, which undermined the US scheme, it also poses a significant political danger. Legislating for trade adjustment assistance concedes an important political principle: that existing producers have the right to something approaching their current income. If change is great, as it is bound to be in the CEECs, it would be hugely expensive to provide assistance. Indeed, it may be impossible as output falls during the transition; then, having once conceded the right, it would be doubly difficult to resist granting protection if this appeared to be the only way of honouring the commitment. Thus, for the CEECs I believe that adjustment assistance must, for now, remain part of the general 'safety net' rather than be written into trade law.

Although escape and less than fair value (LFV) clauses have long been found in trade agreements and trade law, they have become prominent only the last two decades. In part this reflects the reduction in the levels of legislative protection, but in the United States and the EU it mainly reflects two other factors: first, the rules that are administered have steadily been relaxed, making it increasingly easy to obtain protection; and second, politicians have tended to hide behind these rules even when the protection offered is essentially political rather than administered. Both of these factors arise from uncertainty about precisely where responsibility for trade policy lies.

Baldwin (1985) argues that the turf battle in the United States between Congress and the President is the defining characteristic of US postwar trade policy. He argues that, even though administered protection relies on the International Trade Commission (ITC) and various parts of the executive, Congress influences the outcome in at least four non-legislative ways: through annual budgetary review for the agencies concerned; through Committee hearings designed to explore an issue before legislation is framed, which both raise the profile of an issue and make the implicit threat that if the Presidency will not act, Congress will; through Senate's power over appointments to senior executive positions and to the ITC; and through Senate's right to veto any treaty by a blocking minority of one third. Finger (1993) observes that trade policy emanating from the White House, mostly voluntary export restraints (VERs), almost always grows out of a frustrated attempt by a powerful industry to obtain LFV or escape clause protection. The administered protection procedures offer these interests an apparently legitimate public platform; if Congress then provides the political pressure, the executive comes under intense pressure. Nivola (1993) also observes this process, noting the role in it of 'Congressional entrepreneurs', happy to adopt any cause that offers sufficient return in terms of publicity. Similarly, Destler (1992) argues that sufficiently powerful interests always seem to prevail in current US protection debates. He appears to feel that this is not only unavoidable but beneficial in that by making occasional tactical retreats the liberal system survives to impose its rules on the majority of cases. The difficulty lies in being able to tell the difference between a tactical retreat and an incipient rout.

In addition to their non-legislative pressure, and of more consequence, members of Congress can rewrite the rules of administered protection in ways that make them ever more amenable to a protectionist outcome. Indeed, Finger (1992) argues that the principal guiding force behind revisions to the LFV criteria has been to make permissible those arguments that powerful petitioners have previously found excluded. He, Baldwin (1985), Grinols (1989) and Low (1993) all document the gradual loosening of the criteria for receiving protection and the tightening of the constraints on the executive to ensure that Congress's intention of granting protection is not undermined.[8]

It would be easy to conclude that this is a protectionist Congress subverting a liberal executive, and there is much truth in this. There is another dimension however: the tussle over trade policy between parts of government tends, I believe, to bias outcomes towards protectionism. Except following a major catastrophe, such as Smoot–Hawley, it is difficult to dominate trade policy-making processes if one's objective is to make no use of them.

This is well illustrated by the EU's experience over non-tariff barriers on trade with non-member countries. These are dealt with only under the rather unspecific 'Economic Policy' title of the Treaty of Rome, and for many years it was not clear whether the central EU or the national authorities controlled them. Over time the central authorities have prevailed, but at the expense of adopting centrally certain protectionist policies which particular national governments wished to impose. For example, in 1983 the French government threatened controls on all imports of VCRs into France, and started to curtail them by routing them all through the small inland customs office at Poitiers. The EU responded to this challenge by imposing EU-wide restrictions on VCRs from Japan. Similarly, in 1988 the French and Italians sought protection from Korean and Taiwanese footwear and were allowed national VERs, the EU authorities essentially introducing national trade policies despite their mission to create the Single European Market. This embarrassment was soon overcome, however, by extending the policy to the whole of EU imports from Korea and Taiwan. In order to capture and cement its control over trade policy the EU has adopted policies based on those of the most protectionist members and propagated them over the whole EU, albeit somewhat diluted. The moral is that responsibility for trade policy needs to be unambiguously allocated to one agency, subject only to periodic legislative review, at which point the legislature must bear full responsibility.

The deleterious diffusion of responsibility between the US Congress and executive can also occur within an executive. Broadly speaking, in the EU the Commission proposes policy and the Council disposes: there is little Council power to amend the proposals they receive from the Commission. If any progress is to be made, the Commission has to broker compromises between the member states represented on the Council and it has every incentive to do so because it becomes essentially powerless if its proposals are rejected. The outcome of this is an extremely consensual form of policy-making which, I have argued (Winters, 1993, 1994), tends to lead to universalism – policy packages in which each partner prefers to be on the inside, i.e. protected, than on the outside – even though each might oppose protection in principle. Thus if the protection of, say, certain parts if the steel industry is being considered, member governments seek to extend it to those parts of the industry in which they have a large interest as the price for their cooperation. They may do this even if their best outcome would be that the steel industry were not protected at all; this is because the worst outcome is to have an unprotected part of a protected industry, and they are unsure of their ability to block protection in total. Another example: in discussing Agriculture Commissioner McSharry's barely adequate reforms to the Common Agricultural Policy in 1992, UK ministers gave higher priority to ensuring that large farms were eligible for generous set-aside compensation payments than to their professed fundamental aim of reducing the payments themselves. Better have the UK big-farm sector inside the deal than risk being on the outside of it if it passes despite UK opposition.

Universalism afflicts the EU executive in a similar way to which it afflicted the US Congress in 1929. The representatives of the member governments essentially represent geographically limited constituencies and have virtually no concern for other parts of the Union. Thus, like individual Members of Congress, they have very little incentive to act responsibly.[9] The moral is that, if the executive does not bear direct responsibility for the overall outcome of legislation, it will not necessarily be more liberal than a legislature whose members have, at least occasionally, to face consumers. This could even apply to executives which are split along functional rather than geographical lines. If there is no collective responsibility, ministers will openly play to their sectoral interests; no-one will willingly take the overview and an inter-sectoral universalism will tend to emerge. It is overt responsibility for *all* interests which tends to keep executives honest.

2.4 The Bureaucracy

In many respects the EU's executive is a bureaucracy: the Commission comprises bureaucrats directly,[10] while the member states are represented by bureaucrats in most debates. Even when they are represented by politicians, the latter are ministers operating free from parliamentary control. Messerlin (1983) has highlighted a number of serious problems that can arise with bureaucratic protection. The most obvious stems from the fact that bureaucrats are generally unable to reap direct gains from the rents that they create for petitioners.[11] Senior bureaucrats do, however, benefit from having a large and complex sector to administer, both of which features tend to increase the size of their staffs and hence the grading of their posts. These incentives lead bureaucrats to favour industry output-maximizing over industry rent-maximizing tariffs (the former are higher) and to favour complex non-tariff barriers over simple tariffs.

Closely related to the issue of the incentives for different levels of protection is that of agency capture. It is widely recognized that officials charged with managing a particular sector come to identify closely with that sector. Senior and middle-level officials transfer between sectors only infrequently, and hence tend to build up large amounts of sector-specific human capital; their rewards are partly related to the health of their sectors and to how successfully they represent their sectors' interests in government – that is, one manifestation of an official's ability is the vigour and skill with which he fights his corner in bureaucratic debates;[12] only very rarely will bureaucrats earn career credit by running down their sector and subjecting their masters to the resulting political pressure. In addition, if one deals year after year with a particular sector, and the set of individuals in that sector's lobby, it is only human gradually to sympathize with, if not actually to adopt, their outlook. This is particularly true if the lobby can offer the bureaucrat something in return such as data, technical advice, or even help with policy enforcement. One need consider only the role of the steel producers or farm groups in the official management of their sectors to see this.

The factors listed in the previous paragraph combine to make sectoral ministries and particularly their middle-ranking officials (who have important functions but few cross-ministry contacts and no general responsibilities) fiercely protective of their sectors. Messerlin shows how this can lead to intersectoral 'policy wars', whereby each sector pursues its own goals non-cooperatively using the instruments at its command. Since the latter typically include trade policy and other protective devices but not less distortionary policies such as income transfers and retraining budgets, the result is excessive protection. The solution is to induce inter-ministerial cooperation, but that is actually quite hard to do. Even if policy war does not break out, it is difficult to induce negotiators from one ministry (especially at middle levels) to compromise for the sake of those in another. This is one reason (out of several) why arranging trade negotiations along sectoral lines is not sound politics.

Within a bureaucracy the means to obtaining inter-ministerial trade-offs lies in charging the senior, broader, ministries with oversight of policy-making. This is fiercely resisted and resented at the sectoral ministry level, but is none the less important. Thus the Ministries of Finance or of Foreign Affairs should be in a position to impose cooperation on, say, Agriculture and Industry. Moreover, because of their more general briefs – taxation, income distribution, international cooperation etc. – they are usually more liberal than the sectoral ministries; thus recognizing their seniority in trade policy and trade negotiations can be important, at least if these ministries take the trade task seriously enough to employ decent economic advisors. There are parallels here with the discussion above concerning the location of trade responsibility within the executive.

An example of the role of general oversight is agricultural reform. It was only when treasuries became seriously involved in agricultural policy – mainly for budgetary reasons, but also for reasons of efficiency and income distribution – that reform began to take hold in the 1980s. Inside the OECD a joint Agriculture–Trade Mandate study of agricultural support and trade distortions became bogged down by detail and secrecy in the first half of the 1980s. Then, responding to its constituency of Finance Ministries, the Economics and Statistics Directorate took up the issue. It produced a number of reports and in so doing dislodged the earlier detailed study, more or less obliging the national Ministries of Agriculture and Trade to permit its work to be concluded and published. The result has been very useful information and considerably increased pressure for agricultural reform.

The analysis above pertains to industrial countries and should have at least one caveat in its application to the CEECs at present. A major worry for most CEEC governments has been the public sector deficit, and this has led some Ministries of Finance, occasionally encouraged by some international organizations, to view trade policy as a tool of fiscal balance. Not only can tariffs raise money but protection might also postpone adjustment and hence the public sector costs of unemployment support. The latter argument is myopic and should be strongly discouraged. The former may have some virtue over the very short run, but it can be easily undermined by inefficient or corrupt customs procedures and by the raft of exemptions which usually seem to accompany high tariffs. If a Ministry of Finance wishes to pursue a revenue tariff for, say two years – and I would not recommend it – the tariff should be uniform and there should be absolutely no exceptions. Under those circumstances the political attractions are much less than they might first appear to be.

Another difference between the CEECs and the industrial countries is the location of trade policy within its own ministry rather than in association with industry. Thus, while Japan has MITI, the United States the Department of Commerce and the United Kingdom the Department of Trade and Industry,[13] Hungary and Poland each have a Ministry of International (or Foreign) Economic Relations and Romania a Ministry of Trade.[14] This separation of the trade function from industry, energy and agriculture seems desirable because it makes it less easy to concoct anti-trade compromises. It is important, however, that the Ministries of Trade have access to senior ministries and ministers.

2.5 The General Public and the Liberal Lobby

In a democracy trade policy must ultimately stem from the legislature in response to public demands. Thus an important part of the establishment of a liberal trade policy is bringing public opinion to bear in a constructive fashion. Beyond the general perception that openness and internationalism are civilized forms of behaviour, the intellectual case for open borders and free trade is complex and sophisticated. It relies on trading diffuse and abstract benefits – resources flowing to new activities, new jobs being created (and, no, we do not know where they will be) – against concrete and specific costs. It apparently also involves trading 'our people's' welfare against 'theirs'. If the general public is to support liberal policies, it must be given the information and arguments with which to appraise trade policy fairly. This is no easy task intellectually and, for the well-known free-rider reasons, it is unlikely that unbiased information will emerge of its own accord.

Clearly one does not stimulate public debate by requiring, say, that all trade policy decisions be published in the popular press. Rather, one should tell people about their material interest in trade policy – a job for politicians, press and even, possibly, the education service – and then allow access to the means for informed debate. Two sets of suggestions would help in this regard.

First, discussions of detailed trade policy, as well as of grand designs, should be public. The authorities charged with administering LFV and escape clause actions should be required to hear evidence in public, to make all but strictly confidential papers available to both sides and to the public, to produce written analyses of their decisions and to produce annual inventories of distortive policies. Their analyses should include not only repetition of the grounds of the initial petition, but estimates of the costs and benefits of protection nationally and on the various parts of the domestic economy including consumers, users, exporters and non-tradables producers. OECD (1986) and GATT (1985) – the so-called Leutwiler Report – respectively offered indicative checklists of issues to be addressed and protection balance sheets which the trade authorities should be required to complete and publish as a precondition for trade policy action. These would not only inform consumers and other anti-protectionist interests, but also oblige the trade authorities to confront both sides of the issue themselves, at the *same* time and with the *same* set of data.

Leutwiler (GATT, 1985) and the National Consumer Council (1993) both advocate charging an independent body such as the Australian Industries Assistance Commission or US International Trade Commission with the business of collecting, hearing and sifting evidence. The current EU practice, whereby DG I serves as judge and jury is not a good model. It is also desirable that draft recommendations be published prior to implementation in order that public debate may influence the outcome.

The second, and closely related, proposal is to establish a small independent body to represent the consumer interest (see p.24 above) It would be able both to produce general reports highlighting trade policy issues and to fight particular cases, and it should produce an annual report to the parliament or presidency. It would not need resourcing to oppose all trade policy action but rather should select test cases. It must, however, be independent – funded, say, for periods of seven years with a well known, well remunerated but non-renewable Chair – and must have reasonable access to the documents underpinning the cases under discussion. It would be able to monitor the officially produced checklists or balance sheets, but should not be charged with producing them. Overall, this body would be like an 'official opposition', and might possibly operate along the lines of the United Kingdom's Commission for Racial Equality or Equal Opportunities Commission: it would keep the trade authorities on their toes and keep trade policy issues alive in public debate. In trade affairs the closest example is the Australian Industries Assistance Commission (see Long *et al.* (1989)).

As I noted before, when they are pursuing specific political goals, politicians will not welcome interference from such a body. Now, however, before administered protection has taken hold in the CEECs and while there is great interest in market-economy institutions, it should be possible to establish such bodies. Indeed, they would make good cases for technical assistance from the EU or World Bank.

In addition to informing the general public and correcting the market failure which leads the consumer to be under-represented in trade policy forums, institutions must also give scope to industrial anti-protectionist forces. Exporters and import-using firms will frequently have as strong and concentrated interests in trade policy as the protectionist industrial lobbies, and so could offer a natural counterweight. Careless institutional design, however, could undermine their influence. The RTAA and, after it, the GATT were successful partly because they invited exporters into the trade policy debate. By making import liberalization the means to win export expansion, reciprocal trade agreements harness much of the power of mercantilism as a force for good.

When import protection is designed unilaterally, the export interest is as diffuse as the consumers'. Exporting firms, however, will generally lobby only if they are directly and specifically threatened or see direct benefits. For example, in 1984 China suggested that unless it got better MFA quotas in the United States it might buy its wheat elsewhere; suddenly the US farmers became free-traders! Similarly, among the most vocal advocates for the Uruguay Round were the financial services sectors, which thought they saw large market-opening opportunities in the Round. The pernicious element of the United States' 'Super 301' clause, which threatens import restrictions if foreign markets are not opened up to US goods, is that it co-opts exporters to the unilateral import-restricting camp rather than the multilateral, GATT-consistent, import-liberalizing camp. The CEECs, of course, have no potential for such aggressive unilateralism, but the general lesson remains that associating export expansion with threats of import restriction undermines one bulwark against protection.

Similarly, user industries can provide a welcome counter-lobby to protectionism, but only if they see opposition as worthwhile. To crystallize their opposition they should be made to understand that any increased input costs resulting from protection elsewhere in the economy will not be permitted as grounds for protecting or subsidizing them. Such a clause could be written into escape clause law by excluding duties paid on imported inputs from any calculation of injury margins; although such a rule would be viewed as potentially unfair, it would readily point out the costs of the initial act of protection. User industries should have direct and automatic rights of audience in trade policy decision-making. It is not sufficient to argue that they will be heard through a general industrial consultation process, as, for example, Poland and Hungary have for general policy issues (see below). General business forums will be anxious to maintain their solidarity, especially during a transition in which elements hostile to them may still be active, and so will avoid divisive distributional issues. The resulting mutual non-interference will engender universalistic outcomes, as Schattschneider (1935) observed in the interwar United States.

2.6 The CEECs Today

This section briefly summarizes the situation in the three CEECs for which information is available from the GATT's Trade Policy Review Mechanism: Hungary (pertaining to 1991), Poland (1992) and Romania (1992).

To date the CEECs have been moderately liberal in their import policies, although this has begun to look less secure as adjustment pressures have increased. The liberalism has stemmed from the general market-oriented and internationalist sentiment. It has been aided by the fact that trade policy has so far very largely been the preserve of their executives, the rapid speed of transition making it unrealistic for the legislatures to be very active.

In Poland the Sejm (the lower house of the legislature) is responsible for trade policy legislation, 'supervised' by a standing committee. The formulation and implementation of trade policy lies with the Minister and Ministry of International Economic Relations (MIER) acting on behalf of (and, for major issues, subject to the approval of) the Council of Ministers. This Council fixes tariff rates. The MIER is required to cooperate with other ministries and the control of imports is undertaken by an interministerial Special Commission. The Ministry of Agriculture appears to control agricultural trade policy. Policy is subject to judicial review, and to challenge by labour and by business organizations; the Polish Chamber of Commerce is the principal agent for the latter. The importance of these challenges, coupled with the facts that the constitution encourages party fragmentation and a populist style of executive, means that protectionist coalitions could easily emerge. Indeed, since 1991 trade policy has become significantly less liberal. There seems to be no explicit consumer or user representation in administered protection procedures, although the Anti-Monopoly Office makes the preliminary determinations on anti-dumping cases. If this Office is sufficiently independent, this is a useful location for investigations – it essentially starts from the right question.

Poland appears genuinely to split responsibility for trade between the legislature and the executive/bureaucracy. Perhaps for reasons of history its leadership was initially extremely liberal – witness its anxiety to accede to the GATT and sign a Europe Agreement – but this position is now in danger of being eroded. The stalwart use of the Anti-Monopoly Office and consumer representation in LFV cases would help to avoid creeping protectionism, and the GATT and the EU offer some bulwark on tariff and non-tariff barriers. Ultimately, however, there is no antidote to anti-trade legislation other than public opinion, which is currently rather hostile to market-oriented reforms.

The situation in Hungary is somewhat similar to that in Poland, although the GATT records no law on foreign trade later than 1974 (trade instruments are managed by Government Decree) and makes no mention of legislative committees. Trade policy-making is delegated to the Council of Ministers which in turn delegates policy to an Economic Cabinet (under the Minister of Finance) and detailed formulation to the Ministry of International Economic Relations. The latter cooperates with the Ministries of Finance or Foreign Affairs on different aspects of policy, with those of Agriculture and of Trade and Industry in matters of 'concern to them', and with an interministerial Customs Tariff Committee on tariff policy. Representatives of business and consumers attend the latter on an *ad hoc* basis. In addition there is an Advisory Group for trade policy attended by officials, academics and businessmen and a tripartite Council of Conciliation (government, employers and employees) which discusses economic issues and publishes summaries of its plenary sessions. It appears then that trade policy is firmly under executive control and that consumers have much less representation than business. Employee representation is broad based but essentially production oriented, i.e. mercantilist, in focus. It is no substitute for consumer representation.

Of the three illustrative CEECs Romania is at the earliest stage of its transition and appears to have the least developed trade policy-making apparatus. Although parliament is responsible for legislation (subject to professional advice, but apparently not to specialist parliamentary committees), there is no operative foreign trade law at present. Much of the existing, unrepealed law of 1980 has been overruled by Government Decrees, which are frequent and far reaching (TEP, 1994). The executive is, therefore, responsible for trade policy, but it is subject to intense pressures from (state-owned) producer and labour groups. To date this has led more to non-trade measures and the prolongation of export controls, but the potential for import protection at a later stage is obvious. The Ministry of Trade (formerly Trade and Tourism) is responsible for trade policy and for administered protection, but has to cooperate with several other powerful ministries, notably Finance (which is concerned about government revenue), Agriculture and Industry, all of which have interventionist tendencies. The MoT periodically consults economic agents engaged in foreign trade about policy. Business views are not mentioned by the GATT TPR documents, but in fact they are readily transmitted via the Ministries of Industry and Agriculture and the State Ownership Fund for the (small) privatized sector. There seems to be no provision for hearing consumer views.

2.7 Conclusions

This chapter has not defined a unique right way of designing trade policy institutions, but it has set out some principles and identified some pitfalls. The most important of its lessons are as follows.

- Legislatures should avoid product-specific trade policy; sound administrative practice and the use of committees and of rules to limit amendments from the floor help them to do so.
- Detailed trade policy-making should be delegated to the executive.
- Turf-battles about who runs trade policy tend to engender protectionism.
- The executive, and the parts of it which make trade policy, must explicitly take responsibility for *all* the consequences of the policy it makes.
- Administered protection procedures help to diffuse legislative and business fears about trade liberalization, but they must be very tightly managed to avoid creeping protectionism. Among the constraints must be the explicit seeking and recognition of consumer and user-industry views, public hearings and the explicit quantification of the costs and benefits of protectionist measures.
- Officials in sectoral ministries should not have access to trade policy, which should be treated as a whole by a specialized bureaucracy.
- Ministries of Finance and Foreign Affairs should be represented in the formulation of trade policy.
- Public opinion is a vital ingredient of liberal trade; the branches of government should combine to create and support small independent bodies to represent consumer interests and publicize the costs of trade policy; the information on which trade policy is based should be made public; and
- Anti-protectionist forces should be given a specific interest in liberalism: exporters by means of international reciprocity, and user-industries by excluding duties on imported inputs from any calculation of injury margins.
- User industries should have direct and automatic rights of audience in trade policy decision-making.

Notes

1. Even after the CEECs have joined the EU they will have to determine their attitudes towards EU trade policy, despite Brussels' formal competence in the area. All current EU member states continue to devote significant resources to trade policy issues.
2. Bound rates are similarly high for agricultural goods in the other CEECs, but their industrial rates are somewhat lower.
3. Thus one of the two US producers of chloral hydrate in 1929 sought protection, arguing that it employed 'four men in direct operation when in full operation', while the producer of violin chin-rests wrote 'Considering being in this line [purely a speciality of which the writer's father was inventor] the past 42 years being the sole source of income to a family we trust that something will be done,...'.
4. Of course, closing one route to excessive protection is no use if others remain open (Messerlin's substitutability between instruments (see Chapter 3)) so this is a necessary not a sufficient condition for sound policy.
5. Destler argues that the executive's liberalism was strongly underpinned by a liberal elite in Congressional trade policy-making. Thus, while members of Congress were allowed to wax lyrical about their constituents' need for protection, their leaders would prevent most restrictive legislation if the executive failed to. Baldwin takes a less favourable view of Congress.
6. These are safeguards (escape clause) and less than fair value (LFV) protection, the latter in the form of countervailing and anti-dumping duties. Finger, *et al.* (1982), Hoekman and Leidy (1993) and Messerlin (see Chapter 3) all observe that the two forms are highly substitutable, with anti-dumping actions currently the more popular way of gaining protection from imports.
7. In the United States, politicians play no formal role in LFV cases. However, the recourse to voluntary export restraints (VERs) which has now been granted to the US executive as a means of solving trade frictions reduces the de-politicization effect, even if this does not yet seem apparent to the general public. The executive invites the exporters to offer sufficient concessions to enable them to reject a protective recommendation or to persuade the domestic industry to withdraw its complaint. This is basically a political negotiation. VERs, however, will probably be far less important for the CEECs than for the United States.
8. Finger (1992) observes that free trade survived in the loopholes in a protectionist law, not *vice versa*, and that Congress has been busy closing the loopholes.
9. Schapf (1988) notes that, in addition, the EU Council are essentially representatives of their domestic bureaucracies, interested in political and bureaucratic convenience rather than welfare maximization back home.
10. I mean this in a technical rather than a pejorative sense.
11. The increasing tendency in some countries for bureaucrats to drop into lucrative jobs in 'their' sectors when they retire from government service reduces the force of this argument.
12. Wilson (1977) quotes agricultural bureaucrats who say their principal function is to convey agriculture's views to government.
13. The EU does not have a Council for Trade Ministers.
14. Hungary has just abolished its Trade Ministry (see Chapter 4).

References

Baldwin, R. E. (1985), *The Political Economy of US Import Trade Policy*, MIT Press, Cambridge, MA.

Destler, I. M. (1992), *American Trade Politics*, second edition, Institute for International Economics, Washington, DC.

Finger, J. M. (1981), 'Policy research', *Journal of Political Economy*, **89**, 1270–2

Finger, J. M. (1992), 'The meaning of "unfair" in United States import policy', *Minnesota Journal of Global Trade*, **1**, 35–56.

Finger, J. M. (1993), *Anti-dumping: How It Works and Who Gets Hurt*, Michigan

University Press, Ann Arbor, MI.

Finger, J. M., Hall, K. H. and Nelson, D. R. (1982), 'The political economy of administered protection', *American Economic Review*, **72**, 452–66.

GATT (1985), *Trade Policies for a Better Future - Proposals for Action*, GATT, Geneva.

Grinols, E. L. (1989), 'Procedural protectionism: the American Trade Bill and the new interventionist mode', *Weltwirtschaftliches Archiv*. **125**, 501–21.

Hoekman, B. M. and Leidy, M. P. (1993), 'Policy responses to shifting comparative advantage: designing a system of emergency protection', in Stern, R. M. (ed), *The Multilateral Trading System*, Michigan University Press, Ann Arbor, MI. pp. 255–75.

Krehbiel, K. (1987), 'Sophisticated committees and structure-induced equilibria in Congress', in McCubbins, M. D. and Sullivan, T. (eds), *Congress: Structure and Policy*, Cambridge University Press, Cambridge, pp. 376–402.

Long, O. *et al.* (1989), *Public Scrutiny of Protection: Domestic Policy Transparency and Trade Liberalisation*, Special Report, No. 7, Trade Policy Research Centre, London.

Low, P. (1993), *Trading Free: The GATT and US Trade Policy*, Twentieth Century Fund Press, New York.

Messerlin, P. A. (1983), 'Bureaucracies and the political economy of protection: reflections of a continental European', *Weltwirtschaftliches Archiv*, **117**, 461–96.

National Consumer Council (1993), *International Trade: The Consumer Agenda*, National Consumer Council, London.

Nivola, P. S. (1993), *Regulating Unfair Trade*, The Brookings Institution, Washington, DC.

OECD (1986), *International Trade and the Consumer*, OECD, Paris.

Scharpf, F. W. (1988), 'The joint-decision trap: lessons from German federalism and European integration', *Public Administration*, **66**, 239–78.

Schattschneider, E. E. (1935), *Politics, Pressures and the Tariffs*, Prentice-Hall, Englewood Cliffs, NJ.

Shepsle, K. A. (1979), 'Institutional arrangements and equilibrium in multidimensional voting models', *American Journal of Political Science*, **23**, 27–59.

Shepsle, K. A. and Weingast, B. R. (1981a), 'Political preferences for the pork barrel: a generalisation', *American Journal of Political Science*, **25**, 96–111.

Shepsle, K. A. and Weingast, B. R. (1981b), 'Structure-induced equilibrium and legislative choice', *Public Choice*, **37**, 505–19.

Trade Expansion Program (TEP) (1994), *Romania: Restructuring to Face the World Economy*, The World Bank, Washington, DC.

Weingast, B. R. (1979), 'A rational choice perspective on Congressional norms', *American Journal of Political Science*, **23**, 245–62.

Wilson, G. K. (1977), *Special Interests and Policy-Making: Agricultural Policies and Politics in Britain and the USA 1956–70*, John Wiley and Sons, Chichester.

Winters, L. A. (1993), 'The EC and protectionism: the political economy dimension', Discussion Paper No. 865, CEPR, London.

Winters, L. A. (1994), 'The EC and protection: the political economy', *European Economic Review*, **38**, 596–603.

3

Central and East European Countries' Trade Laws in the Light of International Experience*

P.A. Messerlin

3.1 Introduction

In the immediate aftermath of the fall of the Berlin Wall, Central and East European countries (hereafter, CEECs) took dramatic measures in the domain of trade policies. Poland and the former Czechoslovakia (CSFR) eliminated most of their non-tariff barriers. Tariffs became the main instrument of protection of these two countries and they were set or maintained at a very low level: roughly 8% for Poland and 6% for the former CSFR. As a result, in late 1990, these two CEECs enjoyed the most liberal trade regimes in Europe. The same evolution occurred to a lesser extent in Hungary, while Romania and Bulgaria have followed, though with less energy.

The swiftness of these changes in CEEC trade policies mean that most observers did not pay attention to the robustness of the legal background on which these new policies were built. It was commonly assumed that such liberal trade regimes would be rapidly based on an increasingly solid legal basis. The Uruguay Round and, above all, the rapid negotiations of the Association Agreements between the CEECs and the European Community diverted public attention from looking at such an issue more closely.

In late 1990 and early 1991, however, this idyllic 'state of nature' of CEEC liberal trade policies showed increasingly numerous cracks. It became clear that these flaws were greatly increased by a lack of robust trade laws. In early 1991, the first 'GATT Trade Policy Review' devoted to a CEEC (Hungary) provided GATT members the first opportunity to express concerns about certain aspects of

* I would like to thank very much Petros Mavroidis, Peter Naray, Alan Winters and the participants of the CEPR–DG II Joint Seminar on 'Trade Laws and Institutions for Emerging Market Economies' for discussions and very helpful comments on a first draft.

the CEEC trade legal system: the survival of old laws which were merely trimmed of their most direct references to planned economies; and the lack of transparency in the ways effective decisions were taken. Meanwhile, the CEECs' move to less protection was reversed. The former CSFR introduced high temporary import surcharges under a procedure initially unclear (in the end under GATT Article XII). In August 1991, Poland announced a substantial increase in tariff rates which had been reduced only a few months before. In late 1991 and early 1992 more disturbing signals came from changes in CEEC trade policies during the negotiations of the Association Agreements with the Community: the CEECs introduced new trade barriers which targeted certain goods and countries, were rather unpredictable in their timing, and were often large – up to several tens of percentage points in nominal tariffs. Since then, the CEECs' drift towards more protection has continued, as illustrated in this chapter.

How was it possible that CEEC trade policies, which initially were so sound, were so rapidly overturned? This chapter argues that CEEC trade laws suffered from a basic flaw: they did not assess correctly the phenomenon of 'substitutability' in trade matters. First, CEEC trade policies were based on the belief that regional disciplines were a good substitute for nondiscriminatory worldwide disciplines. But, relying on the Association Agreements with the EU (or Europe Agreements, hereafter EAs) and neglecting GATT worldwide disciplines has led CEECs to grant ever expanding privileges – first preferential tariffs, then privileged investment deals, then preferential non-border measures – to an ever narrower set of trading partners: first to all EU-based firms, then to only a few of them.[1] Second, CEEC trade laws ignored the substitutability between the various instruments of protection. Relatively strict anti-dumping rules are useless if safeguards rules are loose or if non-border protection exists: they simply induce CEEC-based firms to use the latter instruments of protection.

The evolution of CEEC trade policies is certainly striking: it is such a dramatic shift concentrated in so few years. But it is not special. It took 20 years for the OECD countries (starting from less open trade regimes) to reach the same point. If nothing is done, the 1990s will probably witness the same evolution among the developing countries which have implemented unilateral trade liberalizations during the late decade.

This chapter looks at trade policies from a liberal point of view. It takes as reference a 'sound' trade policy. It defines such a trade policy as a set of institutions and tools able to produce a cost–benefit analysis of the envisaged trade measures and to take into account the consumers' interests as well as the producers' interests. A 'sound' trade policy is thus not a free trade policy – the chapter recognizes the existence of political costs and acknowledges the necessity to govern under political pressures – but it is a policy which heavily favours an open trade regime because of the focus on consumers' interests.

The chapter is organized as follows. Section 3.2 focuses on substitutability between sources of disciplines by examining CEEC general import laws, including customs laws and rules of origin. Its main conclusion is that regional disciplines were bad substitutes for GATT disciplines. In the CEEC case, this has been exacerbated by the still visible hands of the CEEC states in foreign trade which have been favoured by the low legal status of most of the current CEEC import regulations. Unfortunately, this will have long- term consequences because the CEECs have adopted specific trade measures in order to attract foreign direct investment, causing trade diversion in domestic markets. Section 3.3 examines the substitutability between instruments of protection, including between border barriers and discriminatory non-border taxes. It focuses on contingent protection laws which are likely to be crucial in the future: safeguard, anti-subsidy and, above all, anti-dumping. Despite the fact that cases initiated by the CEECs under such laws are still limited, the CEECs have not escaped the most undesirable outcomes of these laws which have been observed in industrial countries: a few mostly foreign firms are dominant players, the products are similar to those caught in anti-dumping cases in the OECD countries, and cases have been focused on exports from the other CEECs, again exacerbating trade diversion effects. This section suggests a few proposals to keep contingent protection laws under more control in the future. Section 3.4 examines the regulations focusing on exports which have still some importance in the CEECs. The conclusion summarizes the main results and proposals of the chapter.

3.2 General Import Laws and Regulations

Current CEEC general trade laws date back to the period of planned economy: 1974 for Hungary, 1980 for Romania and 1988 for the former CSFR. The most recent general trade law is the Polish Law on Economic Activity adopted in 1988, that is, one year *before* the fall of the Berlin Wall and the collapse of the centrally planned economies.

All these laws have been purged of provisions closely related to the centrally planned system, such as state monopolies on foreign trade or special provisions for trade agreements between planned economies. But none of these laws has been repealed: once truncated, they have been completed on an *ad hoc* basis, with three major consequences.

3.2.1 Low Legal Status under High State Surveillance

The first consequence is the low legal status of existing import rules because of the way the truncation of existing trade laws has been done. If certain provisions have been superseded by more recent laws of higher rank, such as the Constitution, most of the obsolete rules have been simply replaced by governmental decrees or even by mere ministerial regulations. Wide aspects of CEEC foreign trade are thus ruled by legal tools having a very low rank in the legal apparatus of a typical market economy. The CEECs offer a wide range of illustrations of these difficulties, from mild forms to stark illustrations. For instance, the Romanian legal system on foreign trade is a mix of three laws (the Constitution and the laws on foreign investment and on free trade zones), of many governmental decrees (20 decrees between August 1990 and September 1992 ranging from the tariff schedule to tariff quotas) and of a host of ministerial decrees on issues as crucial as contingent protection regulations.

This low legal status of most CEEC trade regulations has an essential corollary: it leaves ample room for highly discretionary decisions from many parts of the executive branch of the government, including from low levels of the bureaucracies. The dismantling of provisions closely linked to centrally planned economies has clearly eliminated the risk of direct and open interventions of state authorities in CEEC foreign trade activities. But it has not eliminated (to say the least) the risk of feudal powers associated with specific sources of rule-making. All these aspects have been well captured by the GATT *Trade Policy Review Report on Hungary* (GATT, 1991, p.8): '...While the most outdated regulations [of Hungary's basic trade law] have been abrogated, its provisions include wide discriminatory competence for the Government in trade-related matters, and a strict separation between foreign and domestic trade.'

This legal structure favours an impenetrable system of relations and coalitions, including between some CEEC public authorities and *foreign* firms. Such a system is capable of both long resistance to change and swift reversals of alliances, of both lasting rigidities and brutal changes. This situation is extreme in the CEECs. But it is not special and it has been observed (and to a large extent is still observed) in OECD countries with heavily bureaucratic states, such as France. This similarity casts some doubt about the possibility of rapid change in the CEECs.

3.2.2 Regional Disciplines: a Bad Substitute for GATT Disciplines

When trade policies are run by governmental decrees which can be quickly changed, strong external disciplines are particularly valuable. The CEECs could rely on two sources of disciplines: the EAs and the GATT.

The EAs could not offer a strong support to CEEC legal disciplines because their rule-making sections include provisions imposing loose (to say the least) constraints, as illustrated by the provisions on anti-dumping and safeguards. In these circumstances, strict constraints on CEEC trade policies would only come from the EU on a case-by-case basis. It is hard to see, however, why it would be so. If EU interests are not at stake, why would the EU want to struggle with CEECs about trade disciplines? And if EU interests are at stake, how could the EU suddenly find the will to impose a clear interpretation on unclear provisions, when it has been unable to impose from the outset a strong and clear wording of the EAs' provisions on the CEECs and on its own member states and firms?

This leaves the GATT as the main external source of trade discipline for the CEECs, who are all GATT Contracting Parties, except Bulgaria. During the three past years, however, this membership has not been helpful, except for the former CSFR, and this exception can be seen as a (maybe impressionistic, yet remarkable) test of the irreplaceable role of GATT disciplines.

The transition to stable and sound trade policies could not rely on the existing Protocols of Accession for the CEECs except the former CSFR because they were written in terms adapted to centrally planned economies, as is best illustrated by Poland and Hungary.[2] The Polish Protocol (signed in 1967) defines trade liberalization in terms of import growth rates (instead of declining trade barriers as for market economies). Leaving almost all tariffs unbound imposed no limits on a reversal towards more protection (except straight retaliation from trading partners). Despite appearances, the situation is not different for Hungary. Although its Protocol is closer to the protocols used for market economies, it contains a discriminatory safeguard clause, initially at the request of Hungary's trading partners afraid of 'unfair' competition from Hungarian market socialism. This clause, however, can also be used by Hungary, and since 1990 it has created in Hungary permanent incentives to launch discriminatory safeguard actions (as shown below).

GATT unbound tariffs have fuelled the high volatility of CEEC tariffs observed since the early months of 1991. As soon as imports have increased more rapidly than exports in the CEECs, protection has been deeply restructured by increases of CEEC nominal tariffs or by the introduction of import surcharges. The bolder the initial tariff liberalization was, the higher the later increases of nominal tariffs were. Polish tariffs introduced by the Customs Law were raised 20 months after their initial reduction, with the unweighted average tariff jumping from 5.5% (in 1991) to 18.4% (in 1992) (World Economy Research Institute, 1993, p.198). The average Romanian tariff applied was raised from 12.4% (in 1992) to 18% (in 1993) by the cancellation of almost all the provisional duty suspensions or exemptions granted one year before. There were no large increases in Hungarian regular tariffs because the tariff decreases implemented in 1991 were moderate (the average tariff fell from 16% to 13%).

The only CEEC which could rely on traditional GATT disciplines was the former CSFR: as a founding Contracting Party of GATT, it enjoyed a Protocol of Accession similar to those signed by developed market economies (with many low bound tariffs in 1990). In addition, it is the CEEC with the most stable protection in the manufacturing sector. When the former CSFR increased its tariff protection by imposing import surcharges for 1991 and 1992, it made clear that it was a transitory measure (with announced deadlines). In 1993 it eliminated these surcharges in accordance with its GATT obligations. Moreover, the only sector where the former CSFR has introduced non-tariff barriers is agriculture, where the attraction of EU policy had no counterpart at the GATT level.

All these evolutions suggest two things: a strong link between CEEC stable protection and GATT disciplines (the CSFR case) and a weak link between CEEC stable protection and the EAs (the case of the other CEECs). As trade policy is only one element of the economic policy of a country, it can benefit from GATT support only if other policies are sound. Differences in other policies may explain current divergences between the successor states of the former CSFR (the Czech and Slovak Republics, hereafter the CSRs) which is suggested by the recent evolution of Slovakia (imposing import surcharges again).

3.2.3 Trade Laws and Foreign Direct Investment: a Gordian Knot

The list of the sectors favoured by tariff rescheduling (cars, agri-business such as drinks or tobacco, cars, consumer electronics, etc.) is highly correlated with the presence of foreign direct investments (and barely related to the presence of state-owned companies). For instance, the four sectors listed above represent 73% of the total (actual and committed) foreign direct investment and 42% of the actual foreign direct investment in Poland (World Economy Research Institute, 1993, p.124).

This correlation strongly suggests that the CEECs have used (and are still using) trade policies as a way of attracting foreign direct investment.[3] This evolution is worrisome because it tends to create noncompetitive domestic markets in the CEECs, and to associate privatization with monopolization. In the long run, these noncompetitive markets tend to perpetuate protection.

The clearest illustration of this Gordian knot is provided by the passenger car industry. All the CEECs have inherited inefficient car makers from the central planning regimes. Some of these firms were already joint ventures between EC and CEEC state-owned companies, such as FSM in Poland (with Fiat) or Craiova (formerly Olcit) in Romania (with Citroen). Others were purely state owned, such as Skoda or Karosa in the Czech Republic. In 1990–93, all the CEEC governments have tried hard to attract foreign direct investment in order to rejuvenate their old firms. All the state-owned producers of cars and trucks have been sold to EU firms (if one excepts the Romanian Craiova which is not sold yet): the Polish FSM and FSO to Fiat and GM-Opel, the Czech Skoda and Karosa to Volkswagen and Renault, and the Hungarian Raba to GM-Opel. No foreign investments in the CEEC car industries include green-field plants, if one excepts the Ford and Suzuki plants in Hungary.

Four types of trade measures have been tailor-made for the foreign car makers investing in the CEECs.

First, tariffs on imported new cars are among the highest trade barriers in the CEEC economies (except for products which are traditionally subject to heavy duties, such as tobacco, wines and alcohol). In Hungary, tariff rates on cars (lowered from 40% to 10% by the 1990 Tariff Schedule) were increased (on 11 February 1990) to 13% (for new cars with catalytic converters) and 18% (for new cars without catalytic converters). In Poland, tariffs have been increased to 35% (with a scheduled decrease in this rate over the next decade).[4] Romanian car imports have been subject to a 30% duty rate. All these tariff rates create strong incentives among CEEC consumers to buy new cars which are domestically produced.

Second, the EU firms which have invested in the CEECs have been able to reduce considerably the risk of competition of imports from other EU firms. The EAs have provisions establishing duty-free quotas for EU manufacturers. For instance, the 1992 EC–Polish Agreement specified that 25 000 passenger cars (with catalytic converters) and 5 000 cars (without converters) could be imported duty-free from the EC.[5] Such duty-free quotas are officially available on a 'first come, first served' basis. The legal rules specifying how to apply for a permit to import cars under the duty-free quota system, however, suggest strong biases in favour of EU firms investing in the CEECs, as illustrated by the Polish regulations. These rules specify that the right to apply for a permit to import is only granted to 'authorized' dealers (with long-term contracts with EU car makers established in the CEEC concerned) or the 'authorized' importers of the EU car makers. Applications to obtain the quota, which include confirmation letters by the EU car makers concerned, have to be submitted to the Polish authorities.

Third, complex rules about the quantities to be imported suggest additional biases. For instance, rules for sales made on the dealer's own account are stricter (in this case, a quota is limited to a maximum of 50 cars which can be renewed only after it has been exhausted) than for sales based on contracts concluded with final buyers (in this case, the number of contracts is decisive) (*Polish Foreign Trade*, August 1993, p.30). The impact of these arcane import rules can only be reinforced by the sales strategy generally adopted by EU car makers. This strategy is based on a system of exclusive dealerships. EU car makers which have invested in the CEECs have inherited well-established networks of dealers and they are likely to dominate the CEEC dealers' networks in the foreseeable future. Thus, it is likely that each CEEC car market will be characterized by one strongly dominant EU firm enjoying a highly monopolistic position and *de facto* benefits from all the tariff exemptions granted by the Association Agreements (with the consequence that CEEC tariff revenues are transferred to EU firms investing in the CEECs).

Another aspect of the tariff policy in the car industry concerns prohibitive trade barriers on used cars, which constituted a large portion of annual registrations in the years immediately after trade liberalization (with peaks in 1991 of 51% in the former CSFR and 59% in Poland). For instance, Hungary has imposed a ban on imports of used cars over 6 years old, and Poland and Romania prohibit imports of cars older than 10 years.

The last aspect of the links between tariff policy and foreign direct investment in the car industry concerns trade barriers on car components. In mid 1992, Poland imposed tariff quotas on components for assembly of cars purchased under license from foreign firms and on assembly machines. These quotas are, in zlotys: the 1992 quota on car components was 4.4 trillion zlotys and the 1993 quota was 8.8 trillion zlotys. The obvious effect of these measures is to boost effective rates of protection.

The discriminatory impact of all these measures is considerable. Fiat and GM in Poland, and Volkswagen in the former CSFR, capture roughly 80% of the registrations of new cars in their respective markets. Ford, GM and Suzuki represent 67% of the Hungarian market, despite the absence of domestic producers before 1989 (CMEA rules banned car production in Hungary).

A particularly worrying consequence of discrimination is the quasi-absence of Asian car makers in the CEECs, despite the successes of these producers in reshaping the US and EU car industries. No Asian car makers run plants in the CEECs, apart from the (relatively modest) Suzuki plant in Hungary.[6] CEEC imports of cars produced by Asian car makers are an abnormally low share of CEEC total imports of cars (between 3 and 5%). Indeed, bitter trade disputes are emerging. For instance, India has requested a GATT Panel in order to examine exports of Suzuki cars from India to Poland (after Poland abolished its GSP tariffs on cars). And non-EU trading partners of Poland have been shocked by the fact that Poland excluded all its car tariff items from the tariff negotiations of the Uruguay Round.

Such trade actions for attracting foreign direct investment seriously threaten the emergence of competitive markets in the CEECs. The corresponding static costs of protection are very high because they are a (square) function of high protection rates and because domestic markets shift from competitive to monopolistic. More importantly, dynamic costs are even larger. These include the long-run protection which will inevitably be requested by these noncompetitive markets and the doubts about the merits of a market economy and privatization that such practices will nurture.

3.3 Contingent Import Protection

One of the most difficult problems that a sound trade policy has to solve is to prevent substitutability between alternative instruments of protection. Firms looking for protection will always try to pick up the instrument which offers the same level of protection as all the others but at lower cost (in terms of lobbying, reputation, legal procedures, etc.).

If the CEECs face the same basic problem as the OECD countries, they nevertheless exhibit some special features. It may have been more difficult in the past for the CEECs than for the OECD countries to substitute non-tariff measures imposed at the border for tariffs. Nowadays, however, it seems easier for the CEECs to substitute non-border measures for tariffs (or for non-tariff barriers) but this may not last long.

The substitutability issue between instruments of protection is especially acute when one takes into account contingent protection, i.e. the set of instruments granting protection conditional to specific events (the existence of dumping for anti-dumping, of import surges for safeguard, and of subsidies for countervailing). As a result, this section focuses on this last set of protectionist devices.

3.3.1 Non-tariff Barriers and Non-border Protection as Substitutes for Tariffs

In recent years, the CEECs have adopted border barriers (often highly discriminatory) as a substitute for higher tariffs. A few barriers were similar to taxes. For instance, Hungary has imposed customs fees of 5% for 'administrative and statistical' purposes; in 1997 these fees will be phased out for imports from the EU, but they are expected to stay for imports from non-EU countries. The bulk of the other border barriers are quantitative restrictions (as already illustrated by CEEC protection on car imports described above). For instance, in 1992, Poland imposed temporary permits (restrictions) on a large range of agricultural goods and in 1993 it introduced tariff quotas (in values expressed in US dollars) on ten groups of electronic components (*Polish Foreign Trade*, April 1993, p.27). Since 1991, the Hungarian global quota on imports of consumer goods has been divided into 15 product groups, with group-specific and, in some cases, country-specific ceiling values (GATT Trade Policy Review, 1991, p.13). In 1992, Romania also introduced tariff quotas on certain goods (wood, furniture and paper, machinery of different kinds).

Non-tariff barriers, however, are less prevalent in the CEECs than in the OECD countries. The limited bargaining power of the CEECs, and the reluctance to come back to instruments associated with centrally planned economies, may explain this difference.

Another explanation may flow from the fact that the CEEC's truncated import rules have maintained a distinction between regulations applicable to foreign trade and those applicable to domestic trade, which is much deeper than the distinction that market economies have. This dual legal system creates built-in incentives to grant different treatment for foreign products than for domestic goods, hence there are opportunities for substituting higher *non-border* protection for reduced border protection.

In the CEECs, this possibility has been reinforced by the fact that many goods produced under the centrally planned regimes were cheap compared with Western goods, partly because they were subsidized and partly because they were unsophisticated. The subsidies will disappear slowly, but the second motive is still at work, and tight constraints on CEEC incomes imply that demands for inexpensive goods in the CEECs will survive in the foreseeable future. This makes product differentiation according to the origin of the products easy. CEEC governments can associate foreign goods with 'luxury' versions of products and domestic goods with 'basic' versions more easily that can be done in industrial countries. This higher capacity of discrimination between goods by origin has led CEEC public authorities to impose 'discriminatory' domestic taxes as a substitute for lower border taxes.

Examples from steel to consumer electronics abound in all the CEECs. For instance, foreign tobacco, spirits, liquors, wines and beers are often subject to special taxes (in Romania, it has been estimated that *ad valorem* equivalents of these taxes range between 100 and 233%). Another illustration is provided by the products standards imposed by Poland and Hungary; these countries have refused to accept foreign firms' self-certification of conformance to domestic standards (thus obliging foreign firms to undertake lengthy testing procedures in the importing country).

This, however, may not last long. The CEEC economies will experience increasing product differentiation, making it more and more difficult for their governments to pursue this kind of policy.

3.3.2 Contingent Protection: Basic Issues

So far, unbound tariffs have allowed the CEECs to use instruments of contingent protection, which dominate the trade policy of the OECD countries, sparingly. This situation will change for two reasons.

First, after the Uruguay Round, the vast majority of CEEC tariffs will be bound, making the CEECs eager to introduce the whole panoply of GATT contingent protection. Indeed, the CEECs are currently actively preparing such laws.[7] This is despite the fact that a GATT member could well sign the Uruguay Round without introducing anti-dumping or anti-subsidy regulations in its domestic legal system. This last point should be emphasized: neither the GATT text nor the Uruguay Codes make anti-dumping or anti-subsidy laws mandatory. These texts leave room for the most economically sound attitude in case of flexible economies (such as the CEECs): to benefit as fully as possible from foreign dumping and subsidies.

The second force leading to the adoption of contingent protection regulations by the CEECs is experience from the EAs. In 1992–3, the EC enforcement of EA safeguard and anti-dumping provisions on Czech and Slovak steel has shown the capacity of these instruments to deliver the exact dose and form of protection wanted by EC lobbies. The lesson has been learned by the CEECs.

The instruments of contingent protection are highly undesirable for the CEECs (as well as for the OECD countries) for two reasons. First, their nature will introduce, as a matter of course, an element of perpetual and unforeseeable change in CEEC import regimes. They can be invoked at any time because they rely on complaints lodged by domestic firms, including domestic subsidiaries of foreign firms. In addition, they provide domestic lobbies the fast additional protection that CEEC general import laws (in the process of stabilization after the recent years of dramatic changes) will no longer be able to offer after the signature of the Uruguay Round by the CEECs. In sum, they put domestic firms in the 'driving seat' for designing measures of protection.

Second, the possibility of 'incremental' changes of protection (first an anti-dumping measure for a good, then another one for another product, etc.) modifies dramatically the balance of forces in the debate about the openness of the domestic economy. It boosts the incentives (as well as the power) of protectionist lobbies to lodge complaints (including a powerful 'domino' effect of requesting anti-dumping measures on related goods). Meanwhile, it tends to eliminate incentives among exporting firms to counteract them (why to bother to oppose anti-dumping duties on goods which are far from the exporters' immediate interests?). In contrast, the discussion of a tariff law allows a government to balance pressure groups in favour and against more openness, and a welfare-maximizing government will act so that these two forces are at least roughly equal in order to be able to implement a sound trade policy. Thus, when implementing tools of contingent protection, a government only faces protectionist groups. That is why contingent protection mostly expands and rarely regresses.

Again, the CEECs are not a special case. A large literature has documented all these aspects for the OECD countries, which have so far been the major users of anti-dumping laws. It can be argued, however, that the CEECs will be hurt more severely by these undesirable features. After the huge shocks of the late 1980s, CEEC economies are less stable and much smaller than the mammoth OECD economies. As a result, pressures for protectionist changes in the CEECs will find less counterweights than in OECD countries, which suggests that a series of 'incremental' changes (for instance, anti-dumping measures) will have a more profound impact on the CEEC economies. Moreover, contingent protection is a concept of managed trade which has the capacity to stimulate behaviour already existing in centrally planned economies. It will fit perfectly the old links between CEEC public authorities and state-owned enterprises (thus slowing down the path to a competition-oriented market economy) or the large foreign investors which are often the heirs of the state-owned firms and which have the additional (and dangerous for the CEECs) skills of experts at manipulating anti-dumping regulations in the OECD countries.

3.3.3 The CEEC Cases of Contingent Protection

Hungary, Poland and Romania all have regulations creating instruments for contingent protection, whereas the CSRs did not. Thus, the existing situation in these three CEECs deserves some attention.

Since early 1991, Poland has initiated two anti-dumping cases (fats and oils, and beef meat from EC Member states), but terminated these cases for the lack of sufficient evidence. In 1993, Poland investigated one safeguard case which was terminated by protective measures.

Since 1992, the Romanian authorities have reported three cases handled on the basis of the anti-dumping provisions. The case which seems to be the most representative of possible future cases involves TV tubes imported from the Ukraine and several other states of the former Soviet Union (hereafter, FSU) during the summer of 1992. This case culminated with the abrogation of the tariff reduction granted for 1992 (the applied tariff was 5%) and a return to the statutory tariff rate of 15% (in October 1992).[8]

Since 1992, Hungary has taken about a hundred safeguard measures (if one uses the same criteria for counting these measures as for counting anti-dumping actions taken by OECD countries). This is more than twice the annual number of anti-dumping cases in the United States or EU. This huge number of cases is due to the wide definitions of the products involved and the large number of countries involved: cement from the CSRs, Romania and several states of the FSU (Estonia, Latvia, Lithuania and Georgia); steel from the CSRs, Romania, Russia and the Ukraine (Austria was initially involved in the complaint); a wide range of paper products (imported from all over the world except EU and EFTA countries); a handful of chemical products (carbamide, ammonium nitrate, calcium ammonium nitrate) from the CSRs, Romania, the FSU and Austria; refrigerator compressors from the EU and EFTA; PVC from the all over the world except the EU; bicycles, water meters and rubber products from all over the world. All the actions listed for the first five products have been followed by the imposition of annual quotas, except for the action on paper (because the domestic firm was closed down) and the action on compressors which has been followed by undertakings (*Hungarian Business Herald*, 1993/4). The remaining actions were still pending final decisions in late 1993.

All these cases lead to three general observations. First, there are already signs that only a few firms – in particular, foreign firms – are active in contingent protection cases. For instance, in Hungary Borsodchem was involved as a user in the paper case and as a complainant in the chemical cases. The complainants in the compressor and bicycle cases were foreign firms (Elektrolux from Sweden and Schwinn from the United States) which have been involved in OECD anti-dumping cases.

Second, it seems that decisions taken in some cases were based only on an 'injury' test, defined as mere price undercutting in the CEEC market concerned, which should rather be seen as competition at work. For instance, the major aspect examined in the Romanian TV case seems to have been the fact that import prices were half the prices of TV tubes produced in Romania, whereas little attention was given to the existence of dumping (the fact that TV tubes were sold on the Romanian market at lower prices than in the exporting FSU states).

Finally, the main targets of all these actions have clearly been exporters from the former CMEA members, in particular the other CEECs. EU exporters have been almost entirely excluded from the cases and EFTA firms have received the same favourable treatment to some extent. These different treatments may reflect different pricing strategies from the exporters involved, but an alternative explanation is that they mirror political concerns related to the CEECs' strong desire to join the EU. In fact, regional aspects lead rapidly to many more complications in the context of contingent protection. For instance, the level of protection with respect to other countries than those initially involved may be increased in order to eliminate trade diversion. This is best illustrated by the Romanian TV case, where the combination of the free trade agreement between Moldavia and Romania and the free trade regime between Moldavia and other FSU states induced FSU producers to export TV tubes to Romania through Moldavia as soon as the statutory tariff was reintroduced on exports coming directly from other FSU countries.[9]

3.3.4 Contingent Protection: How to Limit its Protectionist Bias

A few principles could help to reduce the protectionist impact that these laws will inevitably have on the CEEC economies.

'GATT Consistency:' a Wrong Motto

To be 'GATT consistent' is often mentioned as an argument in favour of introducing contingent protection, and it is presented as equivalent to virtuous behaviour. Of course, it may represent some improvement on current CEEC practices because, up to now (mid 1994), CEEC anti-dumping laws have been written in very loose terms, often not GATT consistent. For instance, the basic Romanian text on dumping (Government decision #228/1992) does not mention the existence of injury as a necessary condition for taking action (in the GATT framework, anti-dumping measures can only be taken if dumping causes or threatens to cause material injury to an established industry in the importing country). The Hungarian safeguard law (Government decree #113/1990) makes no reference to crucial GATT conditions, such as the existence of 'unforeseen developments' or the exchange of concessions.

But to look for GATT consistency would be a major mistake from the economic point of view. Consistency with the minimum standards embodied in the Uruguay anti-dumping Agreement means following the economic logic of GATT Article VI, which is basically wrong. This Article looks *only* at the interests of the import-competing producers, which are *not* the only interests to be taken into consideration in a national economy. The interests of the other domestic producers, as well as of the domestic consumers, should also be taken into account by the public authorities which want to take care of the national welfare.

A parallel may be useful. The logic of GATT Article VI is equivalent to the logic of laws which would state that only landlords could vote on urban zoning or that only the wealthy could vote on taxes. Who would introduce such laws just for the sake of 'consistency'?

This remark has two consequences: if a government wants to adopt contingent protection laws, national laws should do *more* than just *fully* incorporate all the GATT provisions.

A Cost–benefit Analysis: the Need for an Institutional Support

What counts is the country's national welfare: national contingent protection laws should take into account the interests of *all* producers and consumers in order to make a 'national' assessment of measures of contingent protection (instead of lobby-biased assessments).

This means the introduction of a 'national interest' clause in domestic anti-dumping laws, which fits well with the economists' approach of a cost–benefit analysis of protection. This clause empowers the government *not* to impose measures (which would have been adopted under mere GATT-consistent procedures) if these measures would harm the whole economy more than they would help the import-competing interests.

The only experience with anti-dumping regulations having such a clause (the EC anti-dumping regulations since 1969) is very disappointing. The EC anti-dumping office has hardly ever used this provision and it has even been used as a tool for favouring protectionist interests (by defining the 'national interest' as the 'necessity' to maintain domestic firms).

This experience reveals a crucial point: in order to be enforced with the necessary conviction and strength, such a provision needs an *institutional* supporter, the best candidate being the competition office, not only because it follows economic logic, but also because it has an intimate knowledge of many domestic markets from the many competition cases investigated.[10] The Polish anti-dumping law is interesting in this respect. According to this law, the anti-dumping procedure is scrutinized by the Polish Anti-monopoly Office which is by nature prone to take into account the harmful impact of dumping and possible anti-dumping measures on competition; that is, on consumers. Although final decisions are taken by the President of the Main Customs Office, final anti-dumping measures are thus likely to be more economically sound than equivalent procedures enforced in the OECD countries without the help of such an institution. Indeed, the minute number of cases initiated in Poland has led to no measures.

The same observation can be made about a second provision (mandatory under the Uruguay anti-dumping Agreement) which has been often suggested for limiting the harm done by anti-dumping measures to the national economy: a 'sunset' clause which imposes an automatic lapse of the measures after five years, except if review of the case suggests maintaining existing measures. As for the national interest provision, such a clause is of little interest if it does not provide a real opportunity for a *fresh* re-examination of the cases. Giving the reviews of the cases to the anti-dumping office which has investigated the initial case makes it likely that measures will be maintained, as shown by the overwhelming number of reviews in the EU followed by renewed measures. A meaningful sunset clause would thus require an appeal institution which would support it forcefully.

'Supportive' vs 'Benevolent' Institutions

The above discussion about 'supportive' institutions suggests that entrusting *one* institution (even be it the anti-monopoly office) with examining such a complex issue as anti-dumping is likely to be a costly mistake.

This conclusion is of special importance for the CEECs which, during the last 40 years, have developed a tradition of 'benevolent' institutions (such as the Planning Offices) more than a tradition of 'checks and balances' between competing institutions. A good illustration of the intractable difficulties faced by 'benevolent' institutions is provided by Article 6 of Romanian Decision 228/1992 which creates a Price Office with two objectives: to provide information on world prices for Romanian exporters and to provide information about the prices of Romanian imports from the rest of the world. The first goal aims at eliminating the risk that Romanian exporters will inadvertently dump and then be caught in foreign anti-dumping procedures. If one leaves aside the problem of getting information accurate enough to be useful, this first goal reveals the first danger. It attempts to compare export and Romanian prices, not merely to look at export prices. As a result, it induces the Price Office to eliminate all situations of 'price undercutting' by Romanian exporters on foreign markets, a task which could end up by *eliminating* competition between Romanian firms in the world markets.[11] The second goal of the Price Office – to give information on prices of Romanian imports from the rest of the world – reveals a second danger. As it is very difficult to provide accurate, timely and exhaustive information on world prices, this procedure may easily lead to abnormally frequent accusations of dumping based on average prices, not on observed prices, and it could easily make the Price Office an administrative substitute to domestic firms generating anti-dumping cases on an *ex officio* basis. This is improper because GATT tradition requires that anti-dumping actions are triggered by firms which are the only judges. (There is a host of reasons as to why domestic firms may not want to lodge anti-dumping complaints when foreign firms dump.)

Stressing the need for two institutions (the anti-dumping office and the competition office) has an additional advantage. It does not put too heavy a burden on the crucial but fragile institutions that are the competition authorities. Granting the enforcement of the whole procedure of contingent protection to these authorities would generate a high risk of ruining their efficiency (and reputation) for two reasons. First, the competition authority does not make the economic policy of a country: the government does. As underlined by the Polish Anti-monopoly Office, 'requests for import protection should be subordinated to the economic policy of the government', a clear limit to the range of actions available to the competition authority (*Bulletin of the Anti-monopoly Office of Poland*, 1994, p.12). Second, CEEC competition laws often have provisions about 'unfair trade' or 'fair business practices' which could be captured by import-competing lobbies.[12]

Substitutability Between Instruments of Contingent Protection

The various instruments of contingent protection – anti-dumping, countervailing (anti-subsidy) and safeguard – 'compete' for providing the level and type of protection wanted by protectionist lobbies. It would thus be worthless to impose strict constraints on one instrument and not on the regulation of the other instruments.

The Polish system of contingent protection may be used as an illustration of this substitutability issue. Safeguard rules were the latest to be introduced in the Polish Customs Law and, in the case of safeguards, the Ministry of Foreign Economic relations is fully in charge. In 1993, the first safeguard action was initiated and terminated by measures. One case does not allow a conclusion but raises a question: does the absence of opinion by the Anti-monopoly Office make a safeguard case easier than an anti-dumping case? It will be interesting to look at the answer to this question provided by future cases.

If substitutability is taken seriously, it implies that all the contingent protection instruments receive *common* treatment, not only in their capacity to balance the interests of the protectionist import-competing industries and of the other producers and consumers, but also in the general legal regime in order to develop the same degree of resistance to legal manipulation. The best illustration of such a common treatment would be the adoption of an unique criterion for defining the field of investigation, for instance the use of the concept of 'relevant market' (coming from the competition enforcement) instead of the *ad hoc* criteria of 'like product' used in contingent protection.[13]

International Legal Support

The last way to minimize the harm done to a domestic economy by contingent protection measures is the adoption of stricter constraints on the use of contingent protection by a group of countries willing to go ahead in this more economically sound direction.

In the case of the CEECs, this solution may be promising because a large portion of their trade is with the EU. The CEECs could thus request the substitution of the articles of the Treaty of Rome dealing with anti-dumping, countervailing and safeguards for the EAs' looser corresponding provisions. This would be huge progress because Article 91 on anti-dumping, Articles 92–93 on anti-subsidy *and* Article 115 on safeguard are politically *and* economically sound.

This can be best illustrated by Article 91. Its first paragraph makes *political* sense for two reasons. It does *not entirely* exclude anti-dumping actions, so that it is acceptable even by protectionist-minded EU members or CEECs. More importantly, it offers a global political long-term strategy for the decade to come: it opens the door of the Union to CEECs able to sign 'parts' of the Treaty of Rome – making those CEECs who wish to do so become *immediate* yet *partial* members of the Union.

The second paragraph of Article 91 reads as follows: 'As soon as this Treaty enters into force, products which originate in or are in free circulation in one Member State and which have been exported to another Member State shall, on reimportation, be admitted into the territory of the first-mentioned State *free of all customs duties, quantitative restrictions or measures having equivalent effect*. The Commission shall lay down appropriate rules for the application of this paragraph.' (Author's emphasis.)

This paragraph of Article 91, which is often called the 'boomerang' provision, makes *economic sense* both for EU members and CEECs for two reasons. First, it is likely to discipline EU exporters to the CEECs. The emerging intra-CEEC protection described above may be explained by the surge of CEEC imports from the EU combined with the CEEC fear of lodging anti-dumping actions with EU exporters. As a result, CEECs tend to heap safeguards on imports from the rest of the world. Article 91:2 will allow each CEEC to pre-empt 'dumping' by EU firms in their own market and it will contribute to relaxation of protectionist pressures in the CEECs. Second, Article 91:2 will also impose stricter market disciplines in the CEECs. Firms from CEECs often say that their products are dumped in the EU by 'unknown and unscrupulous' intermediaries. Article 91:2 eliminates this excuse: under the authority of such a provision, a CEEC firm will be induced to keep track of its products in the EU markets if it does not want to find them in its own market.

Lastly, the anti-dumping cases which would be handled under Article 91:1 could be subject to the monitoring of competition offices, for instance, by an extensive use of the 'positive comity' approach that the Commission (DG IV) is trying to implement with the United States and Japan. (Indeed implementing the positive comity approach with the CEECs might help to circumvent the difficulties of implementing it with other countries.)

What has been said for anti-dumping could be said with the necessary changes about the subsidy issue: the CEECs could sign another part of the Treaty of Rome, namely Articles 92 and 93.[14] These Articles raise a complex set of issues about enforcement because, in the Treaty of Rome context, enforcing these Articles is devolved to the 'supra-national' Commission. Imposing on the CEECs that the EU Commission alone could assess CEEC subsidies seems difficult. Instead, DG IV (the Directorate in charge of state aids) could be joined by the competition authorities of the CEEC involved when assessing a CEEC's subsidies. Alternatively, DG IV could be joined by a CEFTA competition authority, killing two birds with one stone by creating incentives for direct cooperation between CEFTA members (and moving away from the 'hub and spoke' policy followed by the EU until now). As Articles 92 and 93 are part of the Treaty of Rome which CEECs want to join, the least that the EU could request is that the CEECs behave together, as if they had joined the Union. (Indeed they would have in this domain.)

3.4 The General Export Laws

Centrally planned economies were characterized by barriers on exports that were stricter than barriers on imports. Though most of these barriers on exports have been removed, there are recent signs of the reintroduction of such barriers. For instance, in December 1992 and January 1993 Poland imposed temporary quantitative restrictions on exports of agricultural goods (dairy products, casein) as well as on exports of raw materials (oil, petrol, natural gas). In April 1992, provisions related to the general export regime were adopted in Romania.

Products under export licenses can be divided in two groups: goods subject to quotas for domestic purposes, and products subject to export licenses because trading partners have imposed limited quantities on CEEC exporters through multi-, pluri- and bilateral agreements (dairy, meat, textiles and apparel, iron and steel). The EU, the EFTA countries and, to a lesser extent, the United States and other OECD countries have also done this.

3.4.1 Export Quotas Imposed for Domestic Purposes

There are two major rationales behind this type of export quota: the conservation of natural resources (such as for wood products) and the existence of domestic price controls. The CEECs are generally committed to reducing and eliminating these export quotas through several international agreements, including the Association Agreements with the EU. The list of export quotas for domestic purposes seems still to be long only for Romania. Romanian export quotas range from quotas imposed on raw materials (wood, raw hides), for which the conservationist rationale is dominant to quotas imposed on more sophisticated products (drugs), for which low domestic prices (price controls) constitute the main rationale.

Two general remarks are useful. First, to limit exports puts a cap on the capacity to import. It is thus equivalent to limiting imports. In the situation currently faced by the CEECs, which is marked by an urgent necessity to import equipment and inputs of all kinds, the cost of such export limits is thus extremely high.

Second, alternative instruments may achieve the same objectives at a lower national cost. For instance, nondiscriminatory consumption subsidies on the few drugs considered to be essential could be envisaged. In the case of natural resources, auctioning domestic timber in a nondiscriminatory manner, that is, whether CEEC timber is used for domestic or foreign purposes, would be a more efficient way of satisfying the stated goal of conservation. When property rights on land are more firmly established in the CEECs, auctioning land to enterprises able to take the measures for keeping the stock of timber at the appropriate level could also be envisaged.

3.4.2 Export Restraints Imposed by Trade Partners

Export licences imposed on CEEC exporters by their trading partners (such as the EU) raise the problem of optimal licensing procedures. Currently, the procedures are generally as follows. The authorities announce in some newspapers the list of the customs product codes subject to export licences, the global quantitative limits imposed for each product code, the time limit of validity of the licences (generally six months) and the time limit for getting them. Then, exporters submit applications, in which they give some information on their expected deals: the quantities they have agreed to export and the prices they will be able to charge. In the vast majority of cases, export licences are officially provided on a 'first come, first served' basis and are not 'transferable' (they cannot be sold by the initial beneficiaries of the licences).

This licensing procedure raises two problems. First, it is open to undesirable controls from the public authorities. For instance, the authorities may look at prices indicated in the contracts in order to check whether these prices are close to 'world' prices and/or in order to test the 'seriousness' of the exporters.

Second, and more importantly, these rigid procedures give licences to operators without making them full owners of their licences; that is, without granting the right to sell the licences. Standard economic theory, however, shows that selling rights improves the efficiency of the licensing system, and thus of exporting. The CEEC authorities explain their reluctance to grant such 'transferable' licences by many reasons ranging from morality to credibility. Licence sales, however, are the only way of ensuring that at any time the whole stock of available licences is available for all the potential exporters. For instance, a system of transferable licences allows companies to deal with risk-averse operators (intra-CEEC trade is very risky). Such operators will not hesitate to pay a deposit (if licences are transferable) because they know they could get back the money (or a portion of it) by selling the licences. A system of transferable licences could be combined with a 'first come, first served' procedure for products under nonbinding quotas (that is, with quotas showing low utilization rates). It would be preferable to combine the transferability of licences with a procedure based on 'past performance' of the candidates in exporting products with binding quotas (that is, quotas with utilization rates higher than a threshold, for instance, of 90%).[15]

3.5 Conclusion

This chapter has examined the following question: why did it take only a couple of years for the CEECs' ostensibly liberal trade regimes to be so much undermined by piecemeal protectionism? The chapter argues that the essential obstacle to a stable move towards an open trade regime was the failure of CEECs' trade laws to take properly into account the phenomenon of 'substitutability'. First, the CEECs' trade laws dismissed the fact that relying on disciplines provided by the Europe Agreements was a bad substitute for GATT worldwide disciplines. Second, they have not taken sufficiently into account the potential substitutability between instruments of protection, so that contingent protection represents, and will increasingly represent, a major threat to the existing CEEC trade regimes.

As underlined by Winters in Chapter 2, liberal trade policies were introduced in the CEECs under the pressure of three major forces: the political momentum of reform, the role of certain elites (among them, economists), and the general advice that CEECs were receiving. The two first forces will undergo inevitable changes – some eroding them, other reinforcing them. Liberal trade policies will require actions aimed at keeping these forces as powerful as before.

First, frequent parliamentary elections have a price: losing long-term perspective and increasing the tyranny of short-term interests. As suggested by Winters, there are ways to reduce the intensity of these problems: the use of committees and of rules to limit amendments from the floor will help parliaments to avoid product-specific trade policy. But such rules take time to be implemented, particularly in countries experiencing radical changes in parliamentary majorities in a short period. In Spring 1994, has not the Polish parliament witnessed the introduction of a bill aiming at designing a Polish agricultural policy similar to the disastrous EU Common Agricultural Policy and in collision course with the Uruguay Round Final Act signed at Marrakesh?

Second, the political momentum of reform owed a lot to certain 'elites' (that is, people with some sense of long-term vision) which constituted a kind of 'central bureaucracy' (in the sense that most of these people were not elected). This core group (where economists were influential) which nurtured the consensus about the necessity of new disciplines in economic matters – of liberal trade regimes – will survive only with difficulty.[16] Democracy implies that these elites will be progressively outnumbered by more traditional 'western-style' politicians. And the reversal of the CEECs' trade regimes will speed their fall by exacerbating feudal fights between 'turf bureaucracies.' This problem exists in all countries, but it may be acute in the CEECs where autocratic regimes have generated a tradition of 'turf bureaucracies' particularly able to entrench themselves and to survive in potentially very hostile environments. It will be extremely difficult for markets quickly to eliminate such a feudal system of bureaucratic baronies, as illustrated by Polish Customs. Bitter complaints about the opacity of the Polish Customs have led the government to create 'customs agencies' as a stimulus for customs operations: this use of competition seems to be a mitigated success.

Third, the political momentum of reform benefited initially from huge transitional transaction costs. As it took a while for trade operators to be convinced by the economic and political changes occurring in the CEECs, new trade opportunities have emerged relatively slowly, giving a period of 12 to 18 months to the governments to implement liberal trade reforms without negative reactions. Another illustration of these transaction costs is given by the small number of state-owned enterprises lobbying in trade policies (in sharp contrast to foreign firms investing in the CEECs): many state-owned enterprises have been in disarray when waiting for supposedly imminent privatization, a situation which does not induce them to fight for trade protection, if only because the final set of goods to be produced by the successor privatized firms is largely unknown.[17] Such transitional costs are disappearing, a happy consequence of the CEECs' restored credibility, but a source for future problems.

Finally, it remains to be seen how powerful another challenger of closed markets and turf bureaucracies will become: the courts. As is well known, legal systems are in the CEECs are currently underdeveloped. It will take time to change this crucial feature in countries which have been so much marked by the myth of a 'new era' without conflict. In Hungary, firms excluded from quota allocations can go to court, but they seem not to do so for two reasons. The legal process is slow, so that the costs of going to courts exceed the benefits which could be expected. Second, as import-licensing rules do not contain detailed guidelines about the criteria and procedures for decision-making, it is difficult for complainants to get robust arguments on procedural aspects as well as on substantive issues.[18]

These remarks show how crucial a third force will be for the CEECs: international disciplines, as indeed they were and still are for the OECD countries which have had a long experience of state intervention in trade and industrial matters. This chapter has suggested two ways to make these international disciplines more efficient.

First, the CEECs should aim at minimizing the discriminatory impact of the Europe Agreements in terms of rule-making and rule-enforcing, by using GATT rules instead of Europe Agreement rules as often as possible, including with the EU. Indeed, this is a mere adaptation of the CEEC legal framework of standard economic analysis: uniform tariffs are less harmful than discriminatory tariffs.

Second, the CEECs should also improve EC–CEEC bilateral relations. A powerful move would be to start to improve the Europe Agreement rules by substituting the relevant provisions of the Treaty of Rome for them. In particular, it is suggested that all the existing anti-dumping and countervailing rules of the Europe Agreements be eliminated and replaced by the Treaty of Rome Articles 91 (including 91:2), and 92 and 93 from the Chapter of the Treaty of Rome devoted to competition rules. By signing these parts of the Treaty of Rome, the CEECs will become immediate, yet still only partial, members of the Union.

This last suggestion makes more urgent joint actions among CEECs. The CEFTA Secretariat could receive tasks similar to the Commission, in particular for evaluating state aids, in order to implement the Articles of the Treaty of Rome signed by the CEECs and the Union (with the Commission on behalf of the EU). Moreover, every year, the CEFTA Secretariat could evaluate, under its own responsibility, the trade laws, policies and institutions of the CEFTA countries. As a result, the CEFTA Secretariat would be an institution halfway between the EU Commission (of the early years of the Community) and the GATT Trade Policy Review Mechanism.

Notes

1. For an analysis pointing in the opposite direction (the support that EAs have provided to CEEC trade policies) see Chapter 5.
2. Certain CEECs (in particular, Poland) have understood the danger of the situation: they requested a renegotiation of their Protocols of Accession. It is fair to add that certain GATT Parties have been blocking these renegotiations in order to settle bilateral problems exacerbated by the EAs. Many CEEC trading partners felt that their own interests have seriously suffered from the trade diversion created by the EAs. For instance, the US Trade Representative Office calculated that in 1992, 'US exporters [to Poland] faced a detrimental [tariff] differential of up to 25 percentage points *vis-à-vis* EC exporters.' (USTR, 1994, p.4). As a result, CEEC trading partners were reluctant to offer a botched revision of the Protocols and they felt that the negotiations of the Uruguay Round were the best place for addressing both their bilateral problems with the CEECs and the CEECs' need for new GATT Protocols of Accession.
3. For more detail, see Hindley and Messerlin (1994).
4. According to the *Financial Times* (9 March 1992), it was GM Europe which asked Poland to introduce higher tariffs on cars as a clear condition of establishing its joint venture with FSO.
5. In 1993, these quotas were increased by 5% (Foreign Trade Research Institute, 1993, p.148).
6. And maybe the Korean Daewoo company which is still negotiating with Craiova.
7. According to Czech, Hungarian, Polish and Romanian officials interviewed, contingent protection laws should be ready in all these CEECs by late 1994.
8. The two other cases involved detergents and towels imported from Egypt within the framework of state-trading agreements aiming at reducing the outstanding debt between Egypt and Romania. The import volumes of these two products, however, declined rapidly after the initial import surges; as a result, no official action was initiated and no measures taken.
9. A tariff of 15% was extended to TV tubes exported from Moldavia, illustrating the domino effect of discriminatory measures which increase the costs of a measure that is initially limited. It has been said that this case triggered the fall of the free trade agreement between Romania and Moldavia.
10. In 1990, for instance, the Polish Anti-monopoly Office investigated anti-competitive behaviour in the Polish car market (from FSO) which would have constituted useful background if the Office had been in charge of investigating trade actions in this sector. For an analysis on the

same topic, but from the competition regulation point of view, see Chapter 6.

11. If Romanian authorities were only concerned with 'excessive' price undercutting by Romanian exporters, a better alternative would be to give Romanian exporters detailed information on the risk of undercutting prices by 'too much' in markets protected by frequent anti-dumping actions. Such information could simply consist of summaries of previous anti-dumping cases faced by Romanian firms in the United States or in the EU.
12. For more detail about competition and anti-dumping laws, see Messerlin (1993) and Chapter 6.
13. Competition cases show that defining the relevant market is the most crucial step. Experience with both anti-dumping and competition cases suggests that the improvement coming from the use of such a concept ranges from noticeable (in the case of homogeneous goods, such as basic chemicals) to huge (in the case of differentiated consumer goods). As a result, this improvement will help to minimize the spread of anti-dumping actions in new sectors. In many respects, market relevance may be a strong support to the 'national interest' clause: it comes at an earlier stage of the anti-dumping procedure (when things are still flexible) and it looks a more 'technical' argument – and is thus more efficient for diffusing pressures.
14. As underlined by the Anti-monopoly Office of Poland, 'one of the most important issues the Office faces in the next few years is working out rules for granting state aids.' (*Bulletin of the Anti-monopoly Office of Poland*, p.26).
15. The 'past performance' principle tends to favour well-established exporters and to penalize new competitors who would like to enter the market. If the entry of new firms is seen as a crucial problem for the product considered, an alternative solution is to sell licences to exporters (whether they have exported in the past or not) by auctioning licences. In this case, exporters for whom licences have the highest value (that is, who are able to bid the highest price for them because they are able to extract the highest value from the products exported) will be eager to buy them. It should be recognized that to auction licences requires sophisticated managerial skills from the public authorities because they have to make sure that the auction markets will be efficient.
16. As a result, the future role of the central bureaucracy (in the ordinary sense of the term) will be crucial. Major trade issues could be tackled by a small office under the authority of the Prime Minister. Experience shows that in most cases, a central unit is more open because it is more exposed both to the global realities of the rest of the world and to the wider constituency of the prime-ministership. For a more exhaustive analysis of this type of problem, see Chapter 2.
17. It is fair to add that state-owned enterprises tend to rely on protection based on public subsidies, partly because subsidies were the ultimate system of protection under the former centrally planned regime, partly because this is a form of protection well adapted to firms dominated by labour.
18. Hungary is a good example of transition in these matters. On the one hand, Section 5 of Government Decree 113 (1990) on safeguard measures specifies that 'the provisions of Act IV of 1957 on the general rules of state administration procedures shall be applied with the modifications included in Decree No.1 of 1982 (I.16.)KkM of the Minister of Foreign Trade.' This shows the inertia of the legal system, which plays against an effective role of courts. On the other hand, in the first two years of the Hungarian Office of Economic Competition there have been a reasonable number of cases reviewed by courts, an encouraging sign of an emerging legal order.

References

Anti-monopoly Office of Poland (1994), *Bulletin*, Year 1, No.0, Warsaw.

Foreign Trade Research Institute (1993), *Polish Foreign Trade in 1992*, Annual Report, Warsaw.

GATT (1991), *Trade Policy Review Report, Hungary*, GATT, Geneva.

Hindley, B. and Messerlin, P. A. (1994), 'Attracting Foreign Direct Investment by Trade

Policy', London School of Economics and Institut d'Etudes Politiques de Paris, mimeo prepared for the European Bank of Reconstruction and Development, Office of the Chief Economist.

Hungarian Business Herald, various issues.

Messerlin, P. A. (1993), 'Should Antidumping Rules be Replaced by National or International Competition Rules?', in H. Hauser (ed.), *Competition Policy in International Trade*, Aussenwirtschaft, Heft II/III, September 1994, pp.351–74.

Polish Foreign Trade, various issues.

US Trade Representative Office (1994), *Report on Foreign Trade Barriers.*

World Economy Research Institute (1993), *Poland: International Economic Report,* 1992/93, Warsaw School of Economics, Warsaw, 226pp.

4

The Political Economy of Trade Regimes in Central Europe

László Csaba

4.1 Introduction

The purpose of this analysis is to survey and evaluate the emerging trade institutions in the frontrunner countries of economic transformation. The context of this inquiry is given by the Copenhagen Summit of June 1993, when the EU officially declared full membership of these countries as a commonly shared objective.

With this perspective the following questions seem most pertinent. (1) How robust is the process of trade liberalization launched in 1989 in Central Europe? (2) How important are the Europe Agreements in fostering, supporting and institutionally solidifying this process? Many of those involved, in addition to theorists like Tovias (1994) or Welfens (1993), portray the EU in general and the EAs in particular as a kind of anchor, guiding the entire process of institution building in systemic transformation. (3) What means and institutions are needed to solidify a modern, open market economy in Central Europe and which of them can be employed by the undercurrent of protectionism? Why is the latter so manifest if it is economically so senseless? (4) What – if anything – can the EU do to foster trade liberalization and to counteract reclusive tendencies in the transforming countries? For the time being, there is a danger that those obstacles which will have to be abolished in the case of full membership may be erected in precisely the period of preparation for an Eastern enlargement of the EU.

4.2 Trade Liberalization and Systemic Change

Free trade has a value of its own due to a series of economic and social factors. Very few people with an economic education would doubt this at the theoretical level. Meanwhile, as the fate of the Uruguay Round has clearly indicated, the increasingly *neoprotectionist tendencies* in major trading countries have created a climate which is less than forthcoming to translating this theoretical triviality into commercial policy practices. What emerges here is a hypocritical world, in which customs duties and other transparent trade barriers are bounded by multilateral agreements and are on the *decrease*, while other, non-transparent forms of discriminating against foreign suppliers are on the *increase*. The world over, trade barriers tend to disappear from the shop window of the promulgated trade laws and trade institutions, just to re-emerge reinforced in other forms and areas, which have seemingly nothing to do with international trade, such as consumer protection, observance of health standards or technological prescriptions of various sorts.

In the changing countries of Central Europe a special paradox has emerged. On the one hand, as is both empirically and theoretically demonstrable (Csaba, 1995), economic opening and preserving a free trade regime are at the heart of the transformatory endeavour. It is only free international trade which is able to countervail most of the institutional and other market imperfections in the first transformatory years, from antitrust legislation to creating competition to a heavyweight public sector. Meanwhile, since 1914 the tradition of seeing free trade as a public good has given way to an openly protectionist stance in Central and East Europe, where protecting producer interests and employment, and conserving inherited structures have been elevated to patriotic virtues. Public perceptions have been moulded by this approach for decades. Thus it is unsurprising if the radical opening of 1989–91 is followed by a *swing back towards protectionism* by the mid-1990s.

Opening up these economies after several decades of institutional seclusion was one of the birth pangs the Central Europeans had to undergo when earlier market socialist reforms were radicalized into systemic change. There has always been controversy over whether, and to what degree, such a drastic opening was necessary. Several observers have been of the opinion that opening should have been gradual, quantitative restrictions should have been replaced by customs duties, and even *de facto* convertibility of the currency should have been delayed (Gács, 1991; Szegvári, 1991; Oblath, 1992).

The only country which has more or less followed this gradualist recipe has been the Czech Republic, not known for its radicalism in terms of deliberations. Neither Poland nor Hungary could actually follow this path. In the case of Poland, the accession to power of the first non-communist government was a surprise to everyone. It did not enjoy a parliamentary majority, expectations were running high, and so something dramatic needed to be done which undermined the logic of the planned economy, abolished shortages and imported international price relatives – in short, a clean break with the gradualism of the past needed to be made (Balcerowicz, 1993). This jump, notes Portes (1991), has had the advantage of *precommitting the series of ever-changing governments* to at least the basics of a market-oriented policy line.

In the case of Hungary, gradualism was preached, whereas radicalism was practised. Not because of the particular enlightenment of the socialist politicians of the day, but owing to their total loss of control over processes in 1989. In a tactical effort to rally support behind the ailing Communist party, its general secretary declared the liberalization of tourist travel, with prior consultation of neither with the Ministry of Finance nor with the Ministry of Trade. Since the move was improvised and the credibility of any policy was approximating nil, most citizens were convinced there would be a swift reversal of policy. Thus masses of Hungarians flooded neighbouring Austria to do their shopping as long as the new liberty lasted. Retrospective analyses (Borszéki, 1993, p.49; Pásztor, 1993, p.106;) unanimously talk about a collapse: once the gates were opened and political controls shaken, there was no way back to 'managed opening'.

State monopoly on foreign trade transactions was simply swept away. Due to the dramatic and unplanned nature of this change, there was neither time nor energy left for the bureaucracy to install higher customs tariffs and administer them properly. The reform of foreign trade, doing away with the dominance of 300 large specialized units, was already well under way (Náray, 1989). Therefore there was *no administrative capacity* on hand to control the activities of several thousand already trading companies. Moreover, amendments of the Constitution had just then, in 1989, declared the right of any private agent to conduct basically any activity as a fundamental freedom, and thus the legal base for a reversal was also missing.

One of the interesting outcomes of such an 'inadvertent' opening has been the *lack of disruptive effects on the domestic markets* of the Central and East European countries (CEECs). In the first year of trade liberalization total imports decreased by 20% in the former Czechoslovakia, grew by 1% in Hungary and decreased by 27% in Poland (Gács, 1994). As the same source documents, imports of some items, such as refrigerators, colour TV sets and sanitary chinaware, grew by 4 to 12 times in one leap. It is hardly a surprise that after 40 years of artificial hungering some basic bottlenecks needed to be relieved. In the second year of opening, however, we do not see a surge in importation of these items. As the statistics of Bóc (1993a, p.102) demonstrate, the share of imported commodities in the total retail trade turnover of Hungary accounted for 29.7% in 1991, 27.3% in 1992 and 26.2% in 1993; in terms of value 80% of this in 1993 was derived from changes in the exchange rate. In sum, there is absolutely *no evidence* for imports allegedly crowding out domestic production in the CEECs, which is a surprise in more than one respect. Among other things, it means that it is the level of overall purchasing power rather than any specific trade policy instrument which constrains the growth of imports.[1] This is truly good news, as it used not to be the case in the period of the modified planned economy. It can be taken as an indicator of an emergent real market in Central Europe.

It was political expediency and spontaneity rather than economic calculation or theoretical reasoning which decided the course of opening. Therefore, one should not be taken by surprise that it has been the natural back-swing of the political pendulum rather than anything else which determined the pressures for reverting from the free trade regime. The Europe Agreements played a limited role in the overall process at best. Winters and Wang (1994, pp.32–52) characterize the EAs as an attempt to *minimize* the adjustments the events of 1989 required of the EU. But this thesis applies to the other side as well. Officials in all CEECs have been going out of their way to underline how diligently and skilfully they managed to avoid any sizeable opening which would have done harm to domestic producers, especially in the agricultural sector.

In fact, the EAs have remained much of a side issue. They contained improvements over the pre-1991 *legal* rather than *actual* standing. Further, they contained neither any new financial commitment to be taken up by the EU, nor a firm promise of future membership[2], and there was indeed *no* reason to expect that they should have played other than a marginal role.

As could be expected, the first year of liberalization was a year of enthusiasm and of political consensus: everybody seems to have subscribed to the view that the fallout of CMEA imports and the need to abolish shortages justified an open trade regime. Once the 'honeymoon' was over, however, vested interests – producer lobbies, some political parties and some segments in the state administration – intensified their efforts the 'undo the harm of excessive opening'. This was made possible by the political instability in the region. In fact, none of the CEECs possessed a governmental team and strategy which could have delivered the degree of policy stability which is recommended by modern economic theory.

In Poland governments have been changing every six to nine months since 1989. The October 1993 dismissal of Finance Minister Borowski and his deputy, Kawalec, was followed by a six month interregnum, which is a clear indication of the continued presence of this type of volatility. In Hungary the formally stable coalition government of 1990–94 produced three Ministers of Finance, sharing one common feature: lack of firm backing by the majority of MPs and party gurus. In the new government of Mr Horn, cabinet ministers were airing their deep divisions publicly even before being sworn in, with the new Minister of Industry, Pál, explicitly stating: 'there's no possibility to resolve, only to discuss differences in interest over protecting domestic markets' (Pál, 1994). In Czechoslovakia 1990 was spent discussing what reforms should look like. In 1991, the minimal shock (Williamson, 1991) was introduced, although most of the central government, industry and the Slovaks in particular (Schmögnerová, 1991) have never been particularly convinced of the economic wisdom of the policies advocated by Václav Klaus. Some of them (Adam, 1993) portray these policies as a well-thought-out provocation meant to trigger Slovak secession. Whether or not this is actually true, the fact remains that since the June 1992 elections the breakdown of the federal state has been an accomplished fact.

Managing the breakdown and setting up a new national state rarely entails extreme liberalism in the trade regime, and this held for the Slovak side in particular. Moreover, Slovak political instability has been demonstrated by the quick turnover in key governmental positions and early new elections called for the autumn of 1994. Thus, only in the Czech Republic could one even in theory talk of stability in economic governance (much less in actual policy stances).

A relatively unstable government is of course a call for protectionist forces to come in, and so is a situation in which the rate of exchange is treated as a nominal anchor. Whatever one thinks about the theoretical virtues of 'tying one's hands', the fact remains that stabilization exigencies in Poland and anti-inflationary concerns in Hungary and Czechoslovakia have resulted in deliberately keeping exchange rates stable in the early transformatory phases. With domestic inflation remaining either moderate or high, this resulted in sizeable appreciation of the domestic currency. In Hungary between 1989 and 1993 the Forint appreciated by 47% in real terms. In Poland in 1990–91 17 months produced a 300% appreciation of the zloty (Winiecki, 1993, 1994). The grave trade deficits of 1993 and 1994 both in Poland and Hungary are clear indicators of the dangers of this approach.

All in all, as Tóth (1993) demonstrates in detail, liberalism lasted only for a year and a half. After September 1991, tariff cuts and suspension of duties were discontinued in Poland. Already back in May 1991 a series of tariff and non-tariff barriers to protect agriculture were erected. The new tariff system of August 1991 implied an increase of the overall level of customs and collection was severed. In January 1992 further increases in duties were instituted. The Pawlak government has declared an openly protectionist line, introducing contingent protection and a series of countervailing duties on imported food items. A new interdepartmental anti-dumping office was set up and domestic producers were openly encouraged, even called upon, to make better use of anti-dumping procedures (*Világgazdaság*, 2 December, 1993). The first measures against post-Soviet suppliers of mineral fertilizers have also been passed.[3]

In the Czechoslovak case additional duties were levied on imports, replacing quotas from early 1991 on. These were stepwise reduced as agreed with the GATT in 1991. However, for nine product groups in agriculture new contingents were established in September 1991. From 1 January 1992 coal, textiles and clothing were added to the list of protected areas. In addition, various forms of non-tariff barriers were spreading. Selective protectionist measures were also resorted to (Jindra, 1993, pp.332–34). A 20% extra charge was levied on imported consumer goods in 1991. By and large, the licensing of any transaction in foreign currency remained in effect.

In Hungary agriculture remained protected, especially via licensing and a system of quotas. Since nominal tariffs were still at the low level of 3–15% at the time the EAs were signed, against border rebates of the EU, this was seen to be inevitable. Quota concessions granted to EU suppliers remained mostly below the 1991 levels and for non-traditional commodities only (Meisel and Mohácsi, 1993, pp.121, 130). The pressure of industrial producers to protect their markets resulted in the 1 October 1993 decree of the Minister for Industry, requiring quality controls for all imported commodities to be made at the border of the country. Responding to the uproar of importers even the then Secretary of State for Industry had to concede: his authority failed to notify GATT partners 30 days before the measure, failed to clarify the criteria of evaluation in advance, and even failed to promulgate the measure (Balázs, 1993). This did not invalidate it, though implementation has been softened considerably. Contingent protection for consumer goods is alive and well. Here the increase of procedural protectionism and the use of specifications reflecting some particular producing interest rather than current account considerations have become manifest in the course of 1994 (Borszéki, 1994).

All in all, it was political expediency rather than a firm economic platform which launched trade liberalization. It was equally political motivation that lay behind the move towards protecting the domestic markets. Due to their limited nature, the EAs proved an insufficient deterrent from doing something which ultimately hurts the societies themselves. Well-organized producer lobbies and the bureaucracy searching for its new role proved to be stronger.

4.3 The Lobbies

The role of lobbies in the state socialist period is a well researched subject (Szalai, 1991). Large firms in some sectors of business, especially in priority industries, but also in agri-business, penetrated the highest decision-making organs of the party state. More often than not their interests and priorities were translated into actual decisions, for which ideology provided only a thin camouflage.

With the collapse of Comecon and of the one party state, a peculiar situation emerged in Central and East Europe. Because of their strong integration into the outgoing power structures, priority areas and large firms often found themselves defenceless: subsidies were cut, trade regimes opened and their secure markets gone. In the first months of disarray, reformist governments could indeed make great advances in legislating market-conformable institutions and arrangements: structural adjustment had started. As employment started to follow output losses, however, after a delay of some two years, resistance to the open trade regime started to gather momentum. It is hardly chance that the Czech Republic has encountered the smallest resistance to the open trade regime to date. In this country unemployment is still only about 4% and the drastic devaluation of 1991 still offers considerable across-the-board protection for many sectors in the domestic market.

Old lobbies were soon complemented by new ones. Privatization, or at least top-down privatization conducted by the respective governments of the region, aimed to create new owners via a variety of methods. Whatever the method of creating the class of new owners – voucher privatization, restitution, small investors' programmes, employee stock ownership programmes or leveraged management buy outs – one thing has been common. No new money, management skills or technology have been infused into the new establishments. In other words, these 'real owners' – though much praised in some of the theoretical writings on 'transition' – have a lot in common with the new owners created by the land reforms of the Third World, namely that they have not evolved as the result of market forces, but have been imposed by the state. Thus there are a number of reasons to expect them to be the weak partners in the market game, prone to seeking protection by a public authority, as in infant industry and supply-side arguments for protection

In all four Central European countries, governing parties have shown great concern about creating a 'national' middle class of proprietors tailored to their own tastes. The fight against the *nomenklatura*-managers, the fear of the return of the Germans, and the charge of selling the family silver to aliens all lead to a climate hostile to capital account convertibility.

Market reforms have cut back the room for state discretion. Financial funds of the sectoral ministries have been curtailed or abolished altogether. Meanwhile, employment in the state administration has hardly been reduced. It is not by chance – indeed, it is quite in line with Parkinson's law – that these ministries look for problems that they can take care of.

Inefficient companies are very well suited to becoming subjects for caretaking. In addition, the need to take into account sectoral or regional specificities, to elaborate *transitory solutions*, or operational crisis management are proven ways for the administration to regain its discretionary power. The quality control measures or the high profile of anti-dumping are of course good examples of this. Remaining with the former, there is a world of difference between making a producer liable for any adverse consequences of his product in terms of personal safety or environmental impact, and deciding whether or not the quality of a given product is 'appropriate' for admission to the country.

Analyses of consumer goods markets in Hungary, whether protected or unprotected by quotas, do not show marked dissimilarities, as in both cases it is effective demand rather than anything else which constrains sales. No empirical evidence has been found for the thesis that these quotas were defending the balance of payments rather than *particular producers*. On the contrary: the marked presence of light industry, food industry groups' priorities and commercial policy deliberations were demonstrable (Borszéki, 1993, p.52). The changing parameters and deadlines for decision and the procedure of interdepartmental coordination are well-known levers in the hands of the administration trying to exert discretion in the name of macroeconomic equilibrium.

4.4 The Case for a Special Agency for Free Trade and Harmonization with EU Arrangements

What has been described above is indicative of free trade being a public good under constant threat in Central and East Europe, which is not being taken care of by anybody. Like fair trading, prohibition of child labour, or observance of environmental standards, an open trade regime does not emerge from the spontaneous workings of the market. The Czech Republic and Slovakia do not have a foreign trade agency, and Hungary's MIER was abolished from 15 July 1994. Many observers believe that the Ministry of Finance, the Ministry of Industry, the Competition Office and the Ministry of Foreign Affairs are just enough to take care of the issue. In the following, some arguments are advanced to support a different view, namely, that protectionism does not need an agency to administer its many intricacies, and can in fact flourish among the departments. Meanwhile, a commitment to free trade and the job of orchestrating congruence between domestic and EU legislation does require cross-sectoral overview and organization.

At the start of this chapter a passing remark was made of the new wave of undercurrent or covert protectionism in international trade. The same can be said about the Central European countries. If attention is focused narrowly on trade laws and trade institutions proper, most of the already proliferating protectionist features characterizing a large body of the newly emergent legislation would be lost. In fact, the prospect of eventual full EU membership might be the best way to streamline new legislation and short-cut the already discernible blind alleys.

Let us survey some developments in sectoral legislation which have seemingly nothing to do with trade laws and institutions, but which still have a direct bearing on the scope and on the workings of the latter.

a) *Labour legislation* is part and parcel of the unwritten social contract in any country. In the early 1990s several transforming countries started to import the institutions of tripartite coordination of interests. By and large they imported at least the philosophy behind the Social Chapter of the EU. The new Hungarian and Polish governments are particularly impressed by the virtues of this arrangement.

As is known, corporatist practices of setting wage rates favours the less skilled, the less organized and the low-productivity sectors. These arrangements not only constrain international competitiveness, but nearly always automatically require protection from social dumping of countries with less elaborate labour legislation. If CEECs import these institutions they will not be sufficiently competitive and, moreover, these arrangements will automatically require a protective trade regime, not only against low wage countries, but also against more competitive, more productive nations.

In sum, the premature importation of institutions from the EU may itself become an obstacle to a smooth integration to the EU, whose outer circle is of course trade. As evidenced by the story of Eastern German provinces, early copying of social institutions may lead to output and employment losses as well as to severe constraints on new private ventures, especially in the small-scale sector. Since the CEECs *cannot* expect transfers comparable to East Germany, it would be extremely harmful if the dynamic sectors of their economies were limited by the new labour and, indirectly, trade arrangements. If and when institutional imports in this area become feasible, this will certainly be *after* full membership, i.e. by the time economic adjustment has been mastered. Sequencing mistakes, on the other hand, may backfire in the association phase, i.e. prior to accession. As Hungary formally signed the Social Chapter in December 1991, this is surely not mere speculation.

b) On the employers' side an important arrangement limiting competition can be the *law on chambers of industry*, requiring compulsory membership. This is the case, for example, with the law passed in March 1994 by the Hungarian parliament, effective from October 1994. Depending on the method of application, this arrangement might be a severe limitation on competitors, be they small newcomers or foreigners – just as was the case in the interwar period (Bóc, 1993b). This is of course not a directly commercial issue but, in terms of the four freedoms, or in terms of sectoral discrimination, it certainly can be.

c) *Legislation on land* prohibits foreign ownership in all four countries. This is a greatly emotional issue with very little economics behind it. Knowing the actual conditions of return, few people in their right mind would rush to buy up arable land in the Great Hungarian Plain. But in Bohemia and, to some extent, in Poland an irrational fear of a German *reconquista* of these countries exists. In Hungary, joint ventures can buy everything, and with a special permission from the Ministry of Finance a 100% foreign-owned company can buy all the land it needs. The July 1994 amendment of the Law on Land allows legal persons to obtain land, thereby getting around the restriction mentioned above.

d) *Consumer protection* is normally seen as a perfectly legitimate concern in a civilized market economy. As evidenced by the quality control measures criticized above, however, this may just be a way of erecting non-tariff barriers. For instance, in the new standards introduced in the Polish cosmetics branch, legislators openly aim at protecting, not only consumers, but producers as well: besides quality certificates, an import licence, a certificate from the public health authority and a Polish language description of the product are all required (*Világgazdaság*, 18 January 1994). Likewise, Hungarian producers of yoghurt could impose licensing on imported brands, which they described as having an artificially lengthened life cycle, lacking biological values and 'physiologically ... nothing to do with the notion of yoghurt proper' (quoted in *Világgazdaság*, 6 January 1994). Some analysts (e.g. Török, 1992, 1994) see this form of protecting the market as modern, sophisticated and worthy of emulation across the board. This approach, however, might turn out to be counterproductive earlier than many would think. When some Hungarian industries attempted to go this way, they have found themselves unable to meet their own standards (*Figyelô*, 1993/43). The latter case already foreshadows the dangers inherent in the lack of transparency, i.e. the danger of deals behind closed doors and enhanced discretion by the authorities.

e) *Anti-dumping* is something that needs no advertisement in the EU. Polish and Hungarian producers have tried to make use of this weapon, both against each other and against suppliers from the former Soviet Union. Quotas on cement and steel in Hungary, and on mineral fertilizers in Poland have indeed been imposed. One of the problems which has been found in practice is the need for sophisticated documentation, up-to-date statistics and intelligence in making use of the legal machinery. One of the recurring problems in Hungary was that firms were complaining generally of low prices, or prices lower than their own production costs, rather than that the prices were below the prices of the supplier's domestic market (Juhász, 1993). Proving the latter might not be easy, and thus companies prefer quotas and licensing.

f) Formally, convertibility may appear to render speculation on the *law on currency management* immaterial. But this is not the case, since in practice many restrictions continue to limit the freedom of entrepreneurs, both foreign and resident, whereas the discretionary power of the bureaucrat remains sizeable. The Currency Code elaborated in the National Bank of Hungary (cf. *Napi Gazdaság* and *Magyar Hirlap*, both 4 February 1994) and to be adopted in the second half of 1994, retains a large number of limitations which only serve bureaucratic convenience or may be liable to discriminatory interpretation. For instance, it remains obligatory not only to keep export revenues in Hungarian banks, but also to convert them into Forints. This brings sizeable losses for large exporters, due to the high margins between purchasing and selling rates. Forint accounts for foreigners are allowed, but their uses are still restricted by a number of – easily circumventable – regulations. Establishment of any venture by Hungarians abroad continues to be liable to licensing. Such permission can be declined if the firm had in the preceding five years any arrears in tax, social security or customs payments or was fined by the tax authority in this period. Obviously, if taken literally nearly anybody can be excluded from this activity.

g) *Technological specification* is known to be a means many advanced economies use to filter out unwelcome competitors from abroad. This method has been well digested by the transforming countries, as in the case of Ford Transit vans in 1992. Then Hungarian quotas limiting the imports of cars were specified so that only this particular model was exempted. When the policy produced a public uproar, a high official justified the procedure with reference to international analogies and the need to support serious large investors against non-serious adventurers. In any case, the dormant competition law was activated by the interested parties and the Competition Office restored neutrality by outlawing the discriminatory treatment. This was an example of a procedure that operated when commercial policy was conducted in formally quite unrelated areas.

h) The new *Public Procurement Act* elaborated in Hungary in 1994 and in effect in Poland since 1993 constitutes a prime example of discriminatory treatment against foreigners. The Ministry of Transportation has also issued guidelines requiring public officials to fly national airlines and to buy locally produced cars. Although these malpractices are far from unknown in some of the most advanced nations, one wonders whether it is rational for CEECs to erect barriers which they will have to demolish during or after accession to the EU. The distortionary effects and welfare losses incurred by those indulging in these practices are well known, thus prospective EU membership is probably a potent and convincing argument in pre-empting the emulation of inefficient and trade-distorting practices.

This list is not meant to be exhaustive, but it illustrates our point. For free trade to be crowded out, there is no need of a special agency. To let legal and systemic arrangements evolve in a chaotic fashion, incongruous with both EU practices and among themselves, does not need a visible hand or concentrated mental effort. To do the opposite does. Let us now list some of the agencies which are around in any government and which may be able to do the same job!

1. The *Ministry of Foreign Affairs* used to administer international trade issues in the interwar period. Judging by experience, however, foreign offices are often staffed with economically ignorant people who are, by and large, insensitive to the issue and relevance of free trade. With a non-economic background coupled with an assertiveness on national issues, these people stand a good chance of falling victim to the deceptive arguments of the protectionist lobbies. As seen at the outset, in Central and East Europe being patriotic nearly automatically equals being statist and protectionist on economic issues. This is a typical Olsonian case: producers are always well-organized national constituencies, whereas consumers are by definition disorganized, widely dispersed and cosmopolitan. Left on its own, a traditional foreign office line is almost bound to be forthcoming to protectionist arguments.

2. The *Ministry of Finance* is normally seen as prone to liberalism. One should not, however, neglect the fact that in Hungary in 1993 10% of budgetary revenues stemmed from customs duties, against the 4% average of OECD countries (Kamasz, 1994). Since 95% of customs duties are already bound by multilateral treaties, this relevant source of revenue may fall at a time fiscal overspending has become a problem, as it has in Slovakia and Poland. Thus, the dynamics of domestic debt and its servicing requirement will become an explosive issue soon. It is only right that the Treasuries in all of these countries have a keen interest in retaining and replacing the customs revenues (Beszteri, 1994): a propensity to introduce fees and charges of various sorts, requiring deposits and fines, and levying taxes of various sorts in several phases of turnover will surely not disappear. These enjoy the advantage of not being subject to international coordination and surveillance, unlike subsidies. All in all, there is more than one reason to fear the

re-emergence of a truly baroque fiscal bureaucracy in the place of diminishing tariffs. Therefore there is no reason for us to expect the Treasury to become the guardian of economic liberalism in international trade.

3. It is hard even to conceive theoretically, but 'practical men' do support the idea that the conflicting interests of free trade and protecting domestic industries should be represented jointly by a single *Ministry of Industry*. This line of thinking (e.g. Farkas, 1994) calls for a 'unitary treatment of external and internal markets', and believes that a separate trade agency is intimately related to state trading practices. This is more or less the opposite to what we know and unfold in this chapter. For one, it is a bureaucratic rather than a market system, where the pattern of governmental agencies can be chosen at will. It is there where the institutional separation of domestic and foreign markets makes it irrelevant whether otherwise conflicting interests of home and foreign suppliers are represented in and by a single agency. Only for price-insensitive socialist firms is it unimportant whether supply (producer) or demand (consumer) considerations get institutional backing from a governmental agency. In practice the option of combining trade and industry chosen by the Horn government combines the disadvantages of several solutions.

In the Foreign Office, trade issues will inevitably suffer. Experience taught Hungarian business executives, especially of small and private firms, to keep embassies at arms' length. In the Ministry of Industry and Trade industrial interest is bound to dominate as the latter is organized into lobbies and represented in the tripartite coordination for obvious reasons, whereas gains from free trade seem abstract and long term, and consumer interest is always dispersed, poorly organized, and thus bound to suffer. At a time of depression industrial interest is every bit as protectionist as agri-business.

4. In theory, the *Competition Office* could take over the functions that this analysis would like to be located in a separate governmental agency for free trade and harmonization of legislation. In practice, however, the Competition Office is constrained both by its statute and its philosophy. On the export side, the bigger the better is an established argument for saving any monopoly from persecution. On the import side, gains in market share are more often than not seen as a threat to national interest if registered by foreigners. In major privatization deals this agency is either not or only formally involved. As illustrated by the Ford Transit case, this agency becomes active only if competing interests themselves take care of activating it, which is the inverse of the dynamics required from a free trade agency.

5. Monetary and especially *exchange rate policy* could in theory do a lot. Since there is, however, an inherent tendency to see the rate of exchange as a kind of national symbol (Klacek and Hrncir, 1993) there is a very low probability that this instrument will be manipulated according to free trading concerns. This is probably the most powerful of our arguments favouring a special free trading agency. The requirement of sequencing in the process of approximation to the legal arrangements of the EU is a further argument along the same line.

6. *Legislative organs* in Central and East Europe are quite unlike the US Congress, for good or bad. Discussion of economic issues, be they the budget or international trade, are conducted among empty rows. Thus it is unrealistic to expect that the supreme organ of legislation will take care of legal harmonization and securing the free trade regime. In an institutional vacuum nobody is in charge, and events follow their own logic. This evolves towards protectionism without any proclaimed policy turn, out of the logic of case-by-case political decision-making. The required conceptual clarity can hardly be operationalized without institutional backing, i.e. an agency able and interested in preserving free trade and fighting through this requirement in the daily treadmill of interdepartmental bargains.

7. Our analysis highlights the following findings. First, free trade is not a free commodity produced 'by nature' in unlimited quantities. It requires institutional backing, especially in transforming economies. Second, it is not at all irrelevant what governmental department takes care of this problem. Our far from exhaustive list of possible options cautions against locating the trade agency within the strongholds of competing or conflicting interests, such as the Treasury, the sectoral organs or the Foreign Office. Third, though the considerations advanced above do not suffice for a generalized model of a transition country, the special circumstances of the CEECs seem to make it expedient for them to merge the preservation of liberal trade with their prospective EU accession. This would call for a separate agency.

This could be a Department of European Affairs, possibly a very well staffed and trained International Department in the Ministry of Justice, as much of the actual work of law harmonization entails work on the detail. In this case, however, transatlantic trade, GATT and IMF affairs may become a coordination and competence sharing problem within the administration. Better suited to the latter would be a relatively small trade agency under the Prime Minister's Office, with far reaching decision-making and initiating competencies, but here the legal aspects become problematic. Experiences with similar agencies, especially during the 1980s have demonstrated the relative weaknesses inherent in this choice. Wherever the group is located, however, regular involvement of EU partners of various sorts and the experience of regular encounters with the law harmonization and accession issues may make these agencies more committed to the idea of free trade than their predecessors were, or more committed than if they were located in an office preoccupied with home affairs.

4.5 Agriculture as a Potential Stumbling Block

In the postwar period international trade has been evolving towards liberalization, even though only gradually and with many reversals. The major exception from this general rule is farming. In the end it is the lack of a free market within the major trading nations, even the United States, which explains why international exchanges cannot be liberalized. In the context of the present inquiry our basic thesis is the following. The arrangements of the Common Agricultural Policy (CAP) meet equally non-free-market arrangements on the side of CEECs. *The encounter between two non-market systems is rarely smooth or cooperative.*

Agricultural markets are accepted to be non-self-regulating owing to seasonality, the use of a lengthy chain of cooperation and the perishability of products. Besides, in the EU in particular a definite societal vision has been instrumental in shaping policies (Lányi and Fertô, 1993, pp.35–6): limited fluctuation of prices and a stable income position for the farming population figure high in the aims of policy-makers. In other words, since the mid-1960s a series of non-economic considerations have supplanted business considerations, such as environmental concerns, taking care of human resources, defending the values of local societies, cultural concerns and regional considerations. The problems of urbanization and the resurgence of part-time farming can also be added to these.

The CAP is often portrayed as a reflection of social priorities favouring family farming and the healthy modernization of rural areas. Several analysts are thus of the opinion that the CAP is a success story worthy of emulation. Indeed, representatives of agri-business portray a potential accession to the EU as an unprecedented modernizational push, which would mean a tenfold increase in the subsidization of Hungarian agriculture, thereby creating the foundations for an overall modernization (Varga, 1992, p.60).

This is precisely what frightens opponents. Based on the implausible assumption of an *en masse* CEEC accession to the EU under current unreformed conditions, Anderson and Tyers (1993) arrive at a cost of an extended CAP alone exceeding net inflows from Northern enlargement by 25%. This is yet another indication of the limits to generalizing available EU arrangements in the future. It also reflects a typical outcome when two socially motivated systems meet at the marketplace. But this is merely an intellectual exercise, and not a forecast of any future scenario.

Alternatively, one could conceive a generalization of the Polish model of creating a large number of small farms by a vigorous privatization programme in other CEECs.[4] This results, as could have been expected, in an extremely protectionist stance, which had made its way into Polish trade policy well before Mr Pawlak took office. From this perspective, the failure of Hungary's conservative governments to replicate the Polish model through land reform must be seen as encouraging.

From the perspective of trade institutions the two fundamental issues are the macroeconomic share of agriculture and the forms of market regulation that take the place of commands. Only a much smaller and more market-oriented agriculture allows for more flexible arrangements and policies to evolve. From this particular angle the agricultural slump of the last few years has taken care of much of what would have been politically next to impossible, had there been more stable conditions of rule in Central Europe. For instance, in 1993, according to the data of the National Bank of Hungary, agriculture accounted for only 7.5% of the country's GDP, or half of the 1990 figure.

On the institutional front fewer bright spots are around. Polish agriculture, though privately owned, was known to be an integral part of command structures. Crippled by decades of underinvestment and a lack of institutional and financial infrastructure, Polish farming is more akin to a developing country model than to a West European model. Overemployment and the resultant protectionist pressures are the consequences.

Talking about Hungary, it is often forgotten that farming was basically spared from all socialist reforms, and quantitative growth was achieved while disregarding the needs of external markets (Lányi, 1992). With the collapse of the old regime the Ministry of Farming has centralized foreign trade, supports, quotas and licensing, whereas 'marketing boards' have also become a means of consolidating existing large firms and transmitting bureaucratic priorities.

In 1991 the broad guidelines, and in February 1993 the detailed setup, of the agricultural market order were introduced in Hungary. These employ the entire arsenal elaborated in advanced countries. Very little move towards an actual market infrastructure and an appropriate informational system has been made, however. Analysing the outcomes, Halmai (1993, pp.200–201) noted some fundamental shortcomings. Instead of fostering real market contacts, authorities tend to limit them. Guaranteed prices proved to be expensive and hard to operate. Application of quotas and set prices proved to be a failure. Interventions often amplified rather than mitigated market fluctuations. In the foreign trade area, both exporting and importing possibilities are determined by bureaucratic bargains among the departments and with the marketing boards, and not by efficiency considerations. Until now, reliance was placed on the crudest means of regulating international trade, i.e. licensing and quotas were excessive.

From the latter perspective, the successful conclusion of the Uruguay Round may bring about some favourable change. On the one hand, it will limit the possibility of applying NTBs on the grounds of unproven rumours of epidemics, as was the case in the EU at Easter 1993. On the other hand, in the process of transforming administrative barriers into customs, the average tariff level of Hungarian agriculture may be enhanced to 45% from 20% before tariff cuts start. (Raskó, 1993). Even after the full transitional period Hungary will have some agricultural tariffs in excess of 70%.

There is a consensus view among observers that imports should play a complementary rather than competitive role on the domestic markets of agricultural produce. In order to allow a more flexible trade regime, this philosophy is in need of revision both on the EU and the Central and East European sides. As long as self-sufficiency remains a virtue and only surpluses are exchanged, any liberalizing step is bound to be undermined by two concurring protective safeguard clauses. Needless to say, in the EU it is the interests of taxpayers and the vast majority of consumers which calls for reforms rather than a potential enlargement towards the East. And, conversely, it is basically efficiency considerations and the interest of the vast majority of Central Europeans themselves which call for letting market forces operate in the CEECs. Only this could lay the foundations for a change not only in the forms but also in the level of agrarian protection.

In order to attain this, in the case of Hungary several *reform propositions* have been made (Szabó *et al.* 1994, pp.41–3). These all aim at reducing direct governmental interference, including reducing quotas, price fixing and licensing. A paradox lies in the following: more sophisticated forms of market regulation presume the functioning of a system which is in its infancy at best. The transparency, as well as the institutions typical of modern agricultural markets, are yet to be brought about. One of the important tasks of the state could be to organize these markets and the channels of information. For this, EU assistance in taking over product standards and the system of qualification, quality control and competition rules could indeed be instrumental and mutually beneficial.

One wonders how reasonable is the call voiced by most agrarian specialists in the region that a system of border rebates could, and indeed should, be introduced. If one thinks, however, that it is the future rather than the present EU arrangements which should be targeted, enthusiasm for this option may vanish. Meanwhile, it is not very easy to adjust to a system whose basic qualities still seem to be disputed by the member states of the EU. The present institutional flux can be grounds for some optimism: it may not be inevitable that inward-looking self-sufficient development variants are replicated either side of the continent. Thus the forthcoming reforms and the ongoing spontaneous adjustment may take much of the strain that the mechanistic extrapolation of current arrangements indicates.

4.6 Export Promotion: Limited Efforts, Limited Results

In the Central European countries there is very limited understanding of the uses of the arsenal of export promotion that characterizes contemporary international trade. In a typical view (Jindra, 1993), any special support for sales abroad is distortionary and as such should be avoided; but if it has not happened yet, this is only due to the time needed for any transition to materialize. Since state regulation via a plethora of direct and indirect means used to be a typical feature of command planning, further theoretical models on international trade mostly do not include these instruments. The view of abolishing all state interference in foreign trade has enjoyed much popularity in Central Europe. Others remind us of the potential danger of corruption as well as the threat if these become captured by particular firms or interest groups, as in the United States or in the United Kingdom.

In Hungary, the Ministry of Finance tried to compensate for its unsuccessful fight against the proliferation of special funds administered by various state organs other than the Treasury while subject to very limited parliamentary and public control, by across-the-board cutbacks and recurring attempts to merge all special funds into the Budget, thus concentrating all discretionary power into its own hands.[5] Since the use of trade promotion is not trivial for the general public at times of stagnant real incomes, fighting the special funds of the MIER has become a pet project of the Treasury. Though it has not succeeded in abolishing all relevant funds, the fight left Hungary among the trading nations spending the least, about 0.15% of its GDP, for this purpose.

This is problematic, insofar as (1) it is several times less than the percentage typical of large trading nations; (2) it is insufficient to compensate for the competitive logistic disadvantage of small firms, now dominating external economic activity; (3) it exacerbates problems deriving from the backwardness of overall domestic market infrastructure; (4) it makes it more difficult to enter new, distant overseas markets which expand more dynamically than those in Europe; and (5) it makes it hard to improve export patterns and switch over to the sale of more elaborate products.

Problems of the weakness of the growth in exports and the possibility of a severe decline were forecast by the MIER and by Kopint-Datorg in May–June 1992. These warnings were not taken seriously by other decision-makers. Moreover, the National Bank of Hungary in March 1993 discontinued the provision of export credits and financing. The Export Guarantee Trust with its limited funds of $20 million was ridiculously inadequate for a country selling $10.7 billion worth of commodities in 1992 (the year of its establishment). As could be seen at that time (Kopint-Datorg, 1993) the interplay of a recovering domestic market and the lack of financing and state guarantees have led to a severe drop of exports: 17% in 1993 alone. By the end of that year some commercial banks, e.g. the Hungarian Credit Bank, started to offer financing facilities for deals exceeding $100,000, which was a poor substitute.

Law No. 83/1992 on the special state funds (promulgated in *Külgazdasági Közlöny*, 1993/1) has established two basic funds for export promotion: the Investment Promotion Fund and the Trade Promotion Fund. The first is meant to promote foreign direct investment to projects worth at least 50 million Forints, with 30% foreign ownership and half in cash. For importing technology and for developing physical infrastructure, and particularly utilities, subsidies up to 100 million Forints can be granted. These supports can be requested from a special interdepartmental committee in a public procedure, i.e. criteria for decisions and results are published in the press.

The Trade Promotion Fund is meant to support activities on the foreign market whose costs would exceed the direct interests of business ventures. Likewise, market studies and market presence as well as the various overhead costs of market entry can be subsidized. Product developments and market studies, presence at fairs and exhibitions, PR costs, outlays for registration of patents, quality certificates needed for entering tenders abroad, tuition fees and consulting fees can all be reimbursed on a contractual base, to a maximum of 50% of total outlays. For commodity groups which have suffered particularly severe setbacks in 1993, i.e. a drop of over 25%, in 1994 new collective marketing programmes have been organized by the MIER, i.e. for producers of pharmaceuticals, foodstuffs, meat products and engineering goods.

Through the reorganization of two previously established agencies, ITD Hungary, an investment promotion agency active in marketing new business opportunities in major capital exporting countries as well as in Hungary, has been set up. As new services, besides the previously available investment and export promotion, they offer pre-feasibility studies, organize country and product profiles, and set up export directories and standardized contracts. Further more, they are active in lobbying for the tax rebates which major investors are still able to receive (100% for three years) if the Ministry of Finance decides so (Bánki, 1993).

It might be instructive to provide a brief survey of the Hungarian controversy over the Exim Bank. In the first days of setting up the conservative government in 1990, the ambition to set up such an agency was already publicly formulated by the MIER. For understandable reasons, neither the Central Bank nor the Treasury were enthusiastic about endowing such a ministry with sizeable funds. After several years of futile attempts, in 1993 the atmosphere changed for the better. This time, however, it was the Ministry of Justice which aired second thoughts about an agency, which was to be neither a clear-cut commercial bank, nor an insurance agency, and not quite a classical governmental department either. Finally, a (typical) compromise was struck. The agency was established in February 1994 by a special law, however not in the form the MIER wanted it. It was founded by dividing the previously available Export Guarantee Trust into an Export Insurance Agency, which is a classical agency, and a Bank, with a total founding capital not exceeding the originally available 2 billion Forints ($20 million). Furthermore, as the then Undersecretary of State for Finances was not slow in pointing out, the Bank is unable to secure guarantees for prompt payment, and only later capital infusions will enable it to take more responsibility for larger deals (*Magyar Hírlap*, 22 February 1994).

If we reiterate that Hungary has never resorted to major devaluations for protecting her markets and supporting her exports, neither the pressures for contingent protection nor the pressures for export support schemes are very surprising. What may be astonishing is the very limited results the latter efforts have brought. Indeed, the diversity of forms is in sharp contrast to the minuscule amounts earmarked for these particular purposes.

4.7 Harmonization of Laws with the EU and Other Ways of Fighting Protectionism

The conclusion of the Uruguay Round has resulted in new agreements on anti-dumping and on countervailing measures. Implementation of these may result in a more flexible trade regime on both the EU and the CEEC sides, since the system of border rebates and quotas plus licensing, may be replaced by more transparent and better regulated customs protection, which may in the future be decreased. Adherence to these new agreements may thus significantly contribute to diminishing those institutional rigidities which currently make agriculture so much of a stumbling block. A more streamlined regulation of anti-dumping procedures may also take out much of the current strain from EU–CEEC trade relations.

Harmonization of laws with the EU may be a most efficient way of stopping covert protectionism in the form of technological and procedural prescriptions and other forms of NTB. Of course, here again the question is whether or not the prospect of future membership gives a real economic policy impetus and commitment to the approximation endeavours. If not, the current trend of meeting all formal requirements while playing on the loopholes and other ways of circumventing the substance of market opening, as observed with the EAs on both sides, is bound to continue.

In Hungary the harmonization of laws with the EU is taking place in the framework of a draft programme (Kecskés, 1994). This includes the following priority areas: customs law, company law, banking law, accounting standards, taxation legislation, protection of intellectual property rights, competition law, labour safety standards, food standards, technological norms, veterinary prescriptions, enterprise regulation and environmental norms. All new laws adopted since the signing of EAs will have to conform to EU legislation. The law on insurance and the law on foodstuffs have already been elaborated according to this norm, whereas company law will be approximated in the coming two to three years.

Hungary has got a relatively long history of antitrust legislation. First, law 4/1984 on unfair competition attempted to introduce this instrument into the reform package, and later law 86/1990 on the prohibition of unfair market behaviour extended the scope of action of this legislation. As a detailed analysis of one of the founding fathers of the law (Vörös, 1992, pp.185–190) illustrates, this law is modelled on its German counterpart, and in terms of its techniques and procedures it is already in conformity with the EU standards. If there still is a problem with it, this has to do with the underdeveloped state of competitive conditions in the Hungarian economy. As we have seen in the Ford Transit case discussed earlier, only if there is sufficient pressure and interest on the side of competitors to activate these forms can legislation really bite. Meanwhile, conditions of transformation are not yet identical to those in a mature market economy, where this condition can mostly be taken as given. Therefore it would be worth considering the following: instead of premature copying of options more fitting to a later stage, a more aggressive US-style trust-busting might be appropriate,[6] not only because of existing – inherited – monopolies in some of the subsectors, but also for averting some of the dangers in the unregulated inflow of foreign direct investment. As is easily conceivable, foreign investors may be tempted to buy up entire subsectors or chains in trade, transforming state monopolies into private ones, which later may prove dysfunctional. Among others these will be the vanguard of protectionism: Samsung has won protective duties on colour TV sets, and Suzuki and GM have already gained the reimposition of quotas on the importation of passenger cars from 1994. The guidelines for public procurement discussed above also bear the clear imprint of these pressure groups.

An area where technical assistance from the EU as well as consultations in the Council of Association may be particularly helpful is precisely this: dangers in premature standardization, and especially of copying current rather than prospective EU arrangements. The EU could help a lot in indicating in due time the genre of foreseeable changes, their type and logic, rather than pushing for premature standardization. This might be particularly important in the case of the CAP, since legislation and institution building in Central and East European farming is in its infancy. There is a grave danger in Central and East Europeans' replicating precisely those arrangements which render the external commercial policy stance of the EU so rigid in GATT negotiations.

4.8 On the Robustness of Liberalization

What has been discussed above leaves little room for optimism if events are allowed to follow their own logic. Left on their own, the tendency towards protectionism is bound to roll back the initial enthusiasm for free trade, which is often portrayed by officials as a luxury of theorists. Indeed, the Slovak and the Polish governments have already adopted a series of protectionist measures, and not only in the farming sector. Even in Hungary the degree of trade liberalization has decreased in 1994 by 2% against 1993 owing to protecting some of the farming and consumer markets. Analyses published in the monthly of the Ministry of Industry highlight as an achievement that in the CEFTA agreement all the safeguard clauses included in the EA could be maintained and the protection of home producers secured (Majoros, 1993, p.6). In a similar vein, the 1994 acceleration of implementing the CEFTA agreement contains a large number of exceptions, in the notoriously sensitive sectors of metallurgy, textiles and paper. Interestingly, the bilateral Polish–Hungarian trade protocol contains a pledge to halve customs duties while retaining the right of reimposition of quotas for 50–80% of trade in farm products (as reported in *Világgazdaság*, 1 July 1994).

The bad example of the EU is bound to backfire. EU practices legitimate attempts to protect domestic producers first and foremost, thus reinforcing the underlying protectionist instinct. Any pressure for opening Central European markets may easily be portrayed in the press as one-sided selfishness and may lose its credibility whatever its actual economic merits. As we have seen, the window of opportunity for liberalism was open in 1989–91, and CEEC governments finally have made use of it. It is hardly a surprise, however, that with the crystallization of political forces, lobbies can reorganize themselves. Land reform, the promotion of small business, foreign investors going the easy way and also the emergent political clientele taking some of the commanding heights of the economy may interact to subvert the open trade regime. If the EU leaves room for bureaucratic convenience and pressurizes the CEECs to adopt precisely those arrangements which make the EU itself inflexible in its external trade relations accession may be artificially delayed. Without providing a clear prospect and promise of full membership, economic common sense alone might be insufficient to convince CEEC governments not to give in to protectionist pressures. Taking the spirit of GATT a little more seriously and practising greater largesse when it comes to opening its own markets, rather than staggering sums of transfer payments, may be the assistance the EU could and should grant to its prospective members.

4.9 Conclusions

The political economy approach to trade regimes in Central Europe allows us to identify several of the less trivial of the stumbling blocks before sustained liberalization. A survey of the factors that have given birth to the undercurrent of neoprotectionism indicates that both the grounds and means of this lay increasingly outside the trade sector proper. This is one of the more potent arguments in favour of retaining or creating a separate governmental agency with a direct interest in free trade and suited for harmonization of Central and East European legislation with prospective EU standards. There is a grave danger that NTBs of various sorts, and generally non-transparent means not liable to international surveillance, may continue to proliferate.

Vested interests are numerous and well organized, thus only the credible prospect of full EU membership may provide Central European governments with the political impetus needed to withstand the temptation of protectionism. Multilateral agreements, especially if constrained to tariffs and trade, will not suffice to achieve this. If complemented with palpable gains in terms of market access and coupled with EU technical assistance to mould Central European institutional infrastructure the task of retaining the basically free and open trade regime of the early transition period can realistically be mastered. The Europe Agreements, even complemented by the political promises of the Copenhagen Summit of June 1993, are much too narrow in scope and perspective to serve such a comprehensive objective. As evidenced by the measures and developments of 1991–94, being narrowly conceived trade agreements of limited generosity, the EAs even fall short of creating institutional stability in and for trade in CEECs. For getting better results, it is not a manyfold increase in transfer payments that is primarily required. Competent policies in the Visegrad countries could and should be supplanted by innovative and forthcoming policies of the EU. Technical assistance could focus on help, avoiding the premature standardization of norms and avoiding the creation of new structural rigidities, especially in legislation on farming and on labour markets. In the end, offering perspectives may be much more important than the actual sums to be transferred to any prospective 'Eastern' EU member. Conversely, limited generosity of the EAs or wrong sequencing in the standardization of legal norms may also breed short-sighted and counterproductive answers on the side of the CEECs. The dangers of mutually disadvantageous outcomes from noncooperative games may be coming for the 1990s. Appropriate trade laws and institutions may help to avoid a retrogression into the practices of the 1930s.

Notes

1. Analysis of the developments in sensitive sectors like agriculture, textiles and consumer durables, Bóc (1994) statistically proves this point and disproves crowding-out claims of producers.
2. The June 1993 Copenhagen decisions do imply a change in this respect in terms of potential, but not, however, in terms of the material content of contractual obligations. Thus Balázs (1994, p.18) is quite right in assessing the EAs as, though politically more promising, still financially clearly less generous and inferior to similar EU agreements concluded with Mediterranean countries.
3. It is relatively good news that in the first six months following this initiative only a single Polish firm was actually making use of this option (*Világgazdaság*, 29 June 1994), with others finding it too costly and too time consuming. In Hungary a similar process emerged with a delay of six months.
4. Incidentally, only Romania and later Bulgaria followed this line, whereas Central European countries have not followed suit.
5. The last such attempt took place in June 1994.
6. The recent initiative to set up an EU agency to oversee Central European antitrust practices (cf. *Világgazdaság*, 14 July 1994) may be a useful contribution to activating dormant competition legislation in the region.

References

Adam, J. (1993), 'Transformation to a market economy in the former Czechoslovakia', *Europe–Asia Studies*, **45**(4), 627–46.

Anderson, K. and Tyers, R. (1993), 'Implications of EC expansion for European agricultural policies, trade and welfare', CEPR Discussion Paper No. 829.

Balázs, P. (1993), 'A vizsgálatok nem lassíthatják az importot' (Analyses should not slow down imports) - an interview to Zs Bán in *Világgazdaság*, 11 November.

Balázs, P. (1994), 'Az EK közép-kelet-európai és mediterrán társulásainak összehasonlítása' (A comparison of EU association agreements with East–Central Europe and with Mediterranean countries), *Európa Fórum*, **4**(2), 3–19.

Balcerowicz, L. (1993), 'Az elsô egyenleg' (A first balance sheet), *Valóság*, **36**(1), 33–46.

Bánki, F. (1993), 'It's not only a name that changes', *The Hungarian Economy*, **21**(3), 3.

Beszteri, S. (1994), 'Az új vámtörvényrôl' (On the new customs law), *Pénzügyi Szemle*, **38**(4), 256–63.

Bóc, I. (1993a), 'Szoríts, ha bírsz!' (Squeeze if you can!), *Heti Világgazdaság*, **14**(38), reprinted in *Gazdaság*, **3**(1), 120–3.

Bóc, I. (1993b), 'A magas céh' (The high guild), *Heti Világgazdaság*, **14**(15).

Bóc, I. (1994), 'EK társulás és importliberalizálás' (Association to the EU and liberalization of imports), *Magyar Hírlap*, 16 May.

Borszéki, Zs. (1993), *Egy eszköz, amely túlélte önmagát*, (*A means which has outlived its time*), Kopint-Datorg Foundation for the Research of the Conjuncture, Budapest, February, 91pp.

Borszéki, Zs. (1994), 'Viszik, mint a cukrot?' (A purchasing craze?), *Figyelö*, **38**(27).

Csaba, L. (1995), *The Capitalist Revolution in Eastern Europe*, Edward Elgar, Cheltenham (forthcoming).

Farkas, Gy. (1994), 'Nemzetközi gazdasági kapcsolataink: megérett a felülvizsgálat' (International economic relations: it's time for a change), *Külgazdaság*, **38**(5), 67–78.

Gács, J. (1991), 'Foreign trade liberalization (1968–90)', in A. Köves and P. Marer (eds) *Foreign Economic Liberalization*. Westview, Boulder, CO, pp.185–98.

Gács, J. (1994), 'Liberalization of foreign trade in Eastern Europe: rush and reconsideration', in J. Gács and G. Winckler (eds) *International Trade and Restructuring in Eastern Europe*. Physica Verlag, Heidelberg, pp.123–51.

Halmai, P. (1993), 'Piacszabályozás, piaci rendtartás, válságmenedzselés és kilátások' (Market regulation, market order, crisis management and prospects), *Gazdaság*, **2**, special issue, pp.196–205.

Jindra, V. (1993), 'Die Aussenwirtschaftspolitik der CSFR', in H. Herr and A. Westphal (eds), *Transformation in Mittel- und Osteuropa*, Campus, Frankfurt, pp. 324–42.

Juhász, E. (1993), 'Könnyen célt lehet téveszteni' (It is easy to miss the target), an interview to R. Becsky in *Figyelö*, **37**(43).

Kamasz, M. (1994), 'Százezer forint az értékhatár' (Hundred thousand Ft is the limit – a summary of the draft law on customs), *Magyar Hírlap*, 23 February.

Kecskés, L. (1994), 'A meglévô törvényt nehezebb harmonizálni' (Available laws are more difficult to harmonize), an interview to L. Tóth, in *Világgazdaság*, 1 February.

Klacek, J. and Hrncir, M. (1993), 'Prospects for economic recovery and the role of industrial policy: the case of Czechoslovakia', *Most*, **4**(1), pp.51–62.

Kopint-Datorg, Inc. (1993), *Economic Trends in Eastern Europe*, **4**(1), Spring.

Lányi, K. (1992), 'A hazai agrárgazdaság válságának természetérôl' (On the nature of crisis in Hungarian agriculture), *Kapu*, **5**(5), 10–15.

Lányi, K. and Fertô, I. (1993), 'Az agrárpiacok felépítése afejlett ipari országokban és a magyar rendtartás' (The structure of agrarian markets in advanced industrial countries and the Hungarian market order), *Külgazdaság*, **37**(2), 34–49.

Majoros, P. (1993), 'Csehország, Szlovákia, Lengyelország és Magyarország kapcsolatának új formája: a regionális integráció' (A new form of interrelationship among Bohemia, Slovakia, Poland and Hungary: regional integration), *Kereskedelmi Szemle*, **34**(11), 1–7.

Meisel, V. S. and Mohácsi, K. (1993), 'A társulási szerzôdésés a magyar agrárágazat'

(The association agreement to the EU and the Hungarian farming sector), *Európa Fórum*, **3**(1), 114–33.
Náray, P. (1989), 'The end of foreign trade monopoly: the case of Hungary', *The Journal of World Trade*, **23**(6).
Oblath, G. (1992), 'The limits, successes and question marks of import liberalization in Hungary', *Russian and East European Finance and Trade*, **28**(2), 3–18.
Pál, L. (1994), 'Nem ágazati politikát kell folytatni' (There's no need for sectoral policies), an interview to M. Mink, in *Figyelô*, **38**(28).
Pásztor, S. (1993), '"Szakadt kötelekkel, tört árboccal". Az 1989-ben megkezdett magyar importliberalizálás és elôzményei' (With torn ropes and broken mast. Antecedents and liberalization of imports in Hungary in 1989), in K. Lányi and J. Szabó (eds), *A nyitás gazdaságpolitikája. Importliberalizálási tapasztalatok*, Institute of Economics of the Hungarian Academy of Sciences and the Kopint-Datorg Foundation for the Research of the Conjuncture, Budapest, pp.59–109.
Portes, R. (1991), 'Introduction', in 'The path of reform in Central and Eastern Europe', *European Economy*, special edition No. 2, 1–15.
Raskó, Gy. (1993), 'Mezôgazdaságunk GATT reményei' (Hungarian agricultural hopes after the GATT round), - an interview to P. S. Sz., in *Világgazdaság*, 29 December.
Schmögnerová, B. (1991), 'Privatization in transition from central planning to a market economy in Czechoslovakia', *Most*, **2**(3), 29–38.
Szabó, M., Varga, Gy. and Kapronczai, I. (1994), 'A magyar agrárrendtartás elméleti alapjai és mûködési rendszere, különös tekintettel a belsô piacvédelem szempontjára' (Theoretical background and functioning of Hungarian agricultural market order with special regard to protecting the domestic market), mimeo, Institute for Agricultural Research and Information, Budapest, January, 48pp.
Szalai, E. (1991), 'Integration of special interests in the Hungarian economy: the struggle between large companies and the party and state bureaucracy', *The Journal of Comparative Economics*, **15**(2), 284–304.
Szegvári, I. (1991), 'Systemic change and convertibility: a comparison of Poland, Yugoslavia and Hungary', in L. Csaba (ed.), *Systemic Change and Stabilization in Eastern Europe*, Dartmouth, Aldershot, pp. 33–44.
Tóth, G. L. (1993), 'Foreign economic liberalization in East–Central Europe: the experiences of Poland and the Czech and Slovak Federal Republic', *Acta Oeconomica*, **45**(1-2), 183-196.
Tovias, A. (1994), 'Az EK szerepe a magyar ipari szerkezet korszerûsítésében' (The role of the EU in the modernization of Hungarian industry), *Európa Fórum*, **4**(1), 91–105.
Török, Á. (1992), 'A strukturális alkalmazkodás iparvédelmi eszközei' (Structural adjustment and industrial protection), Parts I and II, *Külgazdaság*, **36**(3), 21–33, **36**(4), 29–41.
Török, Á. (1994), 'Structural adaptations and its mechanisms for protecting domestic industries', *Russian and East European Finance and Trade*, **30**(3), 5–37.
Varga, Gy. (1992), 'A magyar agrárpolitika és a közös piaci csatlakozás' (Hungarian agricultural policy and accession to the Common Market), *Külgazdaság*, **36**(3), 58–64.
Vörös I. (1992), *Az európai versenyjogok kézikönyve*, (*A Handbook of Competition Laws in Europe*), TRIORG Kft, Budapest, 190pp.
Welfens, P. (1993), 'Osterweiterung der EG: Anpassungserfordernisse, Konvergenzprobleme und ordnungspolitischer Reformbedarf in Europa', in H. Gröner and A. Schüller (eds), *Die Europäische Integration als Ordnungspolitische Aufgabe*. G. Fischer Verlag, Stuttgart, pp. 517–49.

Williamson, J. (1991), *The Economic Opening of Eastern Europe*, Institute of International Economics, Washington, DC, 120pp.
Winiecki, J. (1994), 'Macroeconomics of transition in East–Central Europe: Czech Republic, Hungary, Poland and Slovakia in 1993', *Europe-Asia Studies*, **46**(5), 709–34.
Winters, L. A. and Wang, Zh. K. (1994), *Eastern Europe's International Trade*. Manchester University Press, Manchester.

5

The Europe Agreements: Implications for Trade Laws and Institutions*

André Sapir

5.1 Introduction

The liberalization of trade played an important role in the early stages of Central and Eastern Europe's transition process. The high concentration of production in industry necessitated a radical opening of trade. Liberalization was viewed as one of the main tools for imposing the discipline of competition on monopolistic domestic enterprises and, thereby, to improve the efficiency of resource allocation.

Trade liberalization in Czechoslovakia, Hungary and Poland was accomplished in record time. Between 1989 and 1991, these three countries completely abrogated state monopoly in foreign trade, freed over 90% of imports from licences and quotas, and reduced the average tariff rate to less than 15%. This achievement is remarkable in comparison with developing countries where trade liberalization has usually taken place over several decades.[1]

The main factor responsible for the contrasting experiences of Central and Eastern Europe and the developing countries belongs to the realm of political economy. Within each country, trade liberalization is opposed by import-competing interests and is promoted by export interests. Since the losses incurred by the former tend to be more clearly defined and more concentrated than the

* I am indebted to Tibor Baan, Gusztav Bager, Peter Balazs, Imre Boc, Zsuzsa Borzeki, Anne Bucher, Egon Dienes-Oehm, Peter Gottfried, Laszlo Halpern, Eva Havasi, Judit Kiss, Vassili Maragos, Silvano Presa, Emma Toledano Laredo, Marina Varga and Eniko Varsa for helpful discussions during the preparation of an earlier draft. Useful comments were also provided by László Csaba, Bernard Hoekman, Petros Mavroidis, Patrick Messerlin, Joan Pearce, Richard Portes, Adam Török and Alan Winters. I am, however, solely responsible for the opinions expressed in this chapter.

gains obtained by the latter, trade liberalization is usually difficult to implement in normal circumstances. The wave of trade policy reform that hit many developing countries during the 1980s owed a great deal to political changes induced by the acuteness of their macroeconomic-cum-debt crisis. The 1989 revolutions in Central and Eastern Europe were an even bigger political shock, with greater scope for trade liberalization. As Gács (1993) notes, after the changes of 1989 'the usual pressure groups resisting to economic reforms were either nonexistent or virtually ineffective.'

The experience of many developing countries suggests that the main problem regarding trade liberalization is not so much initial implementation as sustainability. Rodrik (1992) questions the credibility of liberal trade policies in situations of intense lobbying by import-competing groups. He insists on the need for liberal-minded governments to enhance the credibility of their policies by building reputation and finding mechanisms of commitment. 'Membership in the GATT, and placing a ceiling on maximum tariff rates by undertaking international obligations, can help'.[2] In this respect, the NAFTA agreement is often regarded as a device 'to lock in ... a set of liberal trade policies that the current [Mexican] government has adopted unilaterally, to make credible to the business community that they cannot be easily reversed by subsequent administrations.'[3]

Sustainability also became a major concern in Central and Eastern Europe as the 'honeymoon of trade liberalization' came to an end in 1991–92.[4] Several problems with the transition process led to increased protectionist pressures. First, it was argued not only by industrialists but also by some academics that the excessively abrupt opening of the economy had unnecessarily exaggerated the initial shock of restructuring. According to this view too rapid and too profound a trade liberalization was endangering the survival of potentially efficient domestic producers.[5] Second, the restructuring involved sales of domestic enterprises to powerful foreign investors who demanded concessions from local governments, including in the form of trade protection. Such demands by multinational companies were soon emulated by domestic companies. Third, the collapse of the CMEA[6] market created additional pressures on those domestic firms already suffering from import liberalization. This situation fits in well with political economy analyses by Hillman *et al.* (1993) and others, which suggest that protectionist pressures are likely to dominate trade opening efforts during the transition from socialism, unless trade policy is credibly non-discretionary. These authors argue that institutional arrangements such as the Europe Agreements (EAs) can play a major role in this respect by limiting the discretion of governments in setting trade policy, like NAFTA is doing for Mexico.

The Europe Agreements offer a potentially powerful mechanism for helping sustain trade liberalization in Central and Eastern Europe by influencing favourably both sides of the protection equation. The EAs should reduce the demand for protection in the countries of the region by expanding their export opportunities. They should also reduce the ability of governments to supply protection by increasing their international commitments. While acknowledging that both sides of the equation are equally important, this chapter will focus entirely on the latter.

The purpose of the chapter is twofold. It will examine the impact of the Europe Agreements on the *process* of trade policy formulation in Central and Eastern Europe. It will also investigate their role in constraining the actual outcome of trade policy. Therefore the central question of the chapter is whether the Agreements are successful in tying the hands of governments in favour of liberal trade policies. A similarly important issue concerns the number of hands which are successfully tied. Tying only one hand would mean that the Agreements have simply led governments in Central and Eastern Europe to shift their supply of protection from all trade partners to those outside the European Union (EU), i.e. those not covered by the EA umbrella.

Two remarks should be made at the outset. First, the chapter is not about the desirability of liberal trade policies in Central and Eastern Europe. Rather, the focus is on their sustainability and, especially, on the role of the EAs in enhancing their credibility. Second, the purpose of the EAs is clearly not to establish free trade in Central and Eastern Europe. Therefore free trade is not the correct benchmark against which EAs should be evaluated. Instead, Europe Agreements must, and will, be judged against their more modest declared objective, namely in helping to sustain trade liberalization in the face of difficulties associated with the transition process and helping achieve membership to the Union.[7]

Comprehensive analysis of the process and outcome of trade policy for all Central and East European Countries (CEECs) covered by Europe Agreements would be a task far beyond the scope of this chapter. It focuses instead on a single country, Hungary, which carries both advantages and disadvantages. A major advantage of selecting Hungary is the GATT (1991) review of its trade policies which constitutes an excellent benchmark for the present study. The main disadvantage is that Hungary's commitment to liberal trade policies probably lies at the far end of the spectrum in the region.

The outline of the chapter is as follows. Section 5.2 is devoted to the process of trade policy formulation and review. It starts with a discussion of the extent to which Europe Agreements might be expected to limit the discretion of Central and East European governments in formulating trade policy. It then analyses trade policy formulation in Hungary and evaluates the actual constraints imposed by the EAs. Section 5.3 examines the actual implementation of trade policies by Hungary with respect to imports from the European Union and other countries. Section 5.4 concludes.

5.2 The Process of Trade Policy Formulation and Review

Europe Agreements impose a certain number of *bilateral obligations* on the CEECs in their trade relations with the European Union. These obligations are in addition to *multilateral obligations* contracted under the GATT.[8] This section will focus on the role of the EAs as an incremental constraint on the process of trade policy formulation in Central and Eastern Europe over and above the constraint already imposed by GATT membership. Because some of the CEECs (including Hungary) have a special status under the GATT, a short presentation of their GATT obligations must precede the analysis of EA obligations. Given the idiosyncratic treatment of individual CEECs under both the GATT and the EAs, the presentation will focus entirely on Hungary.

5.2.1 GATT Obligations[9]

At the time of its accession to the GATT in 1973, Hungary was not a market economy. None the less, GATT's contracting parties accepted accession on the basis of tariff commitments in view of the introduction of Hungary's customs tariffs in 1968.[10] It was judged necessary, however, by contracting parties to include a number of specific provisions in Hungary's Protocol of Accession. Two are especially important. Paragraph 4(a) of the Protocol calls for the progressive elimination of *quantitative restrictions* not consistent with the nondiscrimination clause of Article XIII of the General Agreement. Paragraph 5 of the Protocol includes a specific safeguard clause which, contrary to the general safeguard clause of Article XIX of the GATT, permits *selective safeguard measures*.[11]

According to GATT (1991), 'In the light of the progress registered in the process of transition to a market economy, the Hungarian government has indicated its intention to seek the elimination of all specific provisions of its Protocol of Accession.' As of today, however, these provisions still stand.

The General Agreement has not been incorporated into Hungary's domestic law, but the Protocol of Accession was promulgated by government decree.[12] After its accession to the GATT, Hungary introduced new legislation on foreign trade relations. Act III of 1974 on Foreign Trade is still today the law of the country, although some provisions (such as Section 3 on the State monopoly of foreign trade) were abolished in 1990. Section 20 of the Act gives authority to subject foreign trade to licensing.

Until January 1989, imports of all products into Hungary were subject to licensing, with a distinction between CMEA and non-CMEA countries. This was acknowledged in 1980, when Hungary signed the GATT Agreement on Import Licensing Procedures. It notified its import licensing as 'non-automatic' in the terminology of Article 3 of the Agreement. By virtue of Government

Decree 112/1990, imports into Hungary are no more subject to licensing since 1 January 1991, except in cases explicitly listed in the Decree.[13] At present, the main purpose of the import licensing system appears to be the administration of quantitative restrictions (QRs) on consumer goods. Section 7 of the Decree specifies that 'For the import of products directly serving the supply of the population the Ministry [of International Economic Relations] may set up a six-month quota (consumer goods quota).' The consumer goods quota specifies a global value as well as maximum values for individual products. The latter are further divided into country-specific quotas. This quota, which predates the process of transition to a market economy, has been a regular controversial issue in consultations held by the Working Party on Trade with Hungary instituted by the Protocol of Accession.

Until recently, Hungary did not have any specific safeguard legislation. Being part of the Protocol of Accession, however, Paragraph 5 had legal status. Government Decree 113/1990, which entered into force on 1 January 1991, provides a safeguard legislation based on Paragraph 5. It indicates that safeguard actions are limited to a duration of one year and may be in the form of selective import quotas.

Since the dismantling of licensing requirements for most products, most-favoured-nation (MFN) tariffs have become the principal instrument of trade protection in Hungary. In this respect it is important to note that, since the Tokyo Round, Hungary has had fully bound MFN rates on more than 80% of its tariff lines. More than 90% of the tariff lines for industrial products are bound, against less than 25% for agricultural products.

Hungary has signed the Tokyo Round Agreements, except for the Codes on Government Procurement, Subsidies and Civil Aircraft. The texts signed by Hungary (including the GATT Standards Code and Anti-dumping Code) have been incorporated into Hungary's domestic law.

5.2.2 Europe Agreement Obligations

The Europe Agreement with Hungary was signed on 16 December 1991. Entry into force only took place on 1 February 1994 due to the lengthy process of ratification by all the 13 national parliaments. Nevertheless, the trade related parts of the EA were put into effect from 1 March 1992 by means of an Interim Europe Agreement (IEA).[14] Since entry into force of the Agreement, its application is monitored, at ministerial level, by the Association Council aided by the Association Committee.[15]

Title III of the EA ('Free Movement of Goods') includes provisions for establishing a free trade area between the European Community (EC) and Hungary over a transitional period of maximum ten years starting from 1 March 1992. In principle, these provisions limit considerably the discretion of Hungarian authorities in formulating trade policies with the European Union in the following areas: tariffs and para-tariffs, QRs, and safeguard and anti-dumping procedures.

Tariffs and Para-tariffs

Article 10 of the EA imposes the gradual elimination of tariffs on imports into Hungary of industrial products originating in the EU. For most products, the reduction will start on 1 January 1995 and be completed on either 1 January 1997 or 1 January 2001. Special protocols lay down the arrangements applicable to textiles and clothing, steel and coal, and processed agricultural products.

For industrial products, Article 11 of the Agreement also imposes the abolition of tariffs of a fiscal nature, although no schedule is specified. Article 12 further demands that Hungary abolishes on its imports from the EU the following charges having an effect equivalent to tariffs: the 1% licensing fee (by 1 January 1995),[16] the 2% customs clearance fee (by 1 January 1997), and the 3% statistical fee (by 1 January 1997).

Moreover, all tariffs and para-tariffs on industrial products originating in the EU are bound as of 1 March 1992.

In agriculture, tariff reductions are restricted to a small set of products and only apply to limited quantities.

Quantitative Restrictions

Article 10 also calls for all QRs and 'measures having an equivalent effect' on imports into Hungary of industrial products originating in the EU to be abolished. For products subject to import licensing (i.e. those specified in Government Decree 112/1990) and listed in Annex VIa, the abolition will start on 1 January 1995 and be completed on 31 December 2000. For the subset of products also belonging to the consumer goods quota and listed in Annex VIb, Hungary has opened from 1 March 1992 import ceilings for products originating in the EU.[17] These ceilings are to be progressively increased until the QRs are entirely eliminated. No other QR or measures having an equivalent effect have been permitted since 1 March 1992. Special protocols govern the arrangements applicable to textiles and clothing, steel and coal, and processed agricultural products. Moreover, all QRs and measures having an equivalent effect on imports originating in the EU are bound as of 1 March 1992. In agriculture, QRs have been either increased or abolished for a small set of products.

Exceptional Measures

Article 28 of the EA allows 'Exceptional measures of limited duration which derogate from the provisions of [the Agreement to be] taken by Hungary in the form of increased customs duties.'

Unfortunately, the scope of Article 28 is extremely vague. Paragraph 2 merely specifies that exceptional measures 'may only concern infant industries, or certain sectors undergoing restructuring or facing serious difficulties, particularly where these difficulties produce important social problems.' This stipulation raises at least two serious complications. First, just about every sector of Hungarian industry may claim to be either 'infant', 'undergoing restructuring' or 'facing serious difficulties'. Second, the Agreement provides no definition of 'infant industries' or 'restructuring', nor criteria for evaluating whether a sector is 'facing serious difficulties'.

Exceptional tariffs are subject to further conditions:

- They may not 'exceed 25% *ad valorem*', nor cover more than '15% of total imports from the Community of industrial products'. In addition, exceptional customs duties 'shall maintain an element of preference for products originating in the Community' (Paragraph 3).
- They may not 'be applied for a period exceeding five years' and must 'cease to apply at the latest at the expiration of the transitional period' (Paragraph 4).
- They may not 'be introduced in respect of a product if more than 3 years have elapsed since the elimination of all duties and quantitative restrictions' for that product (Paragraph 5).
- Hungary must inform the Association Council of its intention to take exceptional measures, whereupon the Community may request consultations 'on such measures and the sectors to which they apply before they are applied.' When taking such measures, Hungary must announce a schedule for their elimination (Paragraph 6).

These conditions seem sufficiently strict to avoid any outright protectionist application of Article 28. Exceptional tariffs are time-bound and may only apply to a small fraction of imports. Moreover, the fact that they must maintain 'an element of preference' in favour of the EU implies that other GATT contracting parties must be consulted and acquiesce if the MFN duty is bound. These conditions also create further complications because of their lack of precision, especially with respect to Paragraphs 5 and 6.

Anti-dumping

Article 29 of the Agreement authorizes both Parties to take appropriate measures against dumping in trade with the other Party 'in accordance with the Agreement relating to the application of Article VI of the General Agreement on Tariffs and Trade.' 'Before taking the measures', the Association Council must be supplied 'with all relevant information with a view to seeking a solution acceptable to the two Parties' (Article 33). The final decision, however, is that of the importing Party alone. No arbitration procedure is specified.

Safeguards

Article 30 of the Agreement authorizes both Parties to take appropriate safeguard actions if imports from the other Party cause (a) 'serious injury to domestic producers of like or directly competitive products', or (b) 'serious disturbances in any sector of the economy or difficulties which could bring about serious deterioration in the economic situation of a region'. Winters (1992) is critical of part (b) on the ground that its language is 'ominously innovative' and vague. In particular, no criterion is provided to implement words such as 'could', 'serious deterioration' or 'region'.

The implementation procedure is similar to that for anti-dumping and is also stated in Article 33.

Other Provisions

Additional provisions affecting the free movement of goods between the EU and Hungary are contained in other parts of the Agreement. Only the most important ones will be examined.

Title V of the EA ('Payments, Capital, Competition and Other Economic Provisions, Approximation of Laws') includes provisions relating to balance of payments problems. Article 63 authorizes both Parties, if faced with serious balance of payments difficulties (or threat thereof), to adopt restrictive measures 'in accordance with the conditions established under the General Agreement on Tariffs and Trade'. Their introduction must, however, be accompanied by 'a time schedule for their removal'.

Title VI of the EA ('Economic Co-operation') includes provisions on industrial standards. Article 73 calls for various appropriate measures (such as the adoption by Hungary of Community regulations and European standards and the conclusion of mutual recognition agreements) in order `to reduce differences in the fields of standardization and conformity assessment'.

Overall Assessment: EA vs GATT Obligations

Compared with its multilateral GATT obligations, the European Agreement imposes additional constraints on Hungary's trade policy formulation, but (obviously) these only apply in bilateral trade relations with the European Union. The extent of the added restraints imposed by the EA differs markedly between industrial and agricultural products.

For industrial products, Hungary now has very little room for unilateral manoeuvre with respect to the European Union. All tariffs and QRs on imports from the EU will be eliminated at the latest by 1 January 2001. In the meantime they are, at the very least, bound at their levels of 1 March 1992. Para-tariffs are also bound and progressively abolished.

The situation is rather different in agriculture. Here the EA leaves largely untouched existing tariffs and quotas. Moreover, it does not bind them at their 1992 levels, nor does it prevent Hungary from introducing variable levies.

Derogations from EA obligations in the form of increased tariffs are possible, but only for a limited time and in exceptional circumstances. The requirement that they maintain 'an element of preference' introduces discrimination against third parties, but also necessitates their approval. The safeguard clause also introduces discrimination since EA safeguard actions apply on a selective bilateral basis rather than multilaterally. Recall, however, that selectivity was already permitted under Hungary's Protocol of Accession to the GATT.

Perhaps the main additional constraint imposed on Hungary's trade policy lies in the process of consultation with trade partners. As a GATT member, Hungary is subject to regular consultation held by the Working Party on Trade with Hungary and to periodic review under the Trade Policy Review Mechanism (TPRM). It must also notify new trade policy measures and accept dispute settlement procedures. Together with other GATT obligations, these mechanisms significantly restrict the formulation of trade policy by Hungary. The GATT, however, is also notorious for its lack of enforcement discipline. The World Trade Organization, due to come into being in 1995 as a successor to the GATT, should partly remedy this situation. But the fact remains that bilateral monitoring by the European Union, Hungary's main trading partner, is more likely to be effective than multilateral control.[18] In addition, consultation under the Europe Agreement tends to take place during the process of formulating trade policy, whereas GATT consultations are largely *ex post*.

5.2.3 The Trade Policy Process in Hungary

So far, this section has described the constraints that GATT membership and the European Agreement should, in principle, impose on Hungary's trade policy. It is now time to examine the actual process of trade policy formulation in Hungary and the role played in it by the EA.

In Hungary, overall trade policy is formulated by the government. Within the government, basic trade matters are discussed by an Economic Cabinet which prepares government decisions and actions. The Economic Cabinet has three main components: the Minister of Finance (who chairs the Economic Cabinet); the Minister of International Economic Relations; and the Ministers of Industry (and Trade) and Agriculture. The Ministry of International Economic Relations (MIER) is the main governmental body responsible for trade policy. It chairs the Customs Tariff Committee which plays an important role in formulating and implementing Hungary's tariff policy. The Committee also includes representatives of the Ministries of Finance, Industry and Agriculture as well as representatives of business.

In order to evaluate the actual process of trade policy formulation, two situations will be examined: the consumer goods quota and a safeguard action.

Government Decree 112/1990 does not contain any guidelines for setting up either the global value of the consumer goods quota or individual product limits. No guidelines are provided either in the accompanying MIER Decree 6/1990. During interviews in Hungary it has not been possible to ascertain with precision how the quotas are specified. Industrial policy considerations, however, and lobbying by import-competing interests clearly dominate. This is confirmed by the fact that the Ministry of Industry and Trade and the Ministry of Agriculture appear to be the most active in a decision process which is said to last six months in every year.

In the case of safeguard actions, the Ministries of Industry and Trade (or the Ministry of Agriculture), International Economic Relations and Finance are all explicitly involved in the process. They generally line up as follows. At one extreme, the Ministry of Industry strongly supports the petitions of import-competing producers based on their narrow interests. At the other extreme, the Ministry of Finance tends to reject demands, based on broad considerations of the economy as a whole, although budgetary considerations also play a role. The Ministry of International Economic Relations adopts an intermediate position which takes into account diplomatic relations and existing treaties (especially GATT and EA). The outcome, therefore, depends upon the political weight of the respective Ministers inside the Economic Cabinet.

The role played by the Europe Agreement in the process of trade policy formulation in Hungary can also be appraised in these two situations.

The discretion enjoyed by government authorities in setting up quotas for consumer goods appears to have been greatly reduced by the entry into force of the Interim Europe Agreement. This has come about through a combination of two factors: (a) the imposition by the EA of ceilings for imports from the EU; and (b) the apparent and unilateral decision of Hungarian authorities to grant about 50% of individual product quotas to EU exporters.[19]

On the other hand, the procedure for safeguard actions does not seem to have been considerably affected by the Europe Agreement since selectivity was already present in the Hungarian legislation.

In conclusion, the Europe Agreement appears to play a prominent role in the actual process of trade policy formulation. In view of the EU's status as Hungary's premier trade partner, the Europe Agreement has acquired almost instantly a significance that may even surpass that of the GATT. In any trade matter, Hungarian authorities will probably have to consider their EA obligations prior to their GATT obligations.

5.3 The Trade Policy Outcome

Hungary stands apart among the countries of Central and Eastern Europe for its gradual but steady process of transition to a market economy. The process started in 1968 with the introduction of the so-called New Economic Mechanism. Despite market-oriented reforms, however, many features of a planned economy were retained. Foreign trade remained a State monopoly. Trade relations with other CMEA countries (mostly the Soviet Union) based on intergovernmental agreements (including obligatory delivery quotas at fixed prices) also continued to prevail. Finally, all trade transactions remained subject to licensing.[20]

According to Nagy (1993), the preparation of import liberalization in Hungary started around 1985. In spite of fierce internal opposition, the import liberalization programme was introduced by the government in 1988. Its implementation was accelerated after the political changes in 1990. By 1991, more than 80% of imports were liberalized, i.e. freed from licensing.[21] Also in 1991, the nominal average tariff rate was reduced from 16 to 13%.

Nagy (1993) argues that the ostensible lack of opposition to import liberalization in 1990 can be traced back to two main factors. One was the political change, as a result of which 'the surviving special interest organizations became weaker, less influential or discredited'. The second factor was the poor understanding of the consequences of import liberalization 'based on many illusions concerning the advantages of a market economy in general and of competition in particular'.

This period of grace, however, was short lived. In 1991, the demand for protection rose substantially and by 1992 it was in full swing. Several factors have fuelled the pressure for protection. The transition process produced the expected falls in output and employment. Together with the 50% decline in exports to former CMEA countries, the transition process led to a GDP decline of 12% in 1991 and of 6% in 1992. This generated a massive increase in unemployment, which reached more than 7% in 1991 and 12% in 1992. In 1993, GDP declined by between 1 and 2%, while the unemployment rate remained above 12%.[22]

A second factor was the surge of imports. In 1991, imports into Hungary increased nearly 70% over the previous year. The fastest growth occurred in consumer goods (+110% in 1991) as a result of high pent-up demand. In 1993, imports continued to rise while exports collapsed. As a result, the trade coverage ratio fell to 70% and the trade account registered a $3.2 billion deficit. The last factor was the resurgence of special interest groups, with a clear distinction between foreign and domestic firms. The large foreign investors were the first to successfully campaign for protection. Under the pressure of foreign multinationals, the government raised tariffs in 1991 for three product groups (passenger cars, fertilizers and colour TVs). The following year, large foreign investors set up their own powerful organization (the International Companies

Hungarian Association) outside the Hungarian Association of Enterprises.[23] For their part, domestic producers lacked the lobbying power that multinationals derived from Hungary's need for money, management and technology. Some of them, however, had substantial political weight, especially the agrarian lobby and large-scale state enterprises.

The growing demands for protection facing the Hungarian government were acknowledged in April 1991 by its representative in the GATT Council meeting on the trade policy review of Hungary. The representative admitted that: 'Hundreds of requests had been introduced by domestic industries for the re-establishment of import licensing for products regarded as sensitive by them; pressure was also exercised to increase tariffs and lower the quota for consumer goods; there was a growing number of requests for the initiation of anti-dumping procedures and safeguard actions. For the time being, the government was successfully resisting these pressures, but nobody could predict what actions might become necessary later this year in the light of further trade developments.'[24]

The government's resolve to resist protectionist pressures and sustain import liberalization was strengthened by two complementary decisions. The first was the adoption in March 1991 of the liberal-minded four-year 'Programme of conversion and development for the Hungarian economy'. The second decision was the signature in December 1991 of the Europe Agreement. The previous section concluded that the Europe Agreement has added a significant constraint on the process of trade policy formulation in Hungary. The remainder of this section will examine whether the Europe Agreement has been equally effective in limiting the introduction of new protectionist measures in the face of growing demands for protection. It will also investigate whether the Europe Agreement has resulted in a diversion of protection from EU to non-EU countries. The following trade policy measures will be examined: tariffs, QRs, anti-dumping actions, safeguard actions and other measures.

5.3.1 Tariffs

According to Nagy (1993), hundreds of demands for tariff increases were submitted (mostly by the Ministry of Industry and Trade) to the Customs Tariff Commission in 1992, including after the entry into force of the Interim Europe Agreement. It was 'argued that protection was needed because of severe under-utilization of capacities and large scale unemployment'. Since all tariffs on industrial products are bound under the Agreement, however, the purpose of these demands is not immediately obvious.

The Interim Agreement offered the possibility of tariff increases on industrial products in only two circumstances: as exceptional measures in the sense of Article 28 (Article 22 of the Interim Agreement); or as safeguard measures. A crucial difference between these two measures is that the former can be applied even without an increase of imports.

In February 1993, the Hungarian authorities informed the Joint Committee of their intention to increase tariffs on 17 industrial products as exceptional measures in accordance with Article 28. This was the first proposed application of Article 28 by any of the CEECs. The 17 products and the proposed measures had the following characteristics:

- The products concerned fell into four product categories: chemicals (10 products), paper (3 products), tiles (2 products) and glass (2 products).
- The manufacturers primarily concerned belonged to two groups: purely domestic firms (8 products) and joint ventures (9 products).
- The measures concerned all the three types of sectors contemplated by Article 28: 'infant industries' (3 products), those 'undergoing restructuring' (11 products), and those 'facing social problems' (3 products).
- The current MFN and EU rates fell into two categories: zero rates (11 products), and positive rates (6 products).[25] The positive rates are either 4.9% (4 products) or 10% (2 products). For zero-rated products, the proposed exceptional rates would be, depending on the product: 5%, 8% or 15% for imports from the EU; and, respectively, 10%, 10% and 20% for imports from elsewhere. For products with positive rates, the exceptional tariffs would be: 6.5% for EU products and 8.5% for non-EU products (for the 4 chemical products with 4.9% bound rates); and 20% for EU products and 25% for non-EU products (for the 2 glass products with 10% bound rates). Therefore, the 'element of preference' in favour of the EU, whose principle is required by Article 28, would be rather low: either 2 percentage points (for 5 products) or 5 points (for 12 products).

In response to the information provided by Hungary, and in view of the test-case nature of its proposal, the Community delegation at the Joint Committee raised a number of objections centring on three issues. The first involved the concepts of 'infant industries', 'restructuring' and 'social difficulties' which the Hungarian authorities were asked to define. The second was the proposed measures and sectors concerned, for which supplementary information was requested. The third was the issue of products with bound zero MFN rates. The Community claimed that no exceptional measures could be introduced for these products (which accounted for the majority of the Hungarian list) by virtue of Article 28 (Paragraph 5).[26] Both Parties agreed to continue consultations in the framework of an *ad hoc* working group.

Despite several meetings of the *ad hoc* working group, consultations had not been concluded after one year of discussions. Some Hungarian officials bitterly complained of the length of the procedure. They regretted that their government had chosen to 'ask the Community's permission' rather than 'inform the

Community of its decision' to apply exceptional measures. These officials felt that their government should adopt a more aggressive attitude now that the Europe Agreement had been ratified and had entered into force. Others, however, seemed not at all unhappy that the long consultations had prevented tariff increases in Hungary.

The issue of Article 28 measures was again taken up in April 1994 at the first meeting of the Association Committee which followed the first EU–Hungary Association Council held in March 1994, a few weeks after entry into force of the Europe Agreement. There the EU delegation proposed to accept the Hungarian request for 6 products, provided the request was dropped for the remaining 11 products. Further consultations were held in May, but no agreement has been reached as yet. In the end, it seems that an agreement will be reached and that exceptional measures will be introduced for 7 products (4 chemical products, 2 glass products and 1 paper product). Meanwhile, the Hungarian authorities have refrained from implementing any unilateral measures. As a matter of fact, it appears that no tariff increase has been implemented by Hungary against imports of industrial products from either the EU or elsewhere since the Interim Agreement came into effect on 1 March 1992.

Finally, note that the primacy of the EA over GATT obligations, which was hypothesized at the end of the previous section, appears to be confirmed by the behaviour of the Hungarian authorities in this case. The 'element of preference' demanded by Article 28 implies that the implementation of exceptional measures requires the consent of GATT. But rather than simultaneously consulting with the EU and seeking GATT's approval, the Hungarian authorities have chosen to concentrate first on the former. They believe, probably rightly so, that agreement by the EU is a prerequisite for obtaining the assent of other GATT members.

5.3.2 Quantitative Restrictions

As already indicated, there is no clear procedure in Hungary for setting up either the global value of the consumer goods quota or individual product limits. By implication, it is difficult to assess the extent of the demands to lower quotas. In any event, the Europe Agreement allows no scope for lowering quotas, since they are bound as of 1 March 1992.

In 1993, the global quota for consumer goods was set at $750 million, up $100 million compared with 1991. The global quota was divided into twenty individual limits corresponding to broad product categories, which fall into eight groups: textiles and clothing (6 product categories), agriculture (6 product categories), transport vehicles (3 product categories, the only ones subject to quantity rather than value limits), household detergent (1 product category), footwear (1 product category), tobacco (1 product category), jewellery (1 product category), and other industrial goods (1 product category).

Detailed examination of the individual product limits does not reveal any tightening of quotas nor any diversion in favour of EU producers during the period 1991–93. Since 1991, the value limits have been increased for all products, with the exception of beverages, where there was a slight decrease. Some product categories have been broken down, implying an increase in restrictiveness. The only new product group subject to quotas has been transport vehicles. The Europe Agreement introduced a quota of 50 000 units for passenger cars originating in the EU in 1992. In 1993, the global quota for vehicles announced by MIER was 160 000 units, broken down into 80 000 new and 80 000 used cars. The quota for vehicles originating in the EU was 80 000 units, broken down into 40 000 each of new and used cars. The 50% share in favour of products originating in the EU applies to nearly all individual global quotas.

5.3.3 Anti-dumping Actions

Until 1991, Hungary had made no recourse to anti-dumping actions.[27] To date, the situation has remained unchanged.

5.3.4 Safeguard Actions

Until 1991, Hungary never applied Paragraph 5 of its Protocol of Accession which authorizes selective safeguard actions.[28] Since then, the situation has somewhat changed.

Since the entry into force of the Interim Agreement, Hungary has never used the safeguard clause (Article 24 of the IEA or Article 30 of the EA) against imports from the EU. According to the *Hungarian Business Herald* (1993), however, since 1992 four actions have been taken against imports from non-EU countries. In accordance with Government Decree 113/1990, which is based on Paragraph 5, the actions were in the form of selective import quotas applicable for one year. The following products and countries are covered by these actions: various cements from the Czech Republic, Slovakia, Romania, the CIS, Estonia, Latvia, Lithuania and Georgia; various iron and steel products from the Czech Republic, Slovakia, Romania, Ukraine and Russia; various paper products from countries other than the EU and Finland; and various chemical products from the CIS, the Czech Republic, Slovakia and Romania.

The limited number of safeguard actions seems to confirm the importance played by the predominantly liberal-minded Ministry of Finance in the trade policy decision process, at least until 1992. It also implies that the diversion in favour of EU producers, although probably real, was not very extensive.

5.3.5 Other Measures

Since entry into force of the Agreement in February 1994 the Hungarian authorities have adopted no restrictive measures under Article 63 despite balance of payments difficulties. So far, Hungary is one of the few CEECs not to have imposed an import surcharge for balance of payments reasons.

On the other hand, Hungary has adopted in January 1993 a government decree on quality control for consumer goods which resembles closely a non-tariff barrier targeted at products belonging to the consumer goods quota. The Community delegation at the February 1993 meeting of the Joint Committee requested that Hungary followed Community procedures in the context of the gradual approximation of the Hungarian legislation to Community law. These procedures distinguish products between those requiring quality controls and those that do not. The Commission demanded that Hungary accept Community certificates of conformity for the former and abandon quality controls for the latter. Much of the dispute centred around footwear and clothing which are covered by the decree but are not subject to quality certification in the Community. The issue remained unresolved and was brought up again at the April 1994 meeting of the Association Committee. There the Hungarian delegation reiterated that the decree was adopted for consumer protection but announced its revision in consultation with the EU.

5.4 Conclusion

Since the 1989 revolutions, countries in Central and Eastern Europe have implemented major trade liberalization programmes, with a swiftness matched only by the rapidity of political changes. The experience of other reforming countries suggests, however, that trade liberalization is often difficult to sustain over a long period, unless governments succeed in building reputation and establishing mechanisms of commitment. GATT obligations can greatly help in this respect, although they lack enforcement discipline. Further international commitment can be obtained by gaining membership in regional groupings dominated by a single partner whose market size is large enough to enforce discipline. A free trade area between a small reforming country and a large country may, therefore, constitute a credible device for sustaining trade liberalization in the reforming partner.

The central hypothesis of this chapter was that Europe Agreements potentially provided a powerful institutional mechanism for sustaining trade opening in the CEECs at a time when the 'honeymoon of trade liberalization' was coming to an end. This potential was related to the ability of the EAs to reduce both the demand for and the supply of protection, even if only the latter was investigated. A secondary hypothesis concerned the potential diversion of protection created by the EAs.

These hypotheses were tested against the experience of Hungary. It was found that the Europe Agreement has had the expected impact on both the process of trade policy formulation and the actual outcome of trade policy. In spite of strong protectionist pressures, Hungary was therefore, able to maintain the course and continue with trade liberalization. At the same time, little evidence of protection diversion was unearthed. There is a clear exception that proves this general rule. The Europe Agreement imposes little discipline regarding the protection of agricultural products. As a result, much of the recent demand and supply of protection in Hungary has taken place in this area.

At the end of the day, the question arises as to whether the Europe Agreement provides a sufficiently solid environment to enable Hungary to continue with trade liberalization despite two major developments. The first concerns the deterioration of the trade balance which has produced liberalization fatigue. In December 1993 the government presented an economic programme aimed at reducing the deficit through a combination of export promotion and import-curtailing measures. The latter included the reintroduction of licences and the increase of import duties for certain agricultural products, as well as the freezing for 1994 of the global quota for consumer goods at the 1993 level. The second development is the May 1994 election which produced a new majority whose commitment to resist protectionist demands remains untested.

The important lesson to be drawn from the Hungarian experience is that Europe Agreements can be successful in tying the hands of the CEECs in favour of liberal trade policies and need not result in protection diversion. But these outcomes cannot be achieved by Europe Agreements alone. Liberal trade policies in the CEECs require a strong internal commitment to trade liberalization, but also a commitment by the EU to improve access to its market. Similarly, preventing protection diversion demands a strong internal commitment to GATT rules.

Notes

1. See Michaely *et al.* (1991).
2. Rodrik (1992). See also Rodrik (1989).
3. See Cooper (1993), and de Melo, *et al.* (1993).
4. See Gács (1993).
5. See, for instance, McKinnon (1991) and Nuti and Portes (1993).
6. Council for Mutual Economic Assistance.
7. It would be absurd for anyone in favour of EU membership for Central and Eastern Europe to judge the EAs against the benchmark of free trade, since the EU has not embraced free trade. I suggest, therefore, to those who insist on the ideal of free trade for Central and Eastern Europe that EU membership may not be desirable. As far as I am concerned I would be satisfied if the EAs could, not so simply, secure continued trade liberalization and EU membership for Central and Eastern Europe.
8. With the exception of Bulgaria, all the CEECs which are party to Europe Agreements are GATT Contracting Parties. Hungary, Poland and Romania became GATT members with special protocols of accession.

9. This section draws heavily on GATT (1991).
10. Other planned economies, such as Poland and Romania, acceded to the GATT on the basis of import commitments which imposed certain minimum import levels.
11. The selectivity clause could operate both ways, on imports into and exports from Hungary.
12. This was due to the peculiarities of the Hungarian legal system.
13. Government Decree 112/1990 has been replaced by Government Decree 173/1993. The new decree modifies slightly the list of products subject to licensing and replaces the 6-month period by a 12-month period.
14. In addition to provisions on trade in goods (Arts 7–36 of the EA), the Interim Agreement also contains provisions on free convertibility (EA Art. 59), competition rules (EA Arts 62–64) and intellectual property rights (EA Art. 65).
15. A lower-level Joint Committee was in charge of monitoring the Interim Agreement.
16. This fee applies only to products subject to licensing.
17. Separate rules apply to textile products and processed agricultural goods belonging to the consumer goods quota.
18. In 1994 (January–May), the EU accounted for 50% of Hungary's exports and 44% of its imports.
19. The 50% figure is slightly above the share of EU exporters in the total imports of Hungary. See Inotai (1993). In some instances, declarations attached to the European Agreement contain explicit obligations for Hungary to grant the EU a share of no less than 50% of a quota.
20. See GATT (1991), Commission of the European Communities (1992), and Nagy (1993).
21. According to figures computed by Dr Borszeki the share of liberalized imports was 84% in 1991, 85% in 1992 and 86% in 1993 (ten months). These figures, which are widely quoted in Hungary, are a very imperfect indicator of trade liberalization. The greater the restrictiveness of licences and quotas, the larger the upward bias. According to Professor Török the share of liberalized imports is now over 90%, based on a tariff line count.
22. European Commission (1994).
23. See Nagy (1993) and Varga (1994).
24. GATT (1991).
25. The tariff rates on products originating in the EU are equal to the MFN rates for all 17 products. The reason is that the tariffs on the 6 products with positive MFN rates will only be reduced, for imports originating in the EU, from 1 January 1995.
26. The Hungarian delegation claimed, instead, that Paragraph 5 only applies to products for which tariffs have been eliminated by the Europe Agreement.
27. See GATT (1991).
28. See GATT (1991).

References

Cooper, R. (1993), 'Round table discussion', in J. de Melo and A. Panagarya (eds), *New Dimensions in Regional Integration*, Cambridge University Press, Cambridge.

Commission of the European Communities (1992), 'Hungary – towards a market economy', *Economic Papers* No. 95, Commission of the European Communities, Directorate-General for Economic and Financial Affairs, Brussels.

European Commission (1994), *Economic Reform Monitor*, May/June, Directorate-General for Economic and Financial Affairs, Brussels.

de Melo, J., Panagarya, A. and Rodrik, D. (1993), 'The new regionalism: A country perspective', in J. de Melo and A. Panagarya (eds), *New Dimensions in Regional Integration*, Cambridge University Press, Cambridge.

GATT (1991), *Trade Policy Review: Hungary*, GATT, Geneva.

Gacs, J. (1993), 'Trade liberalization in Eastern Europe: Rush and reconsideration – Experiences of the CSFR, Hungary and Poland', in J. Gacs and G. Winckler (eds), *International Trade and Restructuring in Eastern Europe*, IIASA, Vienna.

Hillman, A., Hinds, M., Milanovic, B. and Ursprung, B.(1993), 'Protectionist pressures and enterprise restructuring: The political economy of international trade policy in the transition', paper presented at the Tel Aviv–Konstanz Conference on International Economics, 14-15 October, Konstanz.

Hungarian Business Herald (1993), 'Market protection measures initiated in 1992 and in the first half of 1993 in Hungary', 1993/4, 38–39.

Inotai, A. (1993), 'The economic impacts of the Association Agreement: The case of Hungary', Working Paper No. 11, Institute for World Economics, Hungarian Academy of Sciences, Budapest.

McKinnon, R. (1991), *The Order of Economic Liberalization: Financial Control in the Transition to a Market Economy*, The Johns Hopkins University Press, Baltimore.

Michaely, M., Papageorgiou, D. and Choksi, A. (1991), *Liberalizing Foreign Trade – Lessons of Experience in the Developing Countries*, vols 1–7, Basil Blackwell, Oxford.

Nagy, A. (1993), 'Import liberalization in Hungary', Discussion Paper No. 17, Institute of Economics, Hungarian Academy of Sciences, Budapest

Nuti, D. and Portes, R (1993), 'Central Europe: The way forward', in R. Portes (ed.), *Economic Transformation in Central Europe: A Progress Report*, CEPR, London and Office for Official Publications of the European Communities, Luxembourg.

Rodrik, D. (1989), 'Credibility of trade reform – A policy maker's guide', *The World Economy*, **12**, 1–16.

Rodrik, D. (1992), 'The limits of trade policy reform in developing countries', *Journal of Economic Perspectives*, **6**, 87–105.

Varga, M. (1994), 'Trade policy and competitiveness in Hungary', draft chapter of a thesis to be submitted to the European University Institute.

Winters, L.A. (1992), 'The Europe Agreements: Briefing note for "The Association Process –Making It Work for Europe"', mimeo, CEPR, London.

PART 2

Complementary Policies and Institutions

6

Linking Competition and Trade Policies in Central and East European Countries*

Bernard M. Hoekman and Petros C. Mavroidis

6.1 Introduction

Six Central and East European countries (CEECs) – Bulgaria, the Czech Republic, Hungary, Poland, Romania and the Slovak Republic – have negotiated far-reaching Association Agreements with the European Union (EU), so-called Europe Agreements. These Agreements will result in free trade in goods, and include commitments by the CEECs to adopt many of the disciplines of the Treaty of Rome. This chapter focuses on one aspect of the Europe Agreements: competition policy. It does so from the perspective of international trade policy, and from the perspective of the CEECs. The primary goal of the chapter is to explore possible institutional mechanisms that could be implemented by CEEC governments with a view to increasing the sensitivity of competition law enforcement to trade and investment policy.

The outline of the chapter is as follows. We start in section 6.2 with a brief general discussion of the linkages between trade and competition policies. This is followed by a short review of the current state of knowledge regarding 'best practices' in the area of competition policy and the experience of market economies in implementing such policies. Section 6.3 summarizes the requirements of the Europe Agreements in the area of competition policy. Section 6.4 provides an overview of existing competition legislation and institutions in the six CEECs, drawing upon a more detailed country-by-country summary of

* The views expressed in this chapter are personal and should not be attributed to the World Bank or the GATT Secretariat. We are grateful to Kathryn Cusack for excellent secretarial assistance, and David Audretsch, Milan Banas, Alexis Jacquemin, Andras Lakatos, Jan Michalek, Serban Modoran, Peter Palecka, Janusz Piotrowski, Richard Portes, Peter Stefanov and Alan Winters for helpful discussions and suggestions and for providing us with materials.

current laws contained in Appendix 6.2. Almost all the CEECs have passed competition legislation and allocated the responsibility for enforcing their competition rules. They have received substantial technical assistance from OECD members in this connection.[1] Section 6.5 discusses a number of institutional options that would allow competition aspects of trade policy decisions to be taken into consideration by administering authorities and governments. Three situations are distinguished: (1) the transitional period before the entry into force of the Europe Agreement; (2) the period during which the Europe Agreement applies; and (3) eventual accession to the EU. Section 6.6 concludes.

6.2 Trade and Competition Policies: Basic Issues

National competition policy can be defined as the set of rules and disciplines maintained by governments relating either to agreements between firms that restrict competition or to the abuse of a dominant position (including attempts to create a dominant position through merger). The underlying objective of competition policy in most jurisdictions tends to be efficient resource allocation, and thereby the maximization of national welfare.[2] Most competition laws attempt to attain this objective by prohibiting the abuse of dominant positions (either through prohibition or through regulation), and forbidding various kinds of competition-restricting agreements between competitors. The focus of competition laws is on competition, reflecting the belief, which is extensively supported by empirical evidence, that vigorous competition is frequently the best way to foster economic efficiency. Many jurisdictions recognize that specific agreements between firms that may reduce competition could be efficiency enhancing, and make allowance for such agreements. The burden of proof, however, in such instances is usually upon the participants in such arrangements.

The objectives underlying trade policy contrast starkly with those of competition laws. Governments pursue trade policies for a variety of reasons, including as a means to raise revenue, to protect specific industries (whether 'infant', 'senile' or other), to shift the terms of trade, to attain certain foreign policy or security goals, or simply to restrict the consumption of specific goods. Whatever the underlying objective, an active trade policy redistributes income between segments of the population by protecting specific industries and the factors of production employed there, and usually does so in an inefficient manner. Trade policy is consequently often inconsistent with the objectives underlying competition policy. The way this inconsistency is frequently put is that competition law aims at protecting *competition* (and thus economic efficiency), while trade policy aims at protecting *competitors* (or factors of production). The issue facing governments is to ensure that competition prevails. This requires the design of institutional mechanisms that allow governments to explicitly consider the competition implications of particular trade or investment policies.

The more restrictive the trade/investment regime, the more important competition policy becomes to reduce the inevitable negative welfare consequences of the reduction in competition that results from restricting the contestability of markets. From an economic (efficiency) perspective, using competition policy to attempt to offset the competitive distortions created by an active trade policy is of course an exercise in the second best, and may not be welfare enhancing. A preferable policy is to minimize the extent to which trade policy reduces the contestability of markets in the first place. Thus, a liberal external policy stance is a cheap and effective competition policy. Competition from imports is a very important source of discipline upon the behaviour of firms operating in a market.[3] This is the case in particular for the CEECs, given the highly concentrated industrial structures inherited from the past. While a free trade stance greatly reduces the scope of the task facing competition authorities, however, it does not imply that the need for competition rules disappear. Many products are non-tradable (e.g., many services), or, even if tradable, competition may be limited to local markets for other reasons.[4] Free trade must therefore be complemented by the freedom of entry, including the possibility to contest markets through foreign direct investment. Even then, certain products may be produced by (natural) monopolies, by firms with global market power, or by firms where natural or 'unnatural' (government-made) barriers to entry restrict contestability. And, the more open markets are to foreign products, the greater the potential vulnerability to anticompetitive practices of foreign monopolists or cartels. In all such cases competition rules should apply.

In instances where sovereign states have concluded economic integration agreements, the reach of competition policy may be extended to include the behaviour of governments as well as firms. Thus, in the case of the EU, competition policy disciplines also pertain to public monopolies and state-owned enterprises, and governments are restricted in their ability to subsidize firms located in their territory insofar as this affects trade between Member States. It is important to realize that in the EU context, where the ultimate goal is the realization of a common market, competition disciplines are intended not only to enhance efficiency, but also serve as another instrument through which to attain the integration objective. The goal is to ensure that the removal of trade barriers is not nullified by actions on the part of firms or governments to maintain or recreate market segmentation. The 'trade effect' criterion included in the Treaty of Rome's competition policy disciplines implies that in the EU context competition rules are a *complement* to the internal trade policy of the EU, i.e. free trade.[5]

The CEECs have signed far-reaching Association Agreements with the EU that imply a free trade, free foreign direct investment stance towards the EU will exist once the various transitional periods have ended. Trade agreements have also been negotiated with the EFTA countries, and between the CEECs themselves (the Central European Free Trade Association). While the associated trade liberalization reduces the need for an active competition policy stance, it by no means makes competition law enforcement redundant. For one, there is the transition period during which trade or investment barriers remain high for some sectors. More importantly, account needs to be taken of the policy stance towards the rest of the world, of the various safeguard mechanisms built into the EAs that allow for possible intervention to support domestic industries, of the fact that some markets are difficult to contest by foreign firms, and of the actions of other parts of the government that may restrain competition.

6.2.1 Implementing Institutions, Criteria and Procedures

The presumption underlying competition policies is generally that vigorous competition between firms in an industry will foster efficiency. Competition *per se* will not, however, necessarily ensure efficient outcomes. Much depends on the kind of competition that firms engage in, or alternatively, on the objectives underlying agreements between firms in an industry that reduce competition between them. Certain types of agreements between firms may be welfare enhancing for the nation as a whole. Thus, agreements to form an export cartel may allow a domestic industry to raise prices on export markets and improve the country's terms of trade and welfare. Cooperation between firms may also lead to dynamic benefits, e.g., research joint ventures or agreements on the development/use of common standards allowing positive network externalities to be realized. Most competition laws recognize that some agreements between competitors that appear to be competition reducing may in fact not reduce competition, or, even if limiting competition, may be welfare increasing. As a result, a distinction is generally made between *per se* rules and *conditional prohibitions*. The former unconditionally prohibit certain forms of behaviour (agreements). The latter prohibit certain types of cooperation (collusion) in principle, but may permit their existence if the firm(s) involved can convince the competition authorities that the agreement is welfare enhancing.[6] Space constraints prohibit any detailed discussion of competition law theory and principles.[7] What follows is limited to a number of issues that are of particular significance for the CEECs.

A first issue is to determine what types of agreements/behaviour should be subject to *per se* rules. There are only a limited number of competition-reducing agreements between firms that can be rejected on an *a priori* basis (assuming the objective is efficiency), of which price fixing and agreements with similar effects are the most important.[8] Theory suggests these types of arrangements should be subject to *per se* prohibition, and in most jurisdictions they are. A strong political economy argument can be made for a restrictive approach to *per se* rules in the CEEC context. Firms need to have the maximum amount of flexibility to compete in whatever way they see appropriate to their situation. Insofar as there is some uncertainty regarding the legal and institutional environment in an economy in transition, firms may need to be 'creative' in terms of their contractual arrangements.

The majority of countries with active antitrust enforcement identify three types of practices that *may* be prohibited: competition-reducing practices or arrangements between firms; the abuse of a dominant position; and the establishment of a dominant position. Important in this context are not so much the specific legislated rules, but the criteria that apply when implementing the law. For example, in the context of an investigation into abuse of a dominant position, the criteria include those for defining the product and geographical scope of the market, the threshold of necessary market power, and the methods used to determine the feasibility of entry. Experience reveals that the effect and operation of competition laws very much depends on the implementing rules that are applied.

A final issue relates to the design of the institutional mechanisms for enforcing competition rules. This includes the allocation of responsibility for enforcing competition law to an entity, its relationship to the government and legislature, its powers of investigation and sanction, its financing and staffing, and the mechanisms to ensure transparency and consistency, including the availability of an oversight or appeals body (the courts or a tribunal).

The approaches taken by OECD countries towards competition law and policy are quite diverse, reflecting in part differences in economic philosophy, and in part differences in size and openness. A number of lessons can be drawn from both economic theory and experience:[9]

- The focus of the rules and enforcement efforts should be on all sectors, including services, and should centre on the *effects* of agreements between firms, not on their form. The basis for intervening should be market power, not dominance (as measured, e.g., by market shares). A key criterion in investigating whether an arrangement between firms or an action of a firm violates competition rules should be the ease of entry into, and exit from, the industry. Contestability is what matters.
- The number of *per se* prohibitions should be small and focus on horizontal, price-fixing arrangements. Disciplines on vertical restraints should be subject to a well-defined contestability constraint, i.e. a necessary condition for pursuing vertical restraints is significant entry barriers.
- Competition rules should provide *ex post* disciplines on trade policy-created or supported abuse of market power, ideally including a mandate for competition authorities to recommend the removal/reduction of trade barriers and to be consulted in the trade policy formation process.
- The criteria that are used in investigations should be spelled out clearly in

guidelines. *De minimis* rules should be included. Firms should face as little uncertainty regarding potential liability as is possible. Detailed reports of investigations should be published. Procedures should be transparent.
- Civil parties should be able to sue persons (natural and legal) deemed to engage in behaviour violating the competition rules. Enforcement authorities should have the power to levy substantial fines and award damages.
- Both investigating procedures and substantive reasoning should be subject to review by an appeals body that is independent of the enforcement authority.
- An independent body should exist with the mandate to analyse and publicize the costs and benefits to the economy of government created or maintained barriers to entry in individual industries.

6.3 The Europe Agreements' Competition Rules

The Europe Agreements (EAs) foresee the application of the basic competition rules of the EU by the associated countries to practices that affect trade between the EU and each Central and East European country. The rules relate to agreements between firms restricting competition, abuse of dominant position, the behaviour of public undertakings (state-owned firms) and competition-distorting state aids (Articles 85, 86, 90 and 92 of the EEC Treaty respectively). Thus, competition policy is defined widely to include the behaviour of governments as well as of firms. Implementing rules are to be adopted by the Association Council on a consensus basis within three years of the entry into force of the Agreements.[10]

Each Europe Agreement must be ratified by 13 national parliaments plus the European Parliament, because the agreements include issues on which the Commission does not have exclusive competence. To accelerate the implementation of the trade and trade-related provisions of the EAs, interim agreements were signed that entered into force on 1 March 1992 for the so-called Visegrad four (Hungary, Poland, and the Czech and Slovak Republics), 1 May 1993 for Romania and 31 December 1993 for Bulgaria. They will remain in force until the EAs are ratified.[11] As competition policy is a EU competence, it is covered by the interim agreements. The interim agreements revise the language of the EAs as regards the determination of implementing rules by requiring that these be adopted by decision within three years of the entry into force of the interim agreements by the Joint Committee (established under the earlier Cooperation Agreements that had been negotiated with Hungary, Poland and the Czech and Slovak Republics). Subcommittees for competition have been established under auspices of the Joint Committees. It has been agreed that cooperation between the EU and CEEC antitrust authorities is to follow the 1986 OECD Council Recommendation dealing with cooperation on restrictive business practices affecting international trade, and Article V of the agreement between the EU and the United States regarding the application of their competition laws ('positive comity').[12]

The notion of 'positive comity' appears alongside 'traditional' comity in the September 1991 cooperation agreement in antitrust between the EU and the United States.[13] According to the traditional comity principle, sovereign states will consider important interests of other states when exercising their own jurisdiction (Article VI of the agreement).[14] 'Positive comity' shifts the initiative to the state whose interests are affected, which is given the legal option of requesting another state to initiate appropriate enforcement proceedings if this could address the complaining country's concerns (Article V of the agreement). While it clearly goes beyond the traditional principle that is embodied in the OECD Recommendations, the ultimate decision remains at the discretion of the state asked to act. As discussed further below, the notion of positive comity could be exploited further in the trade-competition policy context.[15]

Appendix 6.1 reproduces the relevant Articles pertaining to competition policy from the EA with Hungary. The other EAs contain virtually identical language.[16] As far as disciplines on enterprise behaviour are concerned, the basic rules of the Treaty of Rome have been included. That is, practices that restrict or distort competition and abuses of dominant positions (in either the EU or the relevant CEEC), insofar as they affect trade, are to be assessed on the basis of criteria arising from the application of Articles 85 and 86 EEC. This wording implies that the case law that has been built up in the last 45 years in the EU applies. Article 85 EEC prohibits agreements and concerted practices – both tacit and explicit, whether enforceable or not – that restrict or distort competition in the common market and may affect trade between EU member states. Both horizontal and vertical restraints are covered. The EU applies a version of the 'effects' doctrine: the focus is on distortions of competition within the community, independent of the national origin of the firms involved. Implementation of the conduct within the EU is necessary to assert jurisdiction.[17] Effects on trade may be potential, indirect as well as direct, and involve stimulating as well as restricting trade (e.g., through the use of cross-subsidization). A *de minimis* rule has been established by the European Commission under which firms with relevant market shares below 5% and aggregate annual turnover of less than ECU 200 million are exempted from the reach of competition disciplines. Article 85:3 EEC offers the possibility of exemptions from the general prohibition on competition distorting agreements if it can be shown that the agreement is in the public interest.[18] Certain types of agreements have been granted 'block' exemptions, including those relating to standardization and R&D cooperation, exclusive distribution (as long as parallel imports remain feasible), exclusive purchasing and automobile distribution and servicing. The Commission can self-initiate investigations or respond to complaints and has the power to demand information and levy fines for non-compliance.

Article 86 EEC prohibits abuse of a dominant position. Dominance is determined on the basis of the relevant product and geographic markets. Dominance may relate to the common market as a whole or 'a substantial part thereof'. No quantitative criteria are mentioned in Article 86 regarding the interpretation of substantial, or the market share (or other indicators) required for dominance. Abuse is also left undefined. Article 86 contains an illustrative list of abuses, including unfair trading, price discrimination, tie-ins or bundling, and restricting output or access to markets.

There are some key differences between the rules that apply under the EAs and those that apply to EU or European Economic Area (EEA) Member States. First, the EAs do not reproduce Article 85:3 EEC and thus do not make any allowance for the granting of exemptions. Presumably this will be one of the matters to be addressed by the Association Council/Joint Committee in developing implementation rules. Until then, exemptions granted by national CEEC competition offices do not have to be recognized by the EU (see also Bourgeois, 1993). Second, the EAs do not contain disciplines relating to mergers, and the Commission will presumably apply the relevant regulation unilaterally.[19] Third, they do not spell out what bodies are responsible for enforcement of EA disciplines, the criteria for allocating responsibility, and the options for appeal. These are matters that are left for the Association Council/Joint Committee to determine.

Public undertakings and undertakings to which special or exclusive rights have been granted (e.g., monopolies), are to be subject to the principles of Article 90 EEC within three years of the entry into force of the association agreement. Article 90 requires non-discrimination on the basis of nationality and behaviour consistent with the other competition principles and rules of the EU, including Articles 85 and 86, and 92, insofar as the application of these rules does not impede the realization of the tasks assigned to the public undertaking. State monopolies of a commercial character are to be adjusted within five years to ensure non-discrimination regarding the conditions under which goods are procured and marketed between EU and CEEC nationals (this is analogous to Article 37 EEC).

Turning to disciplines on state aids, until implementing rules are adopted, GATT rules with respect to countervailing of subsidies will apply. State aid, compatible with EU rules for disadvantaged regions (Article 92.3(a) Treaty of Rome), can be applied to the entire territories of the associated states during the first five years. Such regional aid may be given by EU governments to regions in their countries with per capita incomes that are substantially below average, or to areas where there is significant unemployment. The low level of per capita incomes in the CEECs in comparison to those of EU states should ensure that non-industry-specific state aids will be unconstrained in the medium term. The agreements also provide for enhanced transparency of state aids. The adequacy of these provisions are to be determined by the Association Council. State aids to agriculture and fisheries are excluded from competition policy disciplines, and separate rules are to be implemented by the Association Council within three years for the steel sector. The latter are to be based upon Articles 65 and 66 of the Treaty of Paris (European Coal and Steel Community, ECSC), and make allowance for state aids permitted under ECSC auspices.

6.4 Competition Laws and Institutions in the CEECs

Five of the six CEECs currently have competition legislation in force: Bulgaria, the Czech Republic, Hungary, Poland and the Slovak Republic.[20] To a greater or lesser extent CEEC laws are modelled on the EU's approach to competition policy, distinguishing between collusive arrangements (Article 85), abuse of dominant positions (Article 86) and rules for mergers. All the laws apply to goods and service markets (although some services are excluded in some jurisdictions), all appear to follow an 'effects doctrine' approach, and all are based on the conditional prohibition model. While many types of collusive arrangements appear to be prohibited on a *per se* basis, in most cases exemptions are possible. Although superficially similar, there are substantial differences between the various laws. The discussion that follows draws upon the more detailed overview in Appendix 6.2.[21] After the breakup of the Czech and Slovak Federal Republic, the 1991 Federal competition law continued to be enforced in both countries. The Czech Republic adopted an amendment to the 1991 Federal law in November 1993, and a revised law is expected to be submitted to the Slovak Parliament in mid 1994. Until the Slovak Parliament adopts the draft legislation, the Slovak Anti-monopoly Office will apply the 1991 Czech and Slovak Federal law.

6.4.1 *Substantive disciplines*

All the CEEC laws prohibit certain types of anti-competitive practices on a conditional basis. The Czech and Slovak law is the only one to contain an unconditional *per se* prohibition on arrangements that violate legal norms of ethical behaviour and on contracts that obstruct 'in a substantial way economic competition in a market'. It provides an illustrative list of agreements that are prohibited (void) unless an exemption is granted by the competition authorities. Exemptions are automatic for an exhaustive list of types of prohibited agreements if the authority makes no objection within two months of the receipt of the request for an exemption.[22] For other types of agreements explicit exemptions must be granted, the criterion being that this is in the public interest, in turn defined as supporting technological or economic development. The November 1993 Czech amendment to the Federal law gives the Ministry of Economic Competition the right to grant block exemptions along EEC 85:3 lines. The Hungarian law contains a much shorter illustrative list of prohibited practices, relying instead on a general rule: agreements are not to result in a restriction of economic competition. Exemptions can be granted if an agreement is aimed at stopping the 'abuse of economic superiority', or is 'of minor significance' (defined as the firms involved having less than 10% of the relevant market), or if the restriction does not exceed what is required to achieve 'economically justifiable common goals' *and* the resulting economic benefits outweigh the costs. The Office of Economic Competition may present an appeal to the Constitutional Court to express criticism of effective laws and regulations. To date, this option has not been exercised (OECD, 1993c).

The Polish law has an *exhaustive* rather than illustrative list of prohibited 'monopolistic practices'. Exemptions may be granted if the agreements do not significantly restrain competition and are 'necessary to conduct an economic activity'. The Bulgarian law does not list specific collusive arrangements, simply containing a sweeping prohibition on contracts that restrict the choice of a party to the agreement or consumers, unless these are not injurious to consumers. Exemptions can be requested.

All the laws follow the EU approach of prohibiting the abuse of dominant positions. In contrast to Article 86 EEC, the CEECs have specified quantitative criteria defining when a position of dominance exists. The Czech criterion is a market share of 30% or more; in Poland it is 40%; in Hungary 30% (or 50% for the largest 3 firms); and in Bulgaria it is 35%. Firms meeting the criterion are required to notify this to the antitrust authorities. The Czech and Slovak, Hungarian and Polish laws contain illustrative lists of abuses of dominant positions, while the Bulgarian one has an exhaustive list.

Turning to merger disciplines, all the laws require firms to notify mergers that result in a market share exceeding a target level. These levels are those that comprise dominance, i.e. a market share of at least 30, 40, 30 and 35%, respectively, for the Czech and Slovak Republics, Poland, Hungary and Bulgaria. Hungary, however, also requires all mergers where the joint turnover is at least 10 billion Forints (some $100 million) to be notified, even if the market share threshold is not exceeded. More generally, both the Czech and Slovak and Hungarian laws allow mergers that exceed the threshold to be approved if the resulting economic benefits offset the costs. How these terms are defined, however, remains unclear, and usually it will be up to the firm(s) involved to present a case.[23] The Polish and Bulgarian laws do not mention any criteria at all for approving mergers that exceed the market share threshold. In the Czech and Slovak case mergers are automatically approved if no objection is made within three months of notification. In Poland and Hungary this period is two months, and in Bulgaria only one month. Extensions of these time limits are possible.

It is noteworthy that the Czech and Slovak law gives the competition authorities the right to comment on privatization proposals. The law requires the government to analyse the market conditions that are likely to result from a privatization proposal, and ensure that privatization will either result in the abolition of a monopoly if one exists, or not result in a monopoly if one does not exist. The Polish law contains a similar provision that has been actively applied. Over 1 900 'structural decisions' (relating to privatization and transformation of firms) were made in the period 1990–92 by the Polish Antimonopoly Office, of which 89% were approved (OECD, 1993a, p.18). Hungary and Bulgaria do not give their competition offices similar (transitional) powers.

6.4.2 Procedural and institutional provisions

In all cases a separate enforcement agency has been established. The powers of the agency vary substantially across the CEECs. The Bulgarian Commission for Protection of Competition is the weakest. All its members are appointed by the National Assembly for a five year period and can presumably be fired by the same. It cannot impose fines in instances where it finds the law to be violated, having to go through the civil courts to do so. Its main remedy is the right to suggest to the Council of Ministers that it impose mandatory minimum or maximum prices for entities with a dominant position.

The head of the Czech competition office is a member of the government (with the title of Minister of Economic Competition). The Czech antitrust office has the power to levy fines up to 10% of the firm's net turnover or equal to the profits garnered as a result of violating the law. In practice, however, some competition policy decisions are apparently taken in cabinet meetings.

In Poland, two competition bodies were created: an office in charge of investigations, and a court in which decisions may be appealed against. The head of the Polish Anti-monopoly Office is appointed by the Prime Minister. Fines may be imposed by the office up to 15% of after-tax earnings of the firms. Alternatively, firms may be required to reduce prices and firms with a dominant position may be required to divest parts of their operations.

The head of the Hungarian Office of Economic Competition is appointed by the President for six years on the recommendation of the Prime Minister, and can only be fired 'if unfit for office on a lasting basis'. The office is funded from the State budget, and is answerable to the Hungarian parliament. It can impose fines ranging between 30 and 200% of the profits resulting from the violation of the law. The office has three sections: a Board of Experts responsible for investigations, a Competition Council which acts as an arbitration (administrative) court, and a Department of Competition Policy that is responsible for research and policy advice to parliament.[24] The Council does not have competence to judge violations of 'unfair competition' (Chapter 1 of the Act), instead having to file suit in civil court.

The Slovak Anti-monopoly Office is a central government body. Its Chairman is appointed and recalled by the government. Decisions of the Office can be appealed before the Supreme Court.

The antitrust agencies in the CEECs are all required to publish decisions. The Czech, Hungarian and Bulgarian laws allow for hearings to be held, but do not require it. The Hungarian enforcement agency is subject to the strictest time limits for investigations.[25] Decisions by antitrust offices can be appealed against in all the jurisdictions. In Poland appeals go to the special court created for this purpose; in the other three countries appeals go through the civil courts.

The number of cases brought in the Czech Republic, Hungary, Poland and the Slovak Republic have been quite high. In 1992, 255 cases were handled by the Hungarian Office of Economic Competition; in the Czech Republic, out of 1 200 complaints filed in 1992, the Czech Office opened some 100 investigations. In Poland, 113 antimonopoly investigations were launched in 1992, the total for 1990–92 being some 300 (OECD, 1994). The Slovak Anti-monopoly office investigated 158 and 164 cases in 1991 and 1992, respectively, and saw its case load rise to 274 cases in 1993.[26]

6.4.3 Evaluation

A commonality of the CEEC laws is that implementing authorities are given a great deal of discretion as far as interpretation of terms is concerned. Much will depend on the case law that emerges from experience and the guidelines that are developed by the competition offices. Although the leeway given to administering authorities is substantial, this also provides an opportunity to adopt implementing regulations that increase their ability to influence trade/FDI policy stances (see below). As it stands, however, firms operating in the CEECs will face a substantial amount of uncertainty regarding the precise nature of the rules. Only the Czech and Hungarian laws explicitly make use of *de minimis* provisions (5 and 10% share of the relevant market, respectively). Greater use of the concepts of horizontal and vertical restraints would help increase transparency and certainty. Only the Hungarian law makes a clear distinction along these lines, only prohibiting those vertical restraints that involve firms with a dominant position.[27] The reliance on explicit market share thresholds as the main criterion for dominance distinguishes the CEEC laws from Article 86 EEC. While apparently a straightforward indicator that should reduce uncertainty for firms, it may be difficult to monitor for firms. Market share is also not a sufficient indicator of dominance. Much will depend on the definition of the relevant antitrust market and the extent to which entry barriers are found to exist, issues that are generally left open in the various laws. Here the trade policy stance of each country will be important.

The Hungarian office has the greatest independence from the political system, followed by the Polish and Czech offices. In general, it appears that greater emphasis could be put upon procedural requirements and transparency. Hearings are neither mandatory nor necessarily public. Decisions *and* arguments/

reasoning/analysis should be subject to a publication requirement. There is a strong political economy argument to be made for maximizing transparency, as this both increases certainty/knowledge of firms regarding what is allowed and what is not, and reduces the incentive to engage in rent-seeking.

6.5 Competition Rules and Trade Policy: Issues and Options

In the context of the EAs, for each of the CEECs, four distinct time periods can be distinguished that are relevant in terms of the implementation of competition rules: (1) the period up to the entry into force of the competition articles of the Interim Agreement; (2) the period until the entry into force of the EA; (3) the phase during which the EA applies; and (4) the phase during which the country has become a member of the EU.

6.5.1 The Pre-Europe Agreement Phase

Each CEEC in principle has only three years after the implementation of the Interim Agreements in which it is unconstrained regarding its competition policies. Despite EA obligations, substantial discretion remains for national authorities regarding the implementation and enforcement of its competition policy. In this section EA obligations are assumed away. The question of EA compatibility is addressed in the next subsection (and in Appendix 6.2). Taking into account the fact that the majority of the CEECs have competition laws and enforcement bodies, policy issues that arise include: (1) whether the competition rules in force are adequate or appropriate; (2) at the level of implementation, what should be given priority by enforcement authorities, given the substantial amount of discretion implied by the wording of their respective laws; and (3) whether the enforcement agencies have sufficient resources, power and political independence to do their job. In this section the focus will be primarily on the second question. We have only limited information and knowledge on the last question. We simply assume, perhaps heroically, that there are no major problems in this connection. If there are, they should be given priority.[28] As to the first question, many of the CEECs are in the process of amending their laws (see Appendix 6.2), in part with a view to meeting the EA obligations. This is not the place for a detailed discussion of the specific changes to each of the laws that might be considered by the respective governments. Given the wide scope for discretion that is inherent in the enforcement of competition law, decisions that are internal to the implementing bureaucracy will to a great extent determine the effective impact of the laws. What is of key importance then is to enhance the transparency of the process, and minimize to the greatest extent possible any uncertainty market participants might have regarding the criteria that are employed by the competition authorities.

What might be done in addition to what is already being done by competition offices with a view to reducing the scope for protection seeking? First, and foremost, it appears useful to clarify the potential scope of antitrust for local firms by defining terms and criteria used in investigations. Given the great latitude that enforcement agencies have in the CEECs as regards interpretation of the law and the application of criteria, much can be done in this manner to reduce uncertainty and focus the attention of the agency in particular directions. Efforts should be made to specify clearly what practices are *de facto* prohibited on a *per se* basis, thereby publicly announcing what restraints (and those economic effects or results) are considered to be most pernicious. Drawing upon the experience of OECD countries, one procedure could be to distinguish vertical from horizontal restraints, and indicate that specific horizontal agreements will be viewed very critically if requests for exemptions are received, while vertical restraints will be regarded as being much less likely to infringe upon competition principles (Willig, 1992). Those jurisdictions that do not have legislated *de minimis* criteria should adopt and publish relatively high thresholds in their implementing procedures. The EU approach of defining block exemptions can be emulated.[29] This again does not necessarily require formal legislation. As competition offices are responsible for granting exemptions, they can determine the categories of agreements that do not have to be notified. Flassik (1993) has noted that, during the transition, firms and consumers that are negatively affected by restrictive business practices may be unwilling to bring cases given their dependence on existing relationships. It is therefore also important that the competition authorities take a leading role, and exploit their mandate to self-initiate.[30] Finally, transparency can be further improved by publishing not only decisions but also the underlying analysis and reasoning.

Competition authorities can act as the 'conscience' of the government, recognizing and publicizing the costs to consumers of government policies and actions that restrict competition. Trade policy is one obvious area that should be given priority in this connection, the service sector another. Competition policy offices could consider actively applying antitrust law in the light of maintained trade policies (e.g., accounting for the effect of protection on market structure, concentration, etc.). Much can be done in this connection through appropriate wording of criteria and implementation guidelines within the framework of currently existing legislation. For example, trade policy considerations can be linked to the definition of the relevant antitrust market.[31] In principle, the more an industry is protected, the narrower could be the definition of the relevant market, thereby reducing the expected profitability of seeking protection, and thus the incentive to lobby for it. In a similar vein, GATT illegal or 'grey-area' measures such as voluntary export restraint and import expansion agreements should be publicly stated to be unenforceable, and subject to competition policy enforcement.[32] *De minimis* provisions can also be related to the trade policy stance that affects an industry. The more liberal market access conditions are for foreign firms/products, the higher can be the threshold that is applied.

Active scrutiny of petitions for contingent protection should also be pursued by competition authorities. Hungary and Poland already have anti-dumping legislation, while the Czech and Slovak Republics intend to adopt the necessary statutes. Ample experience in the EU and the United States has demonstrated that such measures may be very costly to the economy. Anti-dumping in particular can be used as a tool to substantially reduce competition and enforce collusion. Ideally, no contingent protection should be granted by a government if this would have a substantially negative impact on competition (e.g., strengthen market power or dominance). The decision by the Polish government to give the Anti-monopoly Office the responsibility of implementing anti-dumping investigations is particularly noteworthy. This is laudatory, as it should ensure that competition policy criteria are applied to the firms (industry) applying for protection. Rather than being limited to an *ex post* role, the competition authorities in Poland have an *ex ante* responsibility. Of course, it is important that competition policy criteria are indeed applied, and that *ex post* monitoring remains possible. It is not necessary that competition offices be given the task of applying anti-dumping actions; what matters is that they are able to vet such actions before they are taken. Poland is unique in this regard. The draft Czech anti-dumping statute, however, also gives a role to the competition authorities. While not given a formal responsibility, the draft statute proposes that the decision to apply an anti-dumping action be taken by the government, and not by those administering the statute.[33] As the head of the competition office has Ministerial rank, this at least allows competition concerns to be raised.

The political situation in the CEECs may be somewhat special in this regard as there may be a perceived conflict between vigorous enforcement of competition law and the transition to a market economy. For example, to attract inward FDI a government may be willing to provide 'guaranteed' markets to inward investors, and do so in a way that conflicts with competition policy principles. As noted by Imrich Flassik,

> Foreign companies participating in mergers often demand conditions for the establishment of joint ventures that they would never dare to expect in their home countries. They look for certain concessions for the protection of their desired markets, such as customs privileges. The foreign partners in joint ventures seem surprised by the reaction of the [Federal Czechoslovak Antitrust] office and by the rights that it has, although in their home countries they would not behave in this way....[A]s a new institution ... we find it quite difficult to devise proper measures for the necessary ... strict adherence to the law. But if we demand too severe terms, we may discourage many foreign investors; that would restrict the creation of a competitive environment,

affecting particularly the future relaxation of protectionist measures in relation with the EC (Flassik, 1993, pp.73–74; see also Fornalczyk, 1993).[34]

Notwithstanding active participation in the policy formation process, CEEC antitrust offices have had only limited influence in opposing competition-reducing policies, be they restructuring/privatization-related or trade-related. Thus, in the case of Poland, despite attempts by the Anti-monopoly Office to prevent excessive concentration in privatized industries, often industrial or social policy considerations dominated competition concerns (OECD, 1994, p. 13). Indeed, the Polish Anti-monopoly Office supported substantial reductions in import tariffs for industries that were highly concentrated (monopolized). The resulting adjustment pressures and deterioration of the current account were such that tariffs were subsequently raised in August 1991 (the average tariff rising from 8 to 17%) (Fornalczyk, 1993). The Czech government guaranteed Volkswagen (which acquired a large stake in Skoda) that import tariffs on cars would remain at 19% (15% for vehicles of EU origin) for at least four years.[35] An active stance does, however, have some effect. For example, the Czechoslovak antitrust office was 'absolutely opposed' to the imposition of a high import tariff on cars, and succeeded in lowering the tariff that came to be applied (Flassik, 1993).

The main point to be emphasized is that competition offices have two ways of 'internalizing' trade policy. The first is to oppose trade policies that excessively harm competition on the domestic market; the second is to countervail the anti-competitive effect of trade policy on an *ex post* basis. The first, 'direct', approach has been actively pursued by a number of the CEEC competition offices. In this they compare very well to competition offices in OECD countries, who are much less visible. By commenting on or opposing suggested or existing trade policies, the competition offices ensure that the economy-wide implications of sectoral policies/lobbying are recognized and discussed. The main power of competition offices is, however, of an *ex post* nature. Active enforcement, with guidelines that clearly specify that trade policy will be an important consideration in the implementing competition laws, will help bolster the effectiveness of *ex ante* opposition to policy proposals that restrict access to markets.

Another possibility that could be pursued is to use competition law enforcement as an instrument to reduce the probability of facing contingent protection in export markets. This is an issue that applies during both the pre-EA and the EA phase, given the continued availability of anti-dumping to EU import-competing firms under the EAs. The existence of threats of anti-dumping and safeguard actions on export markets increases the incentive to control state trading, subsidization, and abuse of dominant positions. By enforcing antitrust law and allowing entry, the feasibility for import-competing firms in export markets to argue that unfair trade is taking place is reduced. There are various avenues that can be pursued here. The first is simply an informal 'lobbying' effort on the part of the CEEC government involved, under which it is argued that competition law is being actively enforced, that trade barriers are low and that there is therefore no justification for antidumping. This may have some beneficial impact, depending on the importance of the EU industry concerned. A second, complimentary, approach could be to exploit the 'positive comity' principle (see above). The Commission could be formally requested to examine each anti-dumping petition brought by an EU firm/industry in light of the active enforcement of EU-based competition laws in the CEEC home market of the exporter.[36] A third is to ensure that the country is treated as a market economy by importing nations implementing anti-dumping actions. Active competition law enforcement will help bolster the case for this.[37]

The service sector may be of particular relevance in this connection, as perceived restrictions on access to distribution channels and related services is sometimes held to be one justification for the imposition of anti-dumping measures. More generally, whatever the impact on contingent protection actions in export markets, it is very important that antitrust authorities actively pursue a strategy of fostering the contestability of service markets. Services are especially important in the process of economic development in their role of inputs into the production process generally. Services increasingly comprise the largest share of value added to a manufactured good. Design, the organization of production, inventory and production management, packaging, distribution, marketing and after sales interaction with clients (guarantees, maintenance) are all service activities.

The nature of services are such that markets are often characterized by proximity requirements (prohibiting trade and implying that competition is local), asymmetric information and imperfect competition.[38] Reputation is often crucial in signalling quality to consumers, and as reputation is difficult to establish (being a sunk cost), service markets may be difficult to contest. Pervasive product differentiation may further enhance the market power of incumbent firms. While it may be the case that, for certain regulated services, it is necessary to ensure that quality standards are satisfied, the competition authorities should attempt to ensure that 'consumer safety justifications' do not act to bolster the market power of incumbent firms by having a protectionist effect.

One lesson that can be drawn from the past decade's experience with privatization of service industries in both developed and developing countries is that many services that were (are) provided by the public sector can also be provided by the private sector, often at much lower cost. Of course, this does not necessarily imply transfer of ownership of assets, or the absence of regulatory control. What it does imply is the adoption of institutional forms making such markets contestable. Foreign investors can make a significant contribution to the improvement of the efficiency of 'public' infrastructure services. Development of an efficient economy requires that domestic residents – both final consumers and businesses – have access to high quality services for the lowest possible price. Foreign firms will often offer services that are not provided by domestic incumbents, but for which demand exists. Moreover, because many transnational service firms have an international reputation which they need to maintain, the average quality of the services provided is likely to be both higher and more constant than that which is available from domestic firms. Many of the service products that will be offered in host country markets are likely to have been developed and tested elsewhere, further reducing quality uncertainty. Prices charged will be competitive, however, only as long as care is taken that foreign service corporations do not establish a dominant position and exploit their market power. It is therefore important that efforts are made to ensure that markets remain contestable. In practice this implies that no restrictions should be placed on the number of foreign firms that are allowed to offer specific services. Entry should be free, subject to prudential supervision as deemed necessary, as the most effective source of competition for many foreign service affiliates is likely to be (the threat of entry by) other foreign or local service corporations.

As many service firms possess certain intangible assets that cannot be patented or similarly protected, care must be taken that arrangements involving the transfer of such assets and that may appear restrictive at first sight are not automatically deemed to violate the competition rules. Great care must be taken in determining whether such practices are anticompetitive and, if so, are detrimental to efficiency. In many cases they may simply reflect the need of a firm to safeguard its reputation for quality. What matters is the impact on the contestability of the markets concerned. Free entry can be expected to ensure that markets remain competitive, so that the variety and quality of services are maximized and prices are minimized. Even service industries that have natural monopoly characteristics, so that only one or two firms are able to exist, can be made contestable via the periodic auctioning of operating licenses by the government. The main focus of the competition authorities in this regard should be on the regulatory regime that affects services industries.[39]

6.5.2 The Europe Agreement Phase

This phase has two parts: one transitional, the other the period during which the EA is fully implemented and EU membership is not yet achieved. The transitional period is especially important because competition authorities will have to help ensure that EA-envisaged market access liberalization is realized, and is not offset by private/public actions. Once the EAs are in force, national implementation and enforcement of competition rules must be consistent with the relevant EU principles and the implementation rules agreed to by the Association Councils or Joint Committees.

There are two dimensions to EA competition policy disciplines, one pertaining to firms, the other to governments. As far as the latter is concerned, although far-reaching, EA obligations will only bite gradually. The complete territory of the CEECs will be regarded as a disadvantaged EU 'region' for five years after the entry into force of the EAs. The primary substantive requirement in this period is transparency related: each CEEC government must establish an agency or body responsible for the collection of data on state aids and subsidies more generally. Governments might consider going beyond this EA obligation by establishing (or supporting the creation of) an institution that not only collects data on subsidies/ state aids, but analyses such data and combines them into industry-specific measures of effective support. The Industries Assistance Commission in Australia is an often mentioned example that could be emulated (Spriggs, 1991).

Turning to the classic domain of competition policy, two issues arise: (1) the compatibility of existing laws and procedures with the EAs; and (2) the policy options facing CEEC authorities once the EAs apply. The first question is addressed in Appendix 6.2. In principle the CEEC competition laws are modelled on Articles 85 and 86 EEC. There are inconsistencies, however, with EU language and implementation criteria/guidelines, some of them substantial. An example is the scope for presenting an 'efficiency defence' in merger cases in the Czech and Hungarian laws. This is not possible under the EU Merger Regulation.[40] Another example is the provision in the Hungarian law permitting anti-competitive agreements that are aimed at offsetting 'economic superiority', something that is clearly not possible under the EU rules. In general, there is greater leeway in the CEEC laws for 'public interest' defences. Another example is the possible exemption of cartel agreements on this basis in the Czech and Slovak law. Space constraints prevent a detailed analysis of the various 'incompatibilities' of CEEC laws and EU rules and practice (see e.g., de la Laurencie, 1993). Many of the differences will have to be addressed in the coming years.

Turning to policy, an important question is whether the entry into force of the EAs should lead to a change in the relative weight/attention that is granted to different types of competition law violations. For one, free trade/free establishment for EU firms should be enough to ensure that many markets become contestable. Moreover, once an EA is in force, CEECs may be able to rely in part on enforcement by the European Commission. This will depend to what extent an anti-competitive practice in a CEEC may have (potential) effects on trade between that country and the EU and therefore be subject to EU enforcement. An implication is that less attention may be necessary with respect to potential abuse of dominant positions, as the contestability of markets will presumably increase substantially. Greater priority might consequently be given to non-tradable industries in general, and to those tradable sectors where liberalization occurs most gradually, or not at all. Taking into account Commission resource constraints and the limited significance of CEEC markets in most products, CEEC governments cannot realistically rely on the Commission for the enforcement of EA competition disciplines. Vigorous national enforcement will remain crucial in the EA phase.[41]

EA obligations in the area of trade liberalization are much more far-reaching than those of the GATT, but are of course preferential in nature. Thus, there is still a need for concern about the trade policy stance with the rest of the world. Although freedom of trade and establishment is to be achieved within ten years of the entry into force of the EAs, tariff elimination is gradual, and QRs have been maintained for certain activities during the transition.[42] The binding nature of the EAs should ensure that protection is indeed transitional, and domestic protected industries will presumably realize that they have only a limited period of time to prepare for competition from EU firms. A potential problem that arises is that protection creates vested interests, and these can be expected to lobby the government for continued assistance. One way this might be done within the confines of the EAs is to argue for 'safeguard' actions once liberalization starts to bite. The primary safeguard mechanism embodied in the EAs allows actions to be taken if imports from the trading partner 'cause or threaten serious injury to producers of like products or serious disturbance in any sector of the economy or difficulties which could bring about serious deterioration in the economic situation of a region' (Article 30 of the Hungarian EA). This is very broad language. The concepts (criteria) are also not defined, nor is reference made to the GATT or other treaties for guidance. There are no explicit sunset provisions or time limits.[43]

Competition offices should take into account the antitrust implications of safeguard actions, and actively enforce the law in instances where safeguard actions result in violations. Similar issues may arise as far as establishment is concerned. The CEECs will grant free entry and national treatment to EU firms, subject to negotiated phase-in periods for certain sectors or activities. The modalities and content of these exceptions again differ across CEECs.[44] There is also a need to consider other options through which firms may seek to continue to benefit from government support. As noted earlier, Poland has given EU car producers preferential access to its market, by imposing a tariff quota on imports, and defining criteria for the allocation of this quota that strongly favour European firms that have invested in Poland (see Chapter 3). Tariffs on cars are currently high, standing at some 35%. The provisions of a recent joint venture agreement between FSO, the Polish state-owned car company, and General Motors illustrates the pressures that may arise to maintain the benefits of such arrangements. The Polish government provided assurances in the contract establishing the joint venture that it 'will compensate GM for losses resulting from future changes in tariff and tax conditions.'[45] That is, GM will apparently be able to demand compensation from the government to offset the reduction in the tariff from 40% to zero that is required under the EA over a ten year period. The signal to potential competitors is clear: the costs of contesting the Polish market will be higher. Careful scrutiny should be given to such arrangements so as to ensure that no abuse of a dominant position results, and that markets remain contestable.

An implication of the foregoing is that competition offices need to continue to keep a wary eye on trade policy. The entry into force of the EA should imply that somewhat less emphasis can be given to the behaviour of firms with a dominant position that produce tradables, and that greater priority be given to non-tradables (services) and industries where the transition to free trade and/or freedom of establishment is long or delayed. As already noted, access to many service markets will only be liberalized gradually, on a national treatment basis, with establishment being necessary. The contestability of these markets will largely be determined by the attitude taken by the antitrust authorities. The EAs do not require liberalization of cross-border trade in services, this presumably being kept off the agenda to prohibit regulatory competition. As a result, it remains important that the competition authorities continue to monitor closely the contestability of service markets.

A special complication arises from the continued existence of anti-dumping and safeguard threats under the EAs. This may be an inducement for CEEC firms to collude, if not explicitly then tacitly, with each other and with EU competitors. Continued threats of contingent protection on the part of the EU implies that CEEC firms will face different standards from their EU competitors. EU firms will be permitted to engage in price discrimination or sell below cost on the EU market, whereas CEEC firms will be constrained in pursuing such a strategy by the existence of EU anti-dumping procedures. On EU markets, price discrimination by CEEC firms, in the sense of selling products at prices below those charged at home, may lead to anti-dumping petitions if this injures EU firms. Such dumping is unlikely to be the result of concerted practices or abuse of dominant positions, as these will be difficult to attain by CEEC firms. Nor can it be argued that CEEC firms are unfairly benefiting from a protected home market. Once the EAs are implemented, all tariffs, QRs and restrictions on FDI will have been abolished.

As anti-dumping remains a threat under the EAs, the focus should arguably still be on reducing the likelihood of contingent protection being invoked by the EU. Strict enforcement of antitrust may help convince the European Commission and Member States to be hesitant to pursue complaints of dumping. Advocates of anti-dumping policies often argue it is a justifiable attempt by importing country governments to offset the market access restrictions existing in an exporting firm's home country that underlie the ability of such firms to dump. Such restrictions may consist of import barriers preventing arbitrage, but may also reflect the non-existence or non-enforcement of competition law by the exporting country.[46] Anti-dumping is then defended as an inferior instrument to offset such 'government-made' competitive differences, the optimal solution being held to be elimination of the differences.

The experience that has been obtained with attempts to abolish anti-dumping in the context of regional integration agreements suggests that there are at least three necessary conditions for the abolition of contingent protection: (1) free trade and freedom of investment; (2) disciplines on the ability of governments to assist firms and industries located on their territory; and (3) the existence and enforcement of competition (antitrust) legislation (Hoekman and Mavroidis, 1994). All three elements can be regarded as forming an implicit market access 'guarantee', the objective being to safeguard the conditions of competition on regional markets. As far as the CEECs are concerned it seems that, although these conditions will to a very great extent be satisfied, the EU felt the need to take out insurance. Clearly, the best strategy for the CEECs is to seek the elimination of anti-dumping once the EAs have been fully implemented. This is an issue that could be taken up by the Association Councils.

A second best, possibly transitional, strategy could consist of attempts to secure agreement that anti-dumping becomes the mechanism of last resort. One possibility in this connection is to seek agreement that allegations of dumping are first investigated by the EU's competition authorities (DG-IV). The objective of this investigation would be to determine whether the exporting firm or industry engages in anti-competitive practices or benefits from government-created or supported entry barriers that violate the EAs. If anti-competitive behaviour is found to exist, 'standard' remedies would be applied (i.e. cease and desist orders, fines, etc.). Initiation of an anti-dumping investigation should only be possible if the investigation by the competition authorities has revealed the existence of barriers to entry in the CEEC market that do not violate the EA.

Third best, in the absence of a formal agreement on the matter, is to continue to vocally oppose anti-dumping, especially once the EAs are fully implemented. Given that EU-consistent competition rules will have been implemented, a CEEC government has strong arguments on which to base opposition to EU anti-dumping actions. Continued action against state aids will also help to reduce the scope for contingent protection. The fact that the Commission has somewhat greater discretion on anti-dumping than do administering authorities in certain other jurisdictions further increases the incentives for the CEECs to 'make a case'.

Whatever turns out to be feasible with regard to anti-dumping, it should be remembered that safeguard actions remain a possibility. The elimination of this option should also be on the agenda, a necessary condition again being that the EAs have been fully implemented, and the resulting adjustment has occurred. The main issue in the short run is to reduce as much as possible the scope for EU firms to argue that CEEC firms are trading 'unfairly'. Undercutting the basis for the rhetoric of allegations of unfair trade is important, as protection is then much more easily recognized for what it is.

6.5.3 The Third Phase: Membership of the European Union

It is unclear how long it will take each CEEC to achieve membership of the EU. What matters from the antitrust perspective is not when accession will occur, but what changes will be required in competition policy enforcement. The specifics of the competition legislation and the procedures and criteria that are applied are largely unconstrained by EU membership. The scope of membership is, however, much more far-reaching than the EAs. The EAs are ambiguous regarding the extent to which access to service markets will be liberalized. Disciplines in areas such as the regulation of utilities and telecoms will expand. As a result, the reach of EU competition disciplines is likely to expand. National regulations that may restrict entry into certain industries and that would not be covered by the EAs may become impossible to maintain once the CEEC becomes a member. Another change is that the threat of contingent protection disappears. Intra EU–CEEC anti-dumping, CVD and safeguard actions will become impossible, if not immediately then after a transition period as was the case under the Treaty of Rome (Article 91 EEC). Consequently there will be less pressure on national competition authorities to monitor the effects of threats of contingent protection. More importantly, the government essentially loses control of its trade policy, this being an EU competence. External tariffs will therefore have to be adjusted to the EU's common tariff. The EU (Commission) will also become much more of a factor in enforcing Articles 90 and 92. In short, life becomes much simpler from the perspective of the antitrust authorities. Their main task will be to prevent the exploitation of power on local markets.

6.6 Concluding Remarks

The comparative analysis of the competition laws of the CEECs illustrates that the majority of them have moved towards an, in principle, satisfactory legal framework to promote competition in a relatively short period of time. Although initially under the influence of both the US and the EU competition laws, the CEECs have chosen by and large to adopt legislation that is similar to that of the EU. At this stage the successful protection of competition in the CEECs depends almost entirely on national policies, of which enforcement of competition laws is one important element. But even under the EAs, national enforcement will remain important, both because of the relative insignificance of national CEEC markets, but also because of resource limitations on the part of the Commission.

In a number of areas the CEEC competition laws and enforcement agencies compare very well with those of OECD countries. The 'trade policy awareness' of the authorities is quite high, indeed, much higher than appears to be the case in many OECD comparators. In part this reflects the political importance or weight that is granted to the competition authorities in many of the CEECs (e.g., the Czech decision to give the head of the competition office Ministerial rank) and their willingness to attack trade policy decisions that substantially reduce competitive forces on domestic markets. Although the emphasis that is placed on competition policy in the CEECs is in part a reflection of the need to establish a market economy, OECD governments could enhance competition on their markets by emulating some aspects of CEEC competition law enforcement. Examples are the mandate to scrutinize and comment on the competition implications of government policies generally, and giving the head of the competition office the opportunity to participate in cabinet meetings.

A number of actions have been identified through which competition law enforcement might be strengthened and be made even more sensitive to trade policy. The legislative possibility for antitrust agencies in the CEECs to act *ex officio* does not appear to have been fully exploited, although this may largely be the result of the process of the transition towards private ownership and a market economy. The development of detailed guidelines would help both to reduce uncertainty regarding the priorities given by the competition authorities to types of competition-reducing practices, and clarify what practices will not be pursued. One common denominator in the legislation of all CEECs is the wide discretion that the agencies entrusted with the enforcement of competition laws enjoy. This can have a negative side, in the sense that a number of desirable *per se* prohibitions simply do not exist. An offsetting positive counterpart is that if discretion is exercised in a pro-competition way, the 'jurisprudence' created in this field could further promote the goals of the competition laws. Incorporation of the trade policy stance pertaining to an industry should explicitly be taken into account when defining the relevant market in the enforcement of antitrust. Guidelines to this effect should also be published. Whenever market shares are defined as a threshold (i.e. in the definition of dominant positions) they should be linked to market contestability considerations, i.e. explicit public recognition that what matters is market power. It would prove very useful for the evolution of the competition philosophy in the CEECs, and at the same time enhance transparency, if competent agencies were to publish the reasoning underlying their decisions.

One avenue that could be further explored during the transition phase (i.e. until full implementation of the EAs) is the exploitation of the principle of 'positive comity'. This could provide a link between anti-dumping and antitrust in instances where CEECs are facing anti-dumping threats or actions on the part of the EU. That is, the European Commission could be asked to apply competition policy criteria in anti-dumping investigations against products originating in CEECs, ensuring that there is a threat to competition, not just a threat to an EU competitor. This could be sought on an informal basis during the transitional period. If it proves to be impossible to obtain agreement to phase out anti-dumping once the EAs are fully implemented, a second-best policy could be to formalize the link between competition law enforcement and anti-dumping investigations. More generally, since the CEECs have adopted legislation comparable to that of the EU in the competition field, one can assume that, if they enforce their competition laws vigorously, EU-consistent minimum standards will be respected. This may effectively raise the threshold for EU import-competing industries seeking anti-dumping relief. Vigorous enforcement of competition disciplines in service industries, especially distribution-related, may further help reduce the potential for EU firms to seek contingent protection. In any event, enhancing the contestability of service markets will be very important in the development of a competitive environment. In general it would be desirable to create an independent and objective body that is given the mandate to evaluate government policies from a competition policy perspective. In the absence of such an entity, competition offices should devote resources to building a capacity and reputation for high-quality, objective analysis of the effects of government policies that affect the contestability of markets.

Until the EAs are fully implemented it is important to reduce as much as possible the risk of being treated as an 'unfair trader'. Safeguard actions will always remain possible as long as membership of the EU has not been attained. But safeguard protection is more difficult to seek and obtain if the case for arguing that CEEC firms are benefiting from trade barriers, state aids, or various types of government-maintained entry barriers is weak. From this perspective active competition law enforcement will be of particular importance to the CEECs in the immediate future.

Appendix 6.1 Competition Disciplines in the Europe Agreements

Article 62[47]

1. The following are incompatible with the proper functioning of the Agreement, in so far as they may affect trade between the Community and Hungary:
   (i) all agreements between undertakings, decisions by associations of undertakings and concerted practices between undertakings which have as their object or effect the prevention, restriction or distortion of competition;
   (ii) abuse by one or more undertakings of a dominant position in the territories of the Community or of Hungary as a whole or in a substantial part thereof;
   (iii) any public aid which distorts or threatens to distort competition by favouring certain undertakings or the production of certain goods.

2. Any practices contrary to this Article shall be assessed on the basis of criteria arising from the application of the rules of Articles 85, 86, and 92 of the Treaty establishing the European Economic Community.

3. The Association Council shall, within three years of the entry into force of the Agreement, adopt by decision the necessary rules for the implementation of paragraphs 1 and 2.

4.a For the purposes of applying the provisions of paragraph 1, point (iii), the Parties recognize that during the first five years after the entry into force of the Agreement, any public aid granted by Hungary shall be regarded as an area identical to those areas of the Community described in Article 92.3 (a), of the Treaty establishing the European Economic Community. The Association Council shall, taking into account the economic situation of Hungary, decide whether that period should be extended by further periods of five years.

4.b Each party shall ensure transparency in the area of public aid, *inter alia* by reporting annually to the other party on the total amount and the distribution of the aid given and by providing, upon request, information on aid schemes. Upon request by one party, the other party shall provide information on particular individual cases of public aid.

5. With regard to products referred to in Chapters 11 and 111 of Title 111 [i.e. agriculture] the provision of paragraph 1 (iii) does not apply. Any practices contrary to paragraph 1 (i) should be assessed according to the criteria established by the Community on the basis of Articles 42 and 43 of the Treaty establishing the European Economic Community and in particular of those established in Council Regulation 26/1962.

6. If the Community or Hungary considers that a particular practice is incompatible with the terms of the first paragraph of this Article, and is not adequately dealt with under the implementing rules referred to in Paragraph 3, or in the absence of such rules, and if such practice causes or threatens to cause serious prejudice to the interest of the other Party or material injury to its domestic industry, including its service industry, it may take appropriate measures after consultation within the Association Council or after 30 working days following referral for such consultation.
   In the case of practices incompatible with paragraph 1 (iii) of this Article, such appropriate measures may, where the General Agreement on Tariffs and Trade applies thereto, only be adopted in conformity with the procedures and under the conditions laid down by the General Agreement on Tariffs and Trade and any other relevant instrument negotiated under its auspices which are applicable between the Parties.

7. Notwithstanding any provisions to the contrary adopted in conformity with paragraph 3, the parties shall exchange information taking into account the limitations imposed by the requirements of professional and business secrecy.

8. This Article shall not apply to the products covered by the Treaty establishing the European Coal and Steel Treaty which are the subject of Protocol N 2.

Article 64

With regard to public undertakings, and undertakings to which special or exclusive rights have been granted, the Joint Committee shall ensure that as from the third year following the date of entry into force of the Agreement, the principles of the Treaty establishing the European Economic Community, notably Article 90, and the principles of the concluding document of the April 1990 Bonn meeting of the Conference on Security and Cooperation in Europe, notable entrepreneurs' freedom of decision, are upheld.

Appendix 6.2 An Overview of Competition Legislation in Bulgaria, the Czech Republic, Hungary, Poland and the Slovak Republic

BULGARIA

The 'Law on the Protection of Competition'[48] (published in State Gazette No. 39 of 17 May 1991, Correction State Gazette No. 79/1991) constitutes the legal framework protecting free competition in Bulgaria. According to Article 1(1): 'the object of this law is to guarantee the conditions necessary for free enterprise in manufacturing, trade and services, for a free determining of prices and for the protection of consumers' interests.'

The Act differs not only linguistically (the term 'monopoly position' is used to cover dominant positions as well as monopolies), but also substantially from the laws in force in the other CEECs. The scope of discretion as well as the form of action of the competent authority are much more restricted. The Bulgarian Act comprises a set of definitions and strict prohibitions of behaviour that is deemed to be anti-competitive and leaves little room for the competent authority to exempt specific arrangements. The Act does not make it clear whether the effects doctrine suffices for the authority to assert jurisdiction. Article 1(2) implies this possibility, however, as it states '... which could lead to restrictions on competition in Bulgaria', without explicitly stating the *locus* of the anti-competitive behaviour.

The Act distinguishes between 'monopoly positions' and 'other prohibited practices'. 'Monopoly positions' cover not only monopolies, but also dominant positions and to some extent mergers. 'Other prohibited practices' deal mainly with forms of collusion. According to Article 3, a monopoly position exists if a person either possesses the exclusive right to engage in a certain kind of economic activity by virtue of law or has a market share that exceeds 35% of the relevant market. The threshold set forth in the Act in this second case certainly does not qualify as a monopoly. Indeed, in some jurisdictions it does not even suffice to qualify as a dominant position.

All authorities are prohibited from adopting decisions that might lead to the creation of 'monopoly positions'. This prohibition is only effective, however, to the extent that the aforementioned decisions 'limit significantly the freedom of competition or the free determining of prices' (Article 4). Accordingly, if mergers lead to 'monopoly positions', they are prohibited as well (Article 5). An exemption, however, may be requested from the competent authority. If no opposition is registered within 30 days of notification, authorization is considered granted (Article 6.2).

The Act includes a list of abuses of 'monopoly position'. This list includes classical cases like price-fixing, restricting output or access to markets, tie-ins, monopoly pricing, market sharing, and exclusive distribution agreements. While its wording is wide, the list seems to be an *exhaustive* one.[49] When it comes to the regulation of forms of collusion, the Act contains only one provision that is all encompassing: Article 8(2) stipulates that: 'contractual terms restricting one of the parties with respect to the choice of the market, suppliers, buyers, sellers or consumers, except when the restriction arises from the nature of the contract and is not injurious to the consumers, are prohibited.' The possibility to request an exemption outside the grounds enlisted in Article 8(2) is open, if such a request is deposited to the competent authority. (Article 9).

Procedural Provisions

The competent authority entrusted with the responsibility to ensure that the substantive provisions of the Act will be observed is the 'Commission for the Protection of Competition'. Its tasks are described in the 'Statute on the organization and activities of the Commission for the protection of competition'[50] (published in State Gazette No. 94 of 15 November 1991). Article 3 of the Statute stipulates that the Commission for the Protection of Competition has the following basic functions: (1) preventing restrictions on competition in Bulgaria; (2) applying the measures provided for in the laws against restrictions of competition and against unfair competition; and (3) ensuring protection against abuse of a monopoly position in the market, as well as against other activities which may lead to a restriction on competition.'

The Commission consists of a chairman, two vice-chairmen and eight members. All are appointed by the National Assembly for a period of five years.[51] The guarantees for transparency are expressed through the obligations to publish and notify all decisions as well as through the possibility of having hearings of the interested parties before the Commission.[52] The Commission can self-initiate or respond to complaints brought by natural or legal persons.

The discretionary power of the Commission is, to some extent, curtailed in comparison with those of the authorities in the other CEECs, mainly because of the heavier reliance of the Bulgarian Act on *per se* prohibitions. Much depends, however, on how the Commission makes use of its powers when dealing with these issues, as the wording of the Act still leaves some discretion to the Commission in a number of areas. What the Commission cannot do is to impose fines. If it thinks that this should be the appropriate remedial action, the Commission must submit a case before the competent Bulgarian Court of Law (Article 18.2 of the Act). The Commission does possess one specific remedy that the authorities of other CEECs do not. Article 16 stipulates that 'whenever an abuse of monopoly position occurs and at the initiative of the Commission for the Protection of Competition, the Council of Ministers or a body authorized by it may establish maximum and/or minimum prices which shall be obligatory for the person with a monopoly position.' Although the ultimate decision does not lie within its competence, it is the Commission that sets the process in motion.

CZECH REPUBLIC

The 'Competition Protection Act' of the Czech and Slovak Federal Republic (No. 63/1991 Coll. of law) entered into force in March 1991. It was amended by the Czech Republic in November 1993 (No. 286/1993 Coll. of law). The amendment of the Act implies rather limited changes to the 1991 Federal law. More substantial changes in order to make the legislation fully compatible with EU law are expected to be made by 1996.

The 1991 Act is a comprehensive piece of legislation that resembles, to a large extent, the antitrust rules of the EU. The basic objective of the Act is 'to protect economic competition and create conditions for its further development, and to prevent the creation and maintenance of monopolistic or dominant position of legal and physical persons in their business activities, if it precludes or restricts economic competition' (Article 1). The Act distinguishes between forms of collusion (with special treatment of mergers) and dominant positions. It provides for the establishment of the office of the Czech Republic of Economic Competition, which is entrusted with the responsibility of eliminating anti-competitive measures. Anti-competitive practices in both goods and services markets are covered (Article 3). The November 1993 amendment extends the reach of the law to associations of business, including chambers of commerce.

The Act provides a list of *per se* prohibited practices, that are deemed to be anti-competitive. These practices, listed in Article 3(2), to a large extent reproduce the forms of collusion described in Article 85 EEC, and include price-fixing, market segmentation, barriers to entry, and limitation of production. The list in Article 3(2) is illustrative, not exhaustive.[53] Article 3(1) stipulates that: 'Agreements and other forms of mutual understanding achieved by entrepreneurs which result or, because of their nature, may result by influencing conditions of production or turnover in the goods and services market ... in the elimination or restriction of economic competition, are described as cartel contracts ... which are illicit and void if this Act does not state otherwise or if the body for economic competition ... has not granted an exception.' This wording is wider than the corresponding wording in Article 85(1) EEC.

In the November 1993 amendment, the Ministry for Economic Competition was granted the right to provide block exemptions along the lines of Article 85(3) EEC. Moreover, reference is no longer made to cartel agreements, but to 'agreements distorting competition'. This clearly suggests that both vertical and horizontal agreements will be covered by the law.

Per se prohibitions are tempered by the possibility for parties to such contracts to demand an exception of the competent authority, i.e. the Ministry for Economic

Competition. The Act distinguishes between various forms of collusion for which an exception has been requested. For an exhaustive list (embodied in Article 3(3)), an exception is granted if the authority does not communicate in writing its disagreements with the contract within two months (Article 3(4), 'special procedure'). The list in Article 3(3) consists of: (i) uniform application of conditions of trade; (ii) rationalization of economic activity, particularly specialization agreements; (iii) non-discriminatory rebates granted to customers; and (iv) shares in supplying the market if they are below a certain threshold. For these categories a presumption therefore exists that an exception should be granted. Entrepreneurs may also apply for exception on grounds other than those in Article 3(3). In this case (general procedure), the petitioner has to clarify the reasons in the application and to enclose a draft of the contract in question. The November 1993 Amendment removed non-discriminatory rebates from Article 3(3).

An exception can be granted if the restriction of 'economic competition ... is in the public interest',[54] with particular attention being paid to the interests of the consumers (Article 5(2)). Exemptions are time-limited and cannot have retroactive effect (Article 5(4)). For certain types of contracts no exemption can be granted. Article 5(3) of the Act provides an exhaustive list which includes exclusivity contracts, contracts that violate legal inhibition on ethics of competition or contracts the scope of which obstructs in a substantial way economic competition in the market.

The Czech legislation in this regard is therefore similar to EU-antitrust legislation as it combines *per se* prohibitions with the possibility of specific exemptions. In only a very few cases are exemptions not obtainable. Consequently, the competent authority enjoys a considerable margin of discretion. Even with respect to those contracts where no exemption can be granted, the competent authority still has some leeway, as it must interpret terms. The notion of 'substantial obstruction of economic competition', for example, directly defers judgement to the competent authority that will have to estimate to what extent the proposed obstruction of economic competition is substantial. In applying the law, the Ministry of Economic Competition differentiates between horizontal and vertical agreements. It is gradually introducing criteria for the assessment of horizontal agreements, using OECD guidelines.

With respect to mergers, the 1991 Act establishes 30% of total turnover in the relevant market as the threshold above which mergers are presumed to limit economic competition in the relevant market (Article 8(3)). All mergers that exceed the threshold must be notified to the authority for approval; such contracts were void (illegal) *unless* approved (Article 8(4)). Mergers were regarded as approved if the authority had not decided within three months following notification. The November 1993 amendment no longer makes such mergers void by definition. Instead, they cannot enter into force until approved. Under the new provisions, the focus of the authorities will be solely on the economic effect of the merger, not on the form of the agreement. In judging whether a merger that exceeds the threshold should be approved, the authority must determine whether the economic advantages brought about by the merger outweigh the negative effects created by the restriction of competition (Article 8(4)). The wording of the Act on this point further supports the view that the authority enjoys a considerable amount of discretion.

With respect to dominant[55] positions the Act follows, to a large extent, the approach adopted in Article 86 EEC: it is not the existence or creation of a dominant position that is sanctioned, but the abuse (Article 9(3)). An indicative list of examples of abuse of dominant position (Article 9(3)) draws substantially from the list included in Article 86 EEC.[56] The Act departs on two points from Article 86 EEC: first, it provides a fixed threshold above which an entrepreneur is deemed to be in a dominant position: a market share of at least 30% of supply of identical, comparable or mutually commutable goods of the relevant market in the course of the calendar year (Article 9(2)). No such threshold exists in Article 86 EEC. Second, entrepreneurs who have reached this threshold, including by merger are required to report this to the authority without delay (Article 9(1)). The obligation embodied is one of notification only, since it is not the creation but the abuse of a dominant position that is of concern. The notification will help the authority to better monitor the market behaviour of large entities and determine whether or not abuse occurs. The 1993 amendment gives the Ministry the right to break up dominant firms or monopolies if such entities seriously constrain competition. A basic problem here is that a *de facto* obligation is imposed on entrepreneurs to monitor their market share. Such an obligation might prove to be difficult to meet, especially taking into account that the relevant markets are not well defined.

Article 18 of the Czech and Slovak law gives the authorities the mandate to comment on draft laws and actions of state administrative and local bodies that restrict competition.

Procedural Provisions

Originally the Act provided for an office of Economic Competition and for a Federal Office for Economic Competition dealing with cases that had a bearing on the markets of both the Czech and the Slovak Republic (Article 10). After the two Republics decided to abolish the Federation, the Office of the Czech Republic for Economic Competition is the sole competent authority to deal with competition-related issues in the Czech Republic. Its jurisdiction is circumscribed in Article 10. It has competence ‘in cases concerning protection against, limiting or eliminating competition which may have effects in the territory of the Czech Republic ...’ This wording suggests that the ‘effects’ doctrine constitutes the basis of the Czech jurisdiction. Article 11 of the Act states that the Office is mainly responsible for taking action against anti-competitive behaviour, for approving mergers that are above the set threshold and collusive agreements where the economic benefits offset the costs of the restrictions of competition.

The authority has the competence to impose fines on entrepreneurs for violating the Act. The 1993 amendment strengthened punitive measures against the abuse of a dominant position and agreements restricting competition. The penalty for infringing the law was raised from a maximum of 5% of turnover for the last completed year to a maximum of 10% of net turnover. If violators profited from the breach of obligation, fines can amount to the total profit gained because of the breach (Article 14). All fines are to be imposed within set time limits. Proceedings may be self-initiated or launched upon request. All interested parties have the right to express their views, and, if need be, oral hearings can be organized. All decisions of the authority are subject to appeal before civil courts within 30 days from the date when the decision was handed to the party to the proceeding (Article 13). All employees of the authority are required to maintain confidentiality (Article 16).

Last, but not least, as a transition measure, state administration bodies are required, when transferring state property (privatization), to guarantee the elimination of existing monopolies and/or to disable the creation of new monopolies (Article 19).

HUNGARY

Act LXXXVI of 1990 on the Prohibition of Unfair Market Practices is the legislative framework dealing with the protection of free competition in Hungary. This law was adopted by the Hungarian parliament on 20 November 1990, and entered into force on 1 January 1991. The basic objective of the Act is embodied in the Preamble: 'For the sake of protecting the freedom and priority of economic competition, forms of conduct that are contrary to fair market practices must be banned, and supervision over the structural merger of enterprises must be introduced by creating the necessary organization forms.'

The Act addresses forms of collusion, dominant positions termed economic superiority and mergers. The 'effects' doctrine is again followed: Paragraph 14 prohibits forms of collusion 'which would result in restriction or exclusion of economic competition, irrespective of whether the agreement was concluded on the territory of the Hungarian Republic or not.' The Act applies to both goods and services. The approach taken by the other CEECs is, in principle, also followed here: a list of prohibited practices is included, with the possibility for participants in such practices to request an exemption of the competent authority. The Hungarian Act provides a general rule of what constitutes a prohibited practice and gives only a few examples of what form such practices may take. The general rule is that, for practices not to be prohibited, they should not 'result in restriction or exclusion of economic competition' (Paragraph 14). The wide wording implies that the authorities entrusted with the interpretation of this paragraph enjoy wide discretion.

The examples given in the Act are the classic ones also listed in the other competition laws, i.e. price-fixing, market segmentation, limitation of output, etc. (Paragraph 14). An agreement that falls under the general rule or the examples given in Paragraph 14 is not prohibited if it is aimed at 'stopping abuse of economic superiority' or if it is of 'minor significance' (Paragraph 15). The latter criterion is further explained in Paragraph 16: an agreement is considered to be of minor significance if, in the market in question, the joint shares of the participants do not exceed 10%. For the market in question to be defined (i.e. the relevant market) the goods that form the subject of the agreement (directly competitive but also substitutable) and the geographic area have to be taken into account in accordance with the definition provided for in the same paragraph. Paragraph 17 provides a second rationale for exemption from prohibition if 'the concomitant restriction or exclusion of economic competition does not exceed the measure necessary for attaining economically justifiable common goals; and the concomitant advantages are greater than the concomitant disadvantages.' Again, the wording leaves ample room for discretion when it comes to its interpretation. On this point, however, the Act gives some indication as to what might be a valid reason justifying the exemption (concomitant advantages) and what might be a valid reason justifying the prohibition (concomitant disadvantages).

As advantages the legislation considers the better prices that might result from the implementation of the agreement, the better quality of the products, rationalized production and technological development.[57] Conversely, if the joint shares of the participants to the agreement exceed 30% of the relevant market, it would be considered a disadvantage. The finding of an advantage or disadvantage by the competent authority does not automatically lead to exemption or prohibition; these are rebuttable presumptions. The Act, however, gives the legislator's view as to which agreements are considered pro- and which anti-competitive.

The Hungarian Act prohibits abuse, not the creation of a dominant position (economic superiority). An indicative list of what might constitute an abuse of a dominant position includes unjustified refusal to conclude contracts and erection of barriers to entry (Article 20). The Act also provides an indicative list of what might constitute a dominant position: a share that exceeds 30% in the relevant market (50% if it is joint shares of three entrepreneurs), or a situation where the merchandise of an entity cannot be procured elsewhere (Paragraph 21).

Parties that want to merge are jointly under the obligation to notify the competent authority in order for the latter to grant an authorization if 'the joint share of the participants on a given market as regards any goods sold by them in the previous calendar year exceeds 30%; or the joint returns on sales of the participants in the previous calendar year exceeded 10 billion Forints' (Para.21). In principle, any merger that hampers competition will not be authorized (Paragraph 24.1). A merger, however, can be exempted, notwithstanding Paragraph 24.1, if (a) the advantages of economic competition outweigh the disadvantages; (b) economic competition as regards the larger part of the goods in question is not ruled out; or (c) it promotes transactions on foreign markets which are advantageous from the viewpoint of national economy.[58]

Paragraph 60 of the law requires ministers to consult the competition office on all draft laws that seek to limit competition.

Procedural Provisions

The Office of Economic Competition is the competent authority entrusted with the responsibility to supervise competition as regulated in the Act (Paragraph 52). It is headed by a president and two vice-presidents who are appointed for six years by the President of the Republic at the proposal of the Prime Minister (Paragraph 53). Their mandate is terminated after six years, or following a resignation, death or dismissal. As to the latter, the only case where a subjective judgement by the supervising authority is required for a dismissal concerns the case where 'they become unfit for their office on a lasting basis' (Paragraph 54).

The Office is responsible for prosecuting violators of the Act, but also for granting exemptions. Proceedings may be launched at the request at the interested party or *ex officio* (Paragraph 33). Strict time limits are imposed within which the Office has to make a ruling; transparency of the process is also guaranteed through hearings (Paragraph 34ff). In discharging its responsibilities, the Office may impose fines that are directly connected to the material advantage attained through the unlawful conduct; these can vary between 30 and 200% of such an advantage (Paragraphs 43, 48). Only in exceptional circumstances can the 30% threshold be violated. All rulings of the Office are appealable before the courts within 30 days from delivery of the ruling passed on the matter (Paragraph 41).

Because of 'the drastic restructuring of its economy, and its trial-and-error approach to competition law, the Hungarian government plans to submit draft changes to the 1990 statute to the parliament during the summer of 1994.'[59]

POLAND

The Polish competition law is embodied in the Act of 24 February 1990 on counteracting monopolistic practices, as amended by the Act of 28 June 1991. The objective of the Act is to counteract 'monopolistic practices of economic entities and their combinations that have an effect within the territory of the Republic of Poland.'[60] The 'effects doctrine' is therefore espoused. The Act covers both the goods and the services markets.

The Act distinguishes between 'monopolistic practices' and mergers. The first are, in principle, prohibited. The creation of dominant position or of a monopoly is not prohibited *per se*; what is prohibited is its abuse. Article 7, for example, prohibits 'economic entities in a monopolistic position' from engaging in price-fixing or from charging 'excessively exorbitant' prices. The creation of a monopolistic position is not prohibited; the Act, however, makes it difficult for entities to acquire a monopolistic position, mainly by prohibiting, in principle, 'monopolistic practices'. The abuse of dominant position is considered to be a 'monopolistic practice,' although the term 'monopolistic practices' is not defined, but covers forms of collusion comparable to those covered, for example, in Article 85(1) EEC (with the notable addition of the abuse of dominant position). The 'monopolistic practices' include, *inter alia*, price-fixing, market segmentation and imposition of barriers to entry or onerous contract terms yielding undue economic benefits to the imposing entity. The wording of at least two articles of the Act suggests the list of monopolistic practices embodied in the Act is exhaustive.[61] Articles 4, 5, 7 and 9 are the only articles in the Act covering this subject area. Leaving Article 9 aside, since it deals with a very specific issue (see below), a decision by the competent authority can be taken with respect to the 'monopolistic practices' specified in the other three articles. While the wording is wide, making the list exhaustive is unlikely to prove effective.

If there is a finding that monopolistic practices have occurred, the competent authority will issue a decision ordering their termination and determining the conditions of the termination (Articles 6 and 8). Such practices, however, can be exempted from prohibition if the following two conditions are met: (i) they are necessary to conduct an economic activity; and (ii) they do not result in a significant restraint of competition (Article 6). The burden of proof in this case lies with the party that is claiming the existence of both conditions.

As already stated, abuse of dominant position is considered a prohibited monopolistic practice. Dominance is defined 'as the position of an economic entity if it does not encounter significant competition in a national or local market; it is presumed that an economic entity has a dominant position if its share exceeds 40%' (Articles 2, 7). An indicative list of abuses of dominant position is provided, including price-fixing, market segmentation and refusal to sell (Article 5). Since abuse of dominant position is considered to come under 'monopolistic practices', it is prohibited unless specifically exempted by the competent authority.

Article 9 deals specifically with two practices: specialization contracts and joint sales or joint purchases of commodities. The competent authority is to issue a decision prohibiting such agreements, if they imply a significant restraint of competition and yield no economic benefits to the participants (e.g., a significant reduction in production or sales costs or improvement of the quality of products).

Mergers and 'transformations' are treated separately in the Act. There is an obligation to notify mergers if they lead to a dominant position in the relevant market, or if any of the merging entities already has a dominant position. The competent authority must decide whether the merger will be allowed to go ahead within two months of notification (Article 11).

Procedural Provisions

The Act establishes two bodies (of different hierarchical order) that deal exclusively with competition-related issues: the Anti-monopoly Office and the Anti-monopoly Court. The Anti-monopoly Office is headed by a President who is appointed and recalled by the Prime Minister. The President has extensive powers in organizing the structure of the Office (e.g., by establishing regional offices) (Articles 17, 18), and attends meetings of the Council of Ministers.

The Anti-monopoly Office decides whether certain practices constitute monopolistic practices, whether they should be exempted and whether entities should be allowed to merge, notwithstanding that their resulting market share will exceed the threshold. The Office is entrusted with substantial powers. It has the authority to require the cessation of the monopolistic practice and the conditions thereof (Article 8). In doing so, the Office may order the violating entities to pay fines. Fines can amount to 15% of the after-tax earnings of the entity in the preceding fiscal year. Fines may also be imposed in cases where economic entities fail to execute decisions of the Office (Article 15). Firms with a dominant position may be broken up if they permanently restrain competition. While the Office may object to proposed transformations of firms, it does not have the power to prescribe a particular form of division in transformation cases (Fornalczyk, 1993, p.36).

All decisions of the Anti-monopoly Office may be appealed against within two weeks of the day of the receipt of the decision, to the Anti-monopoly Court. This Court deals exclusively with anti-monopoly cases (Article 27). The procedures followed before this Court are those of the Polish Civil Procedure Code.

SLOVAK REPUBLIC[62]

At the time of writing, the Slovak Republic applies the 1991 Czech and Slovak Federal law on competition (the Competition Protection Act), discussed in the section on the Czech Republic above. A draft law amending the Federal Act was discussed in parliament in January 1994, but was not passed due to political developments. The new government re-submitted the draft law to parliament, which is expected to consider the proposed legislation by mid-1994. Until the draft law is adopted, the 1991 Federal law applies.

The draft law makes safeguarding national welfare the ultimate goal of the competition authorities. This is to be achieved by controlling the abuse of economic power by dominant firms. Agreements restricting competition are prohibited if they have as object or effect restriction of effective competition (where 'effective' is to be interpreted as allowing the market to be contestable). This is an important distinction with the Federal 1991 law, which makes all restraints illicit unless they are approved or exempted by the competition authority because the advantages for the economy offset any costs. The concept of protection of effective competition found in the draft law implies that only those restrictions which harm consumer welfare are prohibited. The test of balance between harm to competition and economic efficiency advantages will be used when evaluating restrictive agreements. It is expected that the law will prohibit an exhaustive list of horizontal agreements on a *per se* basis. Enterprises, however, will have the opportunity to argue that an agreement fulfils the conditions for being granted an automatic exemption (the wording in this connection is the same as is found in Article 85(3) of the Treaty of Rome). A new definition of dominant position in a relevant market is contained in the draft law. Two criteria are proposed: (1) the firm is not subject of substantial competition; or (2) the firm has economic power which allows it to behave independently in the market and it is able restrict competition. A *prima facie* presumption of dominance is established if a firm has a share of 40% or more of the relevant market. The objective underlying the provisions on abuse of dominant positions is also to control economic power of the dominant firm.

The rules regarding concentrations (mergers) are very similar to the provisions of the 1989 EC Merger Control Regulation. The draft law sets two thresholds: SKK 300 million total turnover of the participants, or a 20% market share in the relevant product market in the territory of Slovakia (the latter applies for certain industries where turnover is difficult to calculate). Mergers or concentrations above the threshold are subject to preventive control. The entry into force of an agreement is suspended during one month after its notification to the authorities. A criterion for determining whether the merger is acceptable is the balance between harm to competition – creation or strengthening of a dominant position in the market – and its economic advantages.

Both the existing Czech and Slovak law (1991) and the draft legislation contain a provision (Article 18) mandating the Anti-monopoly Office to analyse actions of state administrative and local bodies having impact on competition (including state aid measures) and may require these bodies to take remedial action. The Anti-monopoly Office is also involved in the privatization process. It is required to provide comments on privatization plans with a view to ensuring the appropriate de-concentration of the state enterprises with a dominant position in the market. In such cases, however, the Office has only an advisory role.

Notes

1. For example, the Antitrust Division of the United States Justice Department and the Federal Trade Commission received a $7.2 million grant from USAID to provide technical assistance to the six CEECs in 1991 (BNA, Antitrust and Trade Regulation Report, May 30, 1991, No. 1518, p.761). Contacts between the CEECs and the European Commission (DG-IV), EU Member State enforcement agencies and the OECD Secretariat have been intense.
2. However, other objectives may also be pursued. Thus, for example, the competition law of the United Kingdom contains a broadly defined public interest objective that, among other things, allows for 'maintaining and promoting the balanced distribution of industry and employment' (Hay, 1993, p.3).
3. This is one of the basic principles of international trade theory, one that applies to both the traditional setting of competitive markets and, in the more recent literature, that allows for imperfect competition. For empirical studies confirming the role of import competition as a source of market discipline in imperfectly competitive markets (reducing price-cost margins), see Levinsohn (1993) and Jacquemin and Sapir (1988).
4. Retail distribution is an often mentioned example in this connection.
5. See, e.g., Ehlermann (1992) or Wheatherill and Beaumont (1993). In the case of the EU, competition policy acts as a discipline on firms that operate in an environment of free trade. Thus, in principle, no conflict arises between competition and trade policy in the EU context, there no longer being a trade policy affecting intra-area transactions.
6. In practice, two approaches can be followed in this regard, of which the rule of reason (pursued in the United States) is one. The rule of reason is based on a case-by-case analysis of the effects of specific situations. The other approach (followed by the EU) is to exempt either specific agreements (along US lines) or *generic* types of cooperative ventures.
7. The literature on competition policy, both economic and legal, is huge. See Hay (1993) for a survey of current economic thinking; and Boner and Krueger (1991) for a summary of the practices of ten countries as well as the EU.
8. Examples of the latter include production (output) sharing, market allocation, exclusionary practices and the exchange of information between competitors on variables such as costs and output.
9. Again, what follows draws upon a large literature. For recent, much more comprehensive discussions of competition rules and experience, see Boner and Krueger (1991), Hay (1993), Neven *et al.* (1993), and the annual reports of the OECD Committee on Competition Law and Policy.
10. For a general review of relations between the EU and the CEECs, see Kennedy and Webb (1993). Pohl and Sorsa (1993) provide a summary of the EAs, and Mastropasqua and Rolli (1994) analyse the economic impact of the trade components of the agreements.
11. As of the end of 1993 only the agreements with Poland and Hungary had been ratified. The respective Association Councils met in early March 1994 for the first time.
12. OECD (1994, pp.14–15). During 1993 several meetings took place between CEEC officials and the European Commission where issues relating to the implementation of competition policy were discussed. These meetings should facilitate agreement on formal implementation rules by the Joint Committees. Presumably these will simply be adopted by the Association Council once the relevant EAs have been ratified. DG-IV of the Commission has interacted with the CEECs with a view to harmonizing antitrust policies (not laws).
13. See, e.g., Ham (1993) for a discussion.
14. The 1986 OECD Recommendation, which replaced the 1979 Recommendation and purports to strengthen international cooperation in this field, encourages OECD members to give effect to the principle of traditional comity.
15. France has challenged the Commission's competence to conclude this agreement, which has been characterized as administrative by the Commission and thus falling within its sphere of competence. The outcome of the case is still pending, although the Advocate General has already pronounced in favour of France's arguments. See Case C-327/91, French Republic *vs* Commission. Even if France wins its case before the European Court of Justice, the 'positive comity' principle can still apply in the EA context as these have been legally concluded by the competent EU organs.

16. The agreements do have minor differences as they were negotiated independently.
17. The 'pure' effects doctrine is therefore not accepted. See van Gerven (1989).
18. Necessary conditions are: (1) that the agreement contributes to improving the production or distribution of goods or to promoting technological or economic progress, while allowing consumers a fair share of the resulting benefit; (2) the agreement is indispensable to achieve this benefit; and (3) it does eliminate competition in respect of a substantial part of the industry involved.
19. The 1989 merger regulation gives the Commission the right to vet mergers with a Community dimension for their impact on competition. Mergers affected are those where the firms involved have a global turnover of at least ECU 5 billion, the aggregate Community turnover of at least two of the firms is above ECU 250 million each, and at least two firms have less than two-thirds of their turnover in the same EU member state.
20. In Romania work is ongoing on the drafting of an antitrust law. At the time of writing the only laws to address some competition-related issues are the 1991 Law on Unfair Competition and the 1990 Law No. 15 concerning restructuring of state economic units. The former includes some principles of free competition; the latter prohibits (on a *per se* basis) certain practices, including price fixing (Chapter V, Association and Free Competition).
21. Gray (1993) and Mastalir (1993) provide complementary summaries of the antitrust legislation in the CEECs.
22. The agreements concerned are uniform application of conditions of trade; rationalization of economic activity, including specialization agreements; non-discriminatory rebates; and all instances where the market share of the firms is below 30% of the relevant market.
23. Arguments that have been used in the Czech context by *foreign* firms that merged with or acquired Czech enterprises to demonstrate that net benefits were positive to the economy include: (i) provision of investment necessary for reconstruction/modernization of plants; (ii) enhancing exports; (iii) improving product quality and competitiveness; (iv) preserving employment; (v) introducing modern management techniques; and (vi) facilitating transfers of technology.
24. Pogacsas and Stadler (1993).
25. Cartel, merger and all other investigations must be concluded within 45, 90 and 60 days, respectively. Maximum extensions allowed for each category are 45, 180 and 60 days (Pogacsas and Stadler, 1993).
26. Financial Times Business Information, *Business Law Brief*, DIALOG database, October 1992, and private correspondence with M. Banas.
27. Poland and the Slovak Republic have drafts of new legislation that makes this distinction, while the November 1993 Czech law does not. In applying the law, however, the Czech Ministry of Economic Competition does differentiate between vertical and horizontal agreements.
28. However, the Czech competition office has been held to be understaffed by a Deputy Minister for Competition. BNA, *Antitrust and Trade Regulation Report*, 24 December 1992, No. 1596, p.787.
29. As was done by the Czech Republic in November 1993, and is also envisaged in the draft Slovak law.
30. Polish and Slovak statistics suggest that complaints account for two-thirds of total investigations (OECD, 1994). In Hungary, the majority of the procedures in 1992 started on the basis of applications (236 cases), the Office of Economic Competition using its right to initiate proceedings *ex officio* in only 17 cases (OECD, 1993b). In part this may reflect the wording of the laws and the transition process. As noted by Fornalczyk (1993), the Polish Anti-monopoly Office was obliged to initiate investigations whenever a complaint was received, and were required to review applications for all mergers/transformations. Resource constraints then 'crowded out' *ex officio* actions.
31. Authorities have substantial latitude in this connection, as the relevant market is not clearly defined in any of the laws. In most jurisdictions the concept is defined through case law and administrative practice.
32. It can be noted in passing that GATT obligations and disciplines have little impact on the pursuit of domestic competition law, even though in principle the linkages between GATT's trade policy disciplines and domestic competition policies are greater than is commonly thought. See Hoekman and Mavroidis (1994).

33. *East–West*, No. 558, 28 October 1993, p.3.
34. The last statement is arguably untrue, as what is being created are rents. Investors may require some inducements, but guaranteed markets should not be one of them. Indeed, a case can be made that attracting foreign direct investment might be given priority over the breaking up of monopolies, but that an overriding concern should be that the government does not maintain barriers to entry.
35. *East–West*, No. 555, 2 September 1993, p.6.
36. A statement by Sir Leon Brittan on 5 February 1994 during an informal meeting of EU Trade Ministers and the European Commission bolsters the importance of establishing that CEEC markets are open and that competition laws are enforced: 'if the countries of Central and Eastern Europe want EU industry to be satisfied to the point that EU markets are further opened, the best assurance they could have is that the same competition laws exist in Central and Eastern Europe' (Europe Information Service, *European Report*, No. 1924, 9 February 1994).
37. This is no longer an issue in the EU context. As of the entry into force of the Interim Agreements, the CEECs are regarded as market economies by the European Commission.
38. See Sapir *et al.* (1993) for a discussion.
39. Many of the CEEC competition offices are sensitive to these issues. For example, the draft Slovak competition law requires the periodic auctioning of operating licenses. The Czech Ministry of Economic Competition has been particularly active in its attempts to enhance competition in the service sector. The Minister opposed a decision by an inter-ministerial commission in the context of the privatization of SPT Telecom to protect it from competition for four years, and supported the idea that foreign entities be able to have 100% control of local telecommunications networks. The Ministry has also challenged the 20-year monopoly that was granted to Eurotel, the provider of cellular phones, and supports imports of electricity (Financial Times Business Information, *Finance East Europe*, 4 March 1994).
40. See Jacquemin (1990) and Neven *et al.* (1993).
41. For example, it is unlikely that many mergers involving EU and CEEC firms will satisfy the EU's criteria for turnover and market share. In practice, EU enforcement can be expected to apply largely in instances where the merger involves a third-country firm.
42. Quotas were to be abolished by the CEECs upon entry into force of the agreements, with a few exceptions for 'sensitive' industries such as automobiles. Poland committed itself to eliminate tariffs on about 30% of its imports from the EU in 1992, and to abolish the remainder over a seven year transition period, with duty reductions taking place during the last four years. Hungary will liberalize 12 to 13% of its imports over a three year period in annual steps of one-third, another 20% between 1995 and 1997, again in steps of one-third and the rest (two-thirds) between 1995 and 2001, in steps of one-sixth per year. The Czech and Slovak Republics will dismantle over a seven year period. A preferential tariff quota was established by Poland for motor vehicle imports from EU producers (25 000 units, to increase by 5% a year, and to be abolished within ten years), and a list of 144 items remain subject to import licensing in Hungary. This includes passenger cars (subject to a preferential quota of 50 000 units, to increase by 7% per year), aircraft, telecommunications equipment, chemicals, pharmaceuticals, plastics, wood and leather products, and footwear. Between 1 January 1995 and the end of 1997, Hungary is to eliminate quantitative restrictions on EU exports of these goods up to an amount of 40% of such imports. All QRs are to be eliminated by the end of 2000, and are to be increased by 10% per year during the transition period.
43. The foregoing refers to the EAs general safeguard clauses: e.g., Articles 29 and 30 of the Hungarian EA. The EAs also contain a safeguard clause allowing temporary entry restrictions and/or trade barriers to be introduced by CEECs during the first stage of the transition period to support industrial and commercial sectors undergoing restructuring programmes, of an 'infant industry' nature, or facing elimination or a drastic reduction in total market share. Tariffs, if used, are not to exceed 25%, EU producers are to be given a margin of preference, quotas, if used, are not to exceed 15% of the total industrial imports from the EU, and actions may only be taken within three years of liberalization of market access and are not to last more than five years.
44. Two EAs are representative. Poland granted immediate freedom of establishment and national treatment for construction and most manufacturing activities, with the exception of mining,

processing of precious stones and metals, explosives, ammunition and weaponry, pharmaceuticals, alcohol, high voltage power lines and pipeline transportation. All but the last two activities are to be liberalized by the end of the first stage of the transition period (five years), at which time most service sectors will also be liberalized (financial, legal and real estate services excepted). By the end of the transitional period (ten years) acquisition of state-owned assets under privatization, ownership, use, sale and rent of real property, real estate agency services, legal services, high voltage power lines; and pipeline transportation will be liberalized. The Czechoslovak agreement liberalized all sectors immediately, except for defence industry, steel, mining, acquisition of state-owned assets under privatization, ownership, use, sale and rent of real property, and real estate service activities, and the financial services industry. These activities are to be liberalized by the end of the ten year transition period. Both countries permanently exclude ownership of natural resources and agricultural land/forests.

45. 'GM and Polish car maker reach assembly deal', *Financial Times*, 14 November 1993, p.5. It was GM Europe that originally asked the Polish government to introduce this high tariff rate, apparently making this a precondition for its joint venture with FSO (See Chapter 3, section 3.2.3).
46. Thus, the United States has claimed that lax Japanese antitrust enforcement permits Japanese firms to collude, raise prices and to use part of the resulting rents to cross-subsidize (dump) products sold on foreign markets. See Garten (1994) for a detailed defence of anti-dumping that emphasizes entry barriers in the exporter's home market.
47. In the Interim Agreements the relevant Article is identical to that in the Europe Agreement, except that each reference to the Association Council is replaced with a reference to the Joint Committee set up by the Agreement on Trade and Commercial and Economic Cooperation.
48. Hereinafter the Act.
49. For example, 'applying an obviously unequitable approach towards different clients or unequitable term ...' (Article 7(1)). Article 7 does not include any word to this respect that would make the list indicative.
50. Hereinafter the Statute.
51. Article 2(2) of the Act; half of the members must be qualified lawyers with a least ten years professional experience.
52. See Articles 9ff of the Statute.
53. This interpretation is dictated by the wording in Article 3(2). 'Illicit, ... , are *in particular* contracts or their parts involving' (emphasis added). The same is true for the list embodied in Article 85(1) EEC.
54. See Article 5(2) of the Act.
55. According to the Act dominant position exists where the entrepreneur is not subject to substantial competition.
56. *A fortiori*, all this is valid in cases of monopoly as well. Monopolies are not deemed to be illegal; they should not, however, abuse their power.
57. These reasons are provided in Paragraph 17(2). The list is indicative.
58. See Paragraph 24(2).
59. Declaration by the Head of Hungary's Office of Economic Competition, 19 March 1993, BNA *Antitrust and Trade Regulation Report*, No. 1607, 25 March 1993, p.330.
60. See Article 1 of the Act.
61. Article 6 stipulates 'The monopolistic practices *specified in articles 4 and 5* are prohibited'; Article 8 further stipulates 'if there is a finding that the monopolistic practices *specified in articles 4, 5 and 7 have occurred...*' (emphasis added).
62. What follows draws on correspondence with Milan Banas.

References

Boner, R. and Krueger, R. (1991), *The Basics of Antitrust Policy: A Review of Ten Nations and the European Communities*. World Bank Technical Working Paper No. 160, Washington, DC

Bourgeois, J. (1993), 'Competition policy and commercial policy', in M. Maresceau (ed.), *The European Community's Commercial Policy after 1992: The Legal Dimension*, Kluwer, Leiden.

de la Laurencie, J.-P. (1993), 'A European perspective on development of competition in transition', in S. Estrin and M. Cave (eds), *Competition and Competition Policy: A Comparative Analysis of Central and Eastern Europe*, Pinter Publishers, London.

Ehlermann, C.-D. (1992), 'The contribution of EC competition policy to the single market, *Common Market Law Review*, **29**, 257–82.

Flassik, I. (1993), 'Priorities of the Czechoslovak Antitrust Office', in C. Saunders (ed.), *The Role of Competition in Economic Transition*, St. Martin's Press, New York.

Fornalczyk, A. (1993), 'Competition policy in the Polish economy in transition,` in S. Estrin and M. Cave (eds), *Competition and Competition Policy: A Comparative Analysis of Central and Eastern Europe*, Pinter Publishers, London.

Garten, J. (1994), 'New challenges in the world economy: the antidumping law and U.S. trade policy', speech presented at the US Chamber of Commerce, Washington, DC, 7 April.

Gray, C. (1993), 'Evolving legal frameworks for private sector development in Central and Eastern Europe', World Bank Discussion Paper No. 209, Washington, CD.

Ham, A. (1993), 'International cooperation in the antitrust field and in particular the agreement between the USA and the Commission of the EC', *Common Market Law Review*, **30**, 571–95.

Hay, D. (1993), 'The assessment: competition policy' *Oxford Review of Economic Policy*, **9**, 1–26.

Hoekman, B. and Mavroidis, P. (1994), 'Competition, competition policy, and the GATT' *The World Economy*, **17**, 121–50.

Jacquemin, A. (1990), 'Horizontal concentration and European merger policy', *European Economic Review*, **30**, 539–50.

Jacquemin, A. and Sapir, A. (1988), 'International trade and integration of the European Community', *European Economic Review*, **28**, 202–12.

Kennedy, D. and Webb, D. (1993), 'The limits of integration: Eastern Europe and the European Communities', *Common Market Law Review*, **30**, 1095–117.

Levinsohn, J. (1993), 'Testing the imports-as-market-discipline hypothesis', *Journal of International Economics*, **35**, 1–22.

Mastalir, R. (1993), 'Regulation of competition in the new free markets of Eastern Europe: a comparative study of antitrust laws in Poland, Hungary, Czech and Slovak Republics and their models', *North Carolina Journal of International Law and Commercial Regulation*, **19**, 61–89.

Neven, D., Nuttal, R. and Seabright P. (1993), *Merger in Daylight: The Economics and Politics of European Merger Control*, CEPR, London.

OECD (1993a), 'Annual report on developments in the Slovak Republic (1992),' DAFFE/CLP(93)25. mimeo, OECD, Paris.

OECD (1993b), 'Annual report on developments in Hungary (1992),' DAFFE/CLP(93)8. mimeo, OECD, Paris.

OECD (1993c), 'Aide memoire of the meeting of May 13, 1993 of the Committee', DAFFE/CLP/M(93)1ADD3.

OECD (1994), 'Annual report on developments in Poland (1992), ' DAFFE/CLP(93)9. mimeo. OECD, Paris.

Pogacsas, P. and Stadler, J. (1993), 'Promoting competition in Hungary', in C. Saunders (ed.), *The Role of Competition in Economic Transition*, St. Martin's Press, New York.

Pohl, G. and Sorsa, P. (1992), *European Integration and Trade with the Developing World*. Policy and Research Series 21, The World Bank, Washington, DC.

Sapir, A., Buiges, P. and Jacquemin, A. (1993), 'European competition policy in manufacturing and services: a two-speed approach?', *Oxford Review of Economic Policy*, **9**, 113–32.

Spriggs, J. (1991), 'Towards aninternational transparency institution: Australian style', *The World Economy*, **14**, 165–80.

van Gerven, W. (1989), 'EC jurisdiction in antitrust matters: the wood pulp judgment', *Annual Proceedings of the Fordham Corporate Law Institute*, Matthew Bender, New York, ch. 21.

Weatherill, S. and Beaumont, P. (1993), *EC Law*. Penguin, London.

Willig, R. (1992), 'Anti-monopoly policies and institutions', in C. Clague and G. Rausser (eds), *The Emergence of Market Economies in Eastern Europe*, Basil Blackwell, Oxford.

7

Industrial and Trade Policies for the Emerging Market Economies*

David B. Audretsch

7.1 Introduction

There are generally two lenses through which to view the interaction between trade and industrial policies. The first lens focuses on the impact that trade policies have on the domestic industrial structure and ultimately the performance of domestic firms. The second focuses on industrial policy as an instrument to promote the international competitiveness of domestic firms. A tension emerges when the interests of the domestic industry seeking protection from foreign rivals and domestic entrants pre-empt the broader and more dispersed social interest for an efficient and competitive domestic industry. Trade policy is particularly likely to be captured by the constituents of industrial policy; that is by industries confronted by a competitive disadvantage and by those which are highly concentrated with only a few large producers. This is exactly the type of industry structure that is prevalent throughout Central and East European countries (CEECs) – highly capital intensive and concentrated – and that tends to have the highest propensity to engage in rent-seeking activities.

The purpose of this chapter is to suggest how institutions can be created and modified to devise and implement industrial policy in the emerging market economies. One of the main issues is how to avoid *regulatory capture*, by which policy makers with a mandate to devise and implement industrial policy become the spokesmen and champions of particular interest groups, and how to make industrial policy consistent with international trade policy.

Section 7.2 links institutions devising and implementing industrial and trade policies to the framework and timetable recently agreed upon in the *Europe*

* I would like to thank L. Alan Winters, Richard Portes and members of the CEPR project on Trade Laws and Institutions for Emerging Market Economies for their useful suggestions.

Agreements. Section 7.3 provides a framework for thinking about industrial policies, their interaction with trade policies, and the institutions charged with policy formulation and implementation. At the heart of this framework is a clear distinction between sectoral policies, which essentially target the economic output of specific industries and even firms, and horizontal policies, which essentially focus on improving the quality of inputs in the production process. There are a number of reasons why industrial policy institutions of this second type are less likely to be subject to regulatory capture than industrial policy institutions of the first type. Regulatory capture is more likely to result when the benefits of industrial policy are concentrated upon a relatively small number of firms, as is the case of industrial targeting. By contrast, regulatory capture is less of a problem when the recipients tend to be more widely dispersed, as is the case for horizontal industrial policies.

Designing institutions of industrial policy and international trade to avoid, or at least to minimize, regulatory capture is the subject of section 7.4. A problem particular to CEECs is that the centralized power and interest groups that are actually promoted through inherited coalition structures can influence the political process and restrict or impede the entry of new firms, including foreign competitors, that would ultimately weaken the prevailing coalition structure. That is, the institutions shaping and implementing trade policies are particularly vulnerable to the special interests represented by a highly concentrated group of large producers. Administrative procedures to diminish the influence of political rent-seeking activities generally fall under the heading of providing *accountability, independence* and *transparency*. The principle of accountability suggests that a greater degree of political scrutiny is required to help compensate for the inevitable imbalance between the concentration of producer interests on the one hand and the relatively dispersed interests of the general public on the other hand. According to the principle of *independence*, administrative agencies should be relatively independent from elected politicians. The principle of *transparency* generally suggests that institutions implementing industrial and trade policies should be charged with revealing to the public the maximum amount of information and reasoning upon which policies are based.

The privatization process poses a special problem involving both industrial and trade policies. Should restructuring occur prior or subsequent to privatization? And whose interests should prevail in the privatization process? The German approach to privatizing the former East German *Kombinante* provides a useful model to the CEECs. Regulatory capture has been avoided to a greater extent because the inevitable bureaucratic nature of the privatization process has been moderated by the *Treuhandanstalt*. In particular, four essential functions have been provided by a central administrative agency, which could easily be adapted in neighbouring countries: (1) creation of supervisory boards and the monitoring of management; (2) evaluation of the potential viability of enterprises and the adjustment of balance sheets in terms of writing off the old debt; (3) reorganization of enterprises, including closure in appropriate cases; and (4) search for and evaluation of potential purchasers, along with the imposition of ancillary conditions. These functions are implemented by a relatively independent (from the government) institution, which has contributed to the avoidance of regulatory capture.

7.2 Industrial Policy and the Europe Agreements

The three largest economies in Central and East Europe, what was at that time Czechoslovakia, Hungary and Poland, signed treaties with the European Community in 1990. At the heart of those treaties was a declaration of cooperation concerning trade, commercial and economic relationships. These agreements anticipated the set of *Association Agreements* involving those countries and the European Community, which were signed in December 1991, and became ratified by the fifteen national parliaments. In the preamble of what has become known as the *Europe Agreements*, a commitment was made to the 'development of trade and investment, instruments which are indispensable for economic restructuring and technological modernization' (CEPR, 1992).[1]

The timing of the association process was divided into two stages, each lasting five years. A key condition upon passage into the second stage is the 'progress to a market economy' (CEPR, 1992, p.14). The first condition for making progress to a market economy is the free movement of goods. This involves the abolition of customs duties on 'most industrial goods originating in the three countries' as well as all quantitative restrictions (Mayhew, 1992, p.14).[2] In addition, an 'anti-dumping' clause was included for protection of domestic industries against serious injury. Finally, under the *Europe Agreements* the Association Countries are held responsible for adhering to the competition laws of the European Union, as mandated under the Treaty of Rome. Similarly, all international trade agreements under the GATT must be adhered to (Mayhew, 1992, p.16).

As Winters (1992) points out, despite the promised trade liberalization inherent in the *Europe Agreements*, iron and steel producers in the European Union were threatening anti-dumping actions against competitors in the Czech and Slovak Republics, Poland and Hungary. In addition, there was pressure that, in terms of institutional structure, 'Eastern and Central Europe must converge towards that practised in the European Union. Similarly, practices involving customs law, company law, banking law, company accounts and taxes, intellectual property, protection of workers at the workplace, financial services, rules on competition, protection of health and life of humans, animals and plants, consumer protection, indirect taxation, technical rules and standards, transport and the environment all need to conform to the analogous practices currently found in the European Union' (Winters, 1992, p.20).

In view of the large number of institutional adjustments that must be rapidly implemented in Eastern and Central Europe, Winters (1992, pp.25–6) states

> It is clear that CHP need the legal framework – the soft infrastructure – to establish a market economy, and that they need it quickly; off-the-shelf institutions seem to make sense in these circumstances and in many cases the EC model is as good as any other. Moreover, given their aspiration to join the EC it seems better to adopt the necessary institutions *ad initium*. The difficulties, however, are two fold. First, CHP have no discretion about the final goal – harmonization – and no influence on the ways in which the EC might move the goal-posts either through new legislation or the interpretation of existing legislation. Second, the timetable for approximation looks unduly quick... In particular, it appears to be intended that approximation precede CHP–EC free trade, which is not due for ten years. This reverses the normal order of integration and leaves a distinct impression that the EC is willing to trade freely only on its own terms. By requiring CHP to adopt the same legal restrictions on economic activity as it has itself, the EC undermines many of the advantages of mutual trade. If CHP feel happy, with, say, lower worker protection, it makes sense for the EC to buy from them those goods for which this offers significant cost reductions. It is far from clear that the EC conventions, developed for countries such as France and Germany, are ideally suited to the needs of the poorer transitional economies, and yet the EAs appear to offer the latter no alternative, even temporary.

In order to meet the trade liberalizations and institutional requirements mandated by the *Europe Agreements*, new institutions are required and a number of existing institutions must be modified. Only within the appropriate institutional landscape can the requisite industrial and trade policies be implemented.

7.3 Framework for Industrial Policy

7.3.1 Institutions for Industrial Targeting

The concept of industrial policy has a number of meanings and applications. Still, what we will define here as the *traditional industrial policy paradigm* can be characterized as focusing on specific outcomes. More specifically, the outcomes are in terms of particular firms and particular industries which comprise the focal point of industrial policies. Under this traditional paradigm the task of public policy-makers is to select those targets, which are generally in terms of *outputs*, and then design instruments which will channel resources to the selected firms and industries.[3]

The theory underlying the traditional paradigm for industrial policy is that the outcomes are assumed to be known. That is, it is implicitly or explicitly assumed that it is known which products should be produced and how they should be produced. And it is also implicitly or explicitly assumed that the firms which potentially could produce those goods, that is the set of players, is also equally well known. Under this paradigm the goal of industrial policy is to devise instruments that channel the necessary resources into the selected firms and industries. Thus, the level of debate typically involves which industry and/or firms should be selected to be targeted for industrial policy.

The traditional paradigm for industrial policy generally follows from two crucial assumptions. The first is that the production process consists of well-defined and well-known inputs. This means that transparency exists in terms of both outputs and inputs. The second major assumption is that the inputs are geographically relatively fixed. This means that assisting any particular firm or industry is concomitant to promoting the domestic economy. The benefits in terms of job creation and high value-added production are presumably bestowed upon the country implementing the industrial policy. That is, it is generally assumed that companies have national affiliations and generally will pass on the benefits of industrial policies to the domestic economy.

The traditional paradigm of industrial policy may have served very well for situations of industrial catch-up, as the case of Japan during the post-war period illustrates. The reason for the success stories, particularly throughout Southeast Asia, is that the assumption of perfect knowledge is more or less valid. That is, in the situation of industrial and technological catch-up, it is well known which products must be produced and even how they should be produced. The major problem is developing the competency in production within domestic firms. But as countries start to actually catch up and approach the technological cutting edge, the traditional paradigm of industrial policy may no longer be so valid. This is because the comparative advantage of leading developed countries at the technological cutting edge involves an increased amount of innovative activity. The higher costs of production in such leading industrialized nations will tend to ensure that manufacturing activities that can be copied relatively inexpensively will shift out of the high-cost advanced industrialized nations to lower-cost developing or less developed countries. This is particularly true in a world where capital and technology are relatively mobile and free to move, but where labour is less mobile and tends to remain in its traditional region. Thus, the source of comparative advantage increasingly becomes new products and new manufacturing techniques that have not yet diffused to less developed nations, or, alternatively, special skills and human capital embodied in the labour force that cannot be easily transferred out of the leading developed nations to less developed countries.

To the extent that innovative activity, which in its most general sense means doing something differently than previously, becomes a relatively more important source for bestowing the comparative advantage, the assumption of perfect knowledge becomes increasingly tenuous. As uncertainty increases, both in terms of what should be produced as well as how to produce it, the danger that *selecting winners*, or targeting specific firms or even entire industries becomes increasingly wrought with danger. This is partly because industries characterized by a rapidly changing technology are typically populated by a multitude of firms, each representing a different *market experiment* in terms of the exact nature of the product offered as well as the manner by which the product is produced (Audretsch, 1995). And as new economic knowledge becomes a more important input as the source of comparative advantage, it becomes increasingly difficult to forecast which potentially new technical knowledge will actually materialize into actual economic knowledge. That is, it becomes increasingly difficult to identify those new ideas and products, and even which firms and industries, that can become successful.

Thus, the limits of the traditional paradigm for industrial policy come when the uncertainty about the outcomes becomes sufficiently great as to raise the likelihood that the wrong sets of economic and technical activities will become targeted is non-trivial, and even becomes likely. This explains why a number of the recent so-called *industrial policy failures* in the European Union, such as the Eureka Project, which is dealing with a very uncertain product and technology, had at best only a small chance of success. Once industrial policy settles on a relatively narrow range of specific outcomes – both in terms of the industry as well as the firm – the chances of success diminish as the degree of uncertainty increases.

Does this mean that there is no longer an intellectual justification for industrial policy? What it does mean is that the intellectual justification for the traditional industrial policy – that is, targeting specific outcomes, or particular industries and firms – is becoming increasingly tenuous. The traditional type of industrial policy may still be justifiable, but only in those cases where new economic knowledge plays a relatively unimportant role. Such industries are becoming more the exception than the rule and will continue to do so as developed nations, including those in Central and East Europe, continue to specialize in products where new economic knowledge is a key input. While there is still an important role for industrial policy, the traditional industrial policy is becoming increasingly less relevant.

7.3.2 Institutions for Horizontal Industrial Policies

The role of industrial policy in West Germany during the last several decades poses something of a paradox. On the one hand, selective industrial targeting, which is consistent with the traditional paradigm of industrial policy, has generally been oriented towards declining industries. There is little evidence to suggest that industrial targeting has contributed to making those industries viable or competitive in an international context. On the other hand, those industries which have exhibited the most success in export markets have not generally been the recipients of industrial targeting. The resolution to this apparent paradox lies in understanding the role of the traditional type of industrial policy, that is industrial targeting, in West Germany. In applying industrial targeting, the German government has generally striven to select industries that need assistance in either maintaining the current level of output or in adjusting to new conditions in the industry. That is, declining industries have generally been targeted for direct government support. Although tax policy in West Germany is more typically oriented to developments in particular regions rather than targeted for specific industries, in certain instances it has been used as an instrument for industrial policy. This may have occurred because the economic welfare of a certain region is tied to that of a particular industry, such as the case in the *Ruhrgebiet*. In particular, the coal, shipbuilding and steel industries have greatly benefited from tax advantages. Tax benefits usually take on two forms, either tax credits or else a special depreciation allowance. In the 1980s, the largest tax benefits in industry were granted to the steel sector.

A more direct tool for targeting industries is financial assistance, which generally takes the form of grants, government guarantees of loans or sub-market-rate loans. The loans are generally implemented through the major banks, such as the Deutsche Bank, Dresdner Bank and Commerzbank. The evidence suggests, however, that this direct industrial targeting has had little impact on promoting the international competitiveness of declining industries (Audretsch, 1989).

Something of a new paradigm with respect to industrial policy seems to have emerged in the 1990s. This new paradigm follows from the assumptions that (1) new economic knowledge is increasingly a key input in the production function, and (2) the factor of production that is the least mobile is labour. All other factors of production, especially capital and even technology, are relatively mobile.

This first assumption suggests that, due to the inherent uncertainty with respect to new economic knowledge, it is increasingly difficult to target specific applications in the production process. As mentioned above, if the outcome is relatively uncertain, targeting actual firms and even entire industries becomes riskier. Under the new paradigm for industrial policy those programmes that are oriented towards enhancing factors of production seem to have the greatest likelihood of success. While it may be increasingly difficult to determine which projects, firms, or even industries will emerge as being viable in the global market, the dynamic comparative advantage of nations is still shaped by the relative endowment of factors of production. By shaping the nature of those factors of production, the new industrial policy can implicitly affect the way in which those factors will be used, if not the specific applications.

The second assumption suggests that, because of its relative immobility with respect to capital and even technology, labour seems to be the factor that lends itself most to quality-enhancing industrial policies. As the Secretary of the Department of Labor in the Clinton Administration, Robert Reich (1990, pp.58–9), points out,

As every economy becomes global, a nation's most important competitive asset becomes the skills and cumulative learning of its work force... Globalization, almost by definition makes this true. Every factor of production other than work force skills can be duplicated anywhere around the world. Capital now sloshes freely across international boundaries, so much so that the cost of capital in different countries is rapidly converging. State-of-the-art factories can be erected anywhere. The latest technologies flow from computers in one nation, up to satellites parked in space, then back down to computers in another nation. It is all fungible: capital, technology, raw materials, information – all except for one thing, the most critical part, the one element that is unique about a nation: its work force.

While the labour force is certainly one input in the production process that can be targeted for industrial policy under this new paradigm, it certainly need not be the only one. Any other factor of production that is either complementary to labour or else is relatively fixed in terms of location may also be appropriate as a target. That is, new economic knowledge is generally embodied in human capital. Thus, the creation and dissemination of new economic knowledge, such as R&D activities, technology transfer, cooperative research arrangements, and education and training all serve to enhance the inputs of human capital and knowledge. In addition, the (public) infrastructure is generally not only fixed in terms of location but also complementary to human capital.

West Germany typifies the type of new industrial policy in its public policies of enhancing the stock of human capital in its labour force at least since the Second World War. The cornerstone of this policy has evolved around the formal system of education, the apprentice system of training workers, a network of retraining programmes, and a social safety net designed to protect all workers exposed to the hazards of industrial restructuring. More than either low-technology or high-technology industries, this type of industrial policy has enhanced inputs that are more important for moderate-technology industries. The strength of the moderate-technology industries in West Germany reflects that the most decisive input in industries such as machine tools, engineering and metalworking is skilled labour and human capital. And West Germany has consistently pursued a public policy of developing the stock of human capital in its labour force since the Second World War.

The goal of the worker training system in West Germany is to instill in the student the general capacity to acquire more skills (*Schlüsselqualifikationen*). Those students not obtaining the *Abitur* (high school degree) attend either secondary technical or vocational school. There are around 400 nationally standardized occupational tracks for which training in a *Lehrstelle*, that is as an apprentice, is possible (Streeck, 1991; Sorge, 1985). Training an apprentice costs roughly US$18 000 per year, and the apprenticeship typically lasts between two and four years. There is no obligation for the apprentice to remain with the firm, or for the firm to hire the trainee subsequent to the apprentice programme, but in fact it is more the rule than the exception that the apprentice remains with the firm, quite often for the remainder of his life. The apprenticeship system effectively forces firms to train workers to a greater degree than they would otherwise.

Government policies and a social environment restricting the (minimum) wage levels, work environment, and forcing employers to invest in a high level of human capital have created a highly skilled labour force that must be deployed in high value-added industries in order for firms to be viable in internationally linked markets. The moderate-technology industries, such as machine tools, are based on such factor endowment. In addition, West Germany has traditionally developed and targeted its so-called *Mittelstand,* i.e., small- and medium-sized firms. That is, firms with fewer than 500 employees account for about 58% of employment in West German manufacturing, while only about 35% of US manufacturing employment is in small- and medium-sized firms (Acs and Audretsch, 1993). Most importantly, about 90% of the apprentices are trained in the West German *Mittelstand*, which accounts for about one-third of all West German exports.[4]

There are numerous government policies directed towards developing the German small- and medium-sized firms. For example, the *Kreditanstalt für Wiederaufbau*, which was originally established following the Second World War to facilitate reconstruction, is devoted towards developing the technological competence of the German *Mittelstand* (Bundesminister für Forschung und Technologie, 1985). Firms with annual sales of less than US$590 million are eligible for grants covering up to 40% of the costs of developing and implementing state-of-the art technology. In addition, small- and medium-sized firms are exempt from many of the anti-monopoly laws in Germany (*Gesetz gegen Wettbewerbsbeschränkungen*), which helps to facilitate joint marketing, purchasing and R&D facilities (Bundesminister für Wirtschaft, 1987).

The success of the West German economy reflects these policies enhancing the quality of the labour force, in that they shape a key factor of production which the nation can deploy. This in turn has influenced those industries in which the country has a comparative advantage, in the case of West Germany the industries where skilled labour and a moderate degree of technological competence are crucial inputs. For example, moderate-technology intensive industries account for 54% of West German exports.[5] By contrast, only 18% of West German exports are in high-technology goods, and 28% are in low-technology goods. Further, while the export share accounted for by moderate technological West German industries rose during the decade of the 1980s, it fell substantially in the United States from 47.0 to 39.9%. More than for any of its European Union counterparts, Japan, or the United States, West Germany thrives on the vitality of its moderate-technology industries (Hughes, 1991).

In conclusion, there are generally two broad approaches to industrial policy which may be applicable to Central and East Europe. The first approach is horizontal, in that it is neutral with respect to specific sectors. A particular virtue of horizontal industrial policies is that no specific industry, sector or enterprise needs to be selected for targeting. Rather, as a result of having access to an enhanced factor of production or a superior infrastructure, enterprises will learn that their competitive advantage lies in industries that best exploit, or take advantage of, that enhanced factor of production. Thus, the decision only has to be made on which type of factor of production is most likely to promote international competitiveness, rather than on any specific industry or particular product.

The emphasis of horizontal policies in Central and East Europe should be on:

1. Strengthening the structural competitiveness of the economy. This is done through promoting efficiency on the supply side of the economy. Policies enhancing factors of production, such as job location programmes, worker retraining programmes, incentive programmes to enhance the mobility of labour, capital market policies, government loan guarantees and competition policies all work towards increasing productivity and reducing the costs of production.
2. Reducing market imperfections and externalities. Numerous imperfections impede the market process. Information remains a particularly scarce resource and the institutions necessary for the transmission of such information are only now being created.
3. Competition in both product and input markets must be increased. This calls not only for a strong competition policy and implementation of the anti-monopoly laws but also for import competition. In particular, entry barriers should be reduced as much as possible.
4. Industrial infrastructure needs to be improved. An important role for the government is to enhance the quality of railways, highways, communications, etc. This also includes non-physical infrastructure, such as human capital. Improvements in the education of citizens and the training of workers will result in longer-run productivity gains.
5. Entrepreneurship and small- and medium-sized enterprises (SMEs). Programmes facilitating the start-up and survival of new firms would inject a key dynamic into a lopsided industrialized structure. Not only would SMEs provide an important mechanism for job generation, but also an engine for technological change and innovation. Experience in the European Union has shown that the new enterprises of today, at least in a few cases, end up as the industrial giants of tomorrow.

The second type of industrial policy which could be pursued is sectoral targeting. Experience in the member nations of the European Union has generally indicated that governments are not particularly adept at separating winning enterprises from losers. Viewed from that perspective, a sectoral approach is especially risky. It is particularly risky in a situation where latent long-term sectoral comparative advantages are hardly identifiable due to the numerous distortions which are still affecting the relative performances of industrial sectors and enterprises. A sectoral approach could, at best, be effective only under certain special and restrictive conditions, such as extreme regional concentration or the existence of a chronic overcapacity in an industry.

7.3.3 Interaction with Trade Policy

As stated in the introduction, there are generally two lenses through which to view the interaction between trade and industrial policies. The first focuses on the impact that trade policies have on the domestic industrial structure and ultimately the performance of domestic firms. This view considers the trade policies to be more or less exogenous and the industrial organization and domestic economic performance to be more or less endogenous. Because trade policies influence the domestic industrial structure and associated economic performance they can therefore be considered to serve as a type of industrial policy.

The second lens focuses on industrial policies as being exogenous and the trade performance as being endogenous. Because an important goal of industrial policy is to improve the international competitiveness of domestic firms, viewed through this lens industrial policies serve as a type of trade policy.

According to the first view, trade policy serves as an industrial policy by providing the spur of foreign competition, where it is deemed to be appropriate. A large and consistent body of empirical evidence has found a systematic tendency for (1) price-cost margins to be lower in the presence of foreign competition (generally measured as import competition); and (2) innovative activity tends to be greater in the presence of foreign competition. Thus, the empirical evidence points to a liberal trade policy as a mechanism for injecting a competitive element into domestic economies.

At the same time, there is at least some evidence suggesting that certain types of industries have a higher propensity to seek out and obtain trade protection as a mechanism for rent seeking or rent protection. Such trade protection is frequently granted under the rubric of providing *industrial adjustment* to an industry severely impacted by foreign competition. By providing an umbrella to protect domestic firms from foreign competition, it is argued that they will have time to make the necessary investments in order to adjust and become viable in global markets. In this sense, trade policy is typically viewed as a type of industrial policy, since the goal is to improve not only the efficiency of the firms but ultimately the international competitiveness of the domestic industry. The evidence from Western countries, however, principally the United States, suggests that certain industries have a greater propensity to seek out and receive trade protection.[6] In particular, Finger (1981) and Finger *et al.* (1982) analyse the determinants of trade policy outcomes. Feinberg and Hirsch (1989) employ a rent-seeking framework to explain the incidence of anti-dumping and countervailing duty complaints brought before the United States International Trade Commission and the United States Department of Commerce. They find that the propensity to file a complaint tends to be the greatest in large capital-intensive industries, particularly those facing employment losses and rising import shares. Companies with the largest economic rents and which benefit the most from protection have the greatest incentive to seek out trade protection. In addition, the empirical evidence suggests that trade protection tends to be greater in industries which are more highly concentrated and where union coverage is more extensive.

The results of studies from Western countries focusing on the process of rent protection suggest that such rent-seeking and rent-protecting activities in CEECs may be particularly severe. It is exactly the type of industry structure found to exhibit the greatest propensity to seek out trade protection – highly capital intensive and concentrated industries – that characterizes the bulk of the industries in the CEECs. Thus, there may be a tendency for not just the firms but also labour and other dependent economic agents to support, and even seek out, programmes of industrial policy that are essentially projectionist in nature.

7.4 Regulatory Capture

7.4.1 Rent Seeking and Institutions of Industrial Policy

In designing institutions of industrial policy and international trade, particular concern has to be undertaken to avoid or at least minimize regulatory capture. Regulatory capture refers to the capture of a regulatory agency by the very constituency that agency is mandated with regulating. As Neven *et al.* (1993, p.164) conclude,

> It is no longer possible to regard government agencies as staffed by selfless and omniscient upholders of the common weal, nor to contrast them with the simple and ruthless pursuit of profits by private firms. For one thing, it has become abundantly clear that government agencies themselves respond to political and economic pressures and incentives, and that limitations on the information available to them may severely constrain the policies they can pursue; for another, the fact that firms may themselves be run by agents with interests of their own other than maximizing shareholder's wealth has become much harder to ignore. One of the tasks, therefore, for both firms and government agencies is to ensure that the individuals running them have incentives to do so in the wider interests of the parties whose welfare they affect.

The theory of regulatory capture is a special case of the more general theory of rent-seeking behaviour, first developed by Tullock (1967) and Krueger (1974).

The standard model of rent seeking identifies a transfer of wealth and loss in allocative efficiency resulting from a restriction in output from the competitive equilibrium price and quality. If the number of sellers in the market is sufficiently small, and if information is widespread among those firms, the organizational costs of obtaining a restrictive policy will be relatively small. Similarly, if only a few parties stand to gain from the transfer of a large amount of wealth, the value of seeking restrictive policies to each member is high. The parties losing from that policy, on the other hand, especially consumers, tend to suffer from high organizational costs and a deficient distribution of information.[7]

Thus, it may be rational and profitable in instances of small coalitions with recognizable gains and low organizational costs to invest collectively in institutional change via the political process. Stigler (1971) predicted that legislatures will respond to special interest group pressure and supply the legal structures necessary to curtail output and maintain the output restriction. In particular, Stigler argued that the state possesses the power to improve the economic well-being of economic coalitions. Such coalitions constitute the demand for regulation. Similarly, the political process, which constructs entry barriers to relatively small groups seeking to obtain such regulation, constitutes the *supply* of regulation.

The process of establishing and maintaining the rent transfers requires two separate mechanisms. The persistence of rents over time depends upon (1) the magnitude of the redistribution of wealth and the allocative efficiency loss, and (2) the ability of the beneficiary group to provide barriers or deterrence to entry. Noll (1989) extended the concept of regulatory capture to include not just regulatory agents but virtually every type of government protection available to special interest groups.

In raising the question, 'Who regulates the regulators?', Laffont and Tirole (1993, ch. 11) suggest that the answer is, 'It depends'. In particular, it depends upon the existence of information asymmetries between the public and the regulators. To the degree that such information asymmetries exist, it is less costly for interest groups and the regulatory agencies to avoid public scrutiny and instead pursue their own interests. Only in the absence of any such information asymmetries, or where the cost of transacting such knowledge is trivial, will the public interest prevail.

7.4.2 Industrial Organization and Regulatory Capture

The fundamental conditions for rent-seeking activities by private interests resulting in regulatory capture seem to be ripe in most of the CEECs. For example, the concentration of economic activities in just a few enterprises is more the rule than the exception. Such a concentration of economic activity tends to increase the pay-off accrued from investment into rent-seeking activities and at the same time reduce the cost of coordination and monitoring. The size distribution of industrial enterprises is highly skewed towards large enterprises, especially when compared to the industrial structure prevalent in the countries of the European Union. Only about 5% of industrial enterprises in the combined Czechoslovakia had fewer than 100 employees. In West Germany, by contrast, about 98.9% of all enterprises, and in Italy about 99% of all enterprises have fewer than 100 employees (Acs and Audretsch, 1993). Similarly, the largest 100 Polish enterprises accounted for 39% of total sales, 43% of income and 18% of all employment. And the largest 500 enterprises accounted for about two-thirds of all sales, 68% of net income and 40% of employment. Johnson and Loveman (1993) report that the average state enterprise in Poland had 1 132 employees. The mean number of employees per plant was 378. By contrast, the mean plant size in the member countries of the European Union is well under 100 employees per establishment (Acs and Audretsch, 1993).

Similarly, in the combined Czechoslovakia, the share of manufacturing employment accounted for by small- and medium-sized firms, or enterprises with fewer than 500 employees, fell steadily from 13.6% in 1956, to 8.8% in 1960, to 2.1% in 1970, and to 1.4% in 1980. By contrast, the share of employment accounted for by large enterprises employing more than 2 500 workers rose from less than one-third in 1956 to well over one-half by 1980. In West Germany, small- and medium-sized enterprises, the so-called German *Mittelstand*, account for 57.9% of manufacturing employment; in the United Kingdom the small- and medium-sized firm share of manufacturing employment is 39.9%; in the Netherlands it is 39.9%, in Portugal it is 71.8%, and in Italy it is 55.2% (Acs and Audretsch, 1993).

Not only is economic activity highly centralized in Central and East Europe, but large administrative agencies have traditionally been linked to each industry. Benacek and Zemplinerova (1995, p.15) refer to this as the 'double' monopoly power in Central and East Europe, which combines a high degree of market concentration with a large bureaucratic political power structure:

> The enterprise in a non-parametrical environmental is a coalition of internal and external participants. The internal participants include the 'control group' – the power center of the enterprise, the worker aristocracy, and the administrative apparatus. The main goal of this group is not to improve efficiency and innovation, but rather to establish close links with all members of the external hierarchical superiors, i.e., planning commission, industry ministries, and regional Party bosses, as well as with key suppliers and customers. These links help to insure the fulfilment of personal interests of the 'control group' – their material and political welfare.

Under the previous political regimes, such coalition structures succeeded in choking off any meaningful entry into the manufacturing industries (Balcerowicz, 1989). As Murrell (1990, p.66) observes, 'Like Sherlock Holmes' dog that didn't bark, the importance of entry to the centrally planned economies might have been somewhat overlooked because of entry's most significant feature – its absence. Lack of entry of new firms could result from the fact that hierarchies like a stable structure.' And, as Kornai (1980) and Granick (1987) emphasized, the refusal to let state-owned enterprises fail along with the guaranteed protection of job rights undoubtedly served to diminish the establishment of new enterprises. Thus, a host of studies ranging from Bulgaria (Puchev, 1990) the Czech and Slovak Republics (McDermott and Mejstrik, 1992, 1993), Hungary (Roman, 1989, 1990), to Yugoslavia (Estrin and Petrin, 1991) and East Germany (Bannasch, 1993) have all identified a conscious policy on the behalf of the incumbent enterprises to restrict entry in the CEECs (Tyson *et al.*, 1994). According to Lipton and Sachs (1990a, pp.84–85),

> The socialist economies also lack adequate procedures for the entry and exit of enterprises. Enterprises are typically founded by ministries or local authorities, which at the same time arrange for the funding to begin operations. Absent of such sponsorship, there is little chance that state enterprise activity can spring up to meet even the most obvious economic needs. On the side of bankruptcy and liquidation state activity has been virtually unknown. In fact, the absence of markets and meaning of relative prices in the economy means that it is difficult, if not impossible, to distinguish between enterprises that should and should not survive.'

Thus, a problem particular to the CEECs is that the centralized power and interest groups that are actually promoted though coalition structures can influence the political process into restricting or at least impeding the entry of new firms – and also foreign competitors – that would ultimately weaken the coalition structure. That is, the institutions shaping and implementing international trade policies are likely to be particularly vulnerable to the special interests represented by a highly concentrated group of several large producers, whose common interest is to block or at least impede the inflow of foreign-produced goods and activities of foreign-based enterprises. At the same time, the group of economic agents who would most benefit from such trade policies – the general public – is generally poorly organized and not well informed. The strength and ability of the public in offsetting highly concentrated political interests is relatively weak. There exists no tradition of consumer and public oriented groups with the requisite resources to offset such special interest groups. Therefore, regulatory capture might be expected to be particularly severe in the CEECs.

Even if some institutions of industrial policy are literally taken off the shelf from the European Union and mirrored in the CEECs, the differential starting point may lead to a greater danger of regulatory capture in Central and East Europe than has been experienced in the European Union. A case in point are the institutions mandated with formulating and enforcing competition policies. Competition policy, as is practised within the European Union, has generally derived from the Treaty of Rome in 1957.[8] While competition policies implemented in the European Union are certainly distinct from the American version of antitrust policy, in fact European competition policy has its roots in the American institutions of antitrust.[9] The core statutes of American Antitrust, Sections 1 and 2 of the Sherman Act, were passed by the United States Congress in 1890 as a reaction to the rapid process of cartelization and centralization of market power prevailing in the United States at the end of the nineteenth century. These legal statutes, as well as their enforcement by the antitrust agencies and interpretation by the judicial system, generally focused on the act of creating monopoly power as constituting a violation of the *Sherman Act* (Section 2).[10] That is, because the concern of public policy was with preventing the creation of monopoly power, policy focused essentially on a verb – *to monopolize* – rather than on a noun, *monopoly*, which would have made the possession of monopoly power a violation of the antitrust statutes. In essentially adapting the American antitrust code, the European Union also implicitly adapted a competition policy that makes illegal the creation of monopoly power through certain specified acts of (illegal) conduct, but not necessarily the *per se* possession of market power. That is, mergers that create sizable market power are generally blocked, while a single firm possessing that same degree of market power is not in violation of the antitrust laws. Similarly, enterprises which engage in aggressive conduct, generally termed *anti-competitive*, in an effort to attain market power are generally found in violation of the antitrust statutes. Enterprises already in possession of market power, however, may not even find it necessary to engage in such *anti-competitive* conduct in order to preserve their market dominance. This asymmetric treatment of the law with respect to the creation of market power on the one hand and firms already in possession of market dominance on the other led John Kenneth Galbraith (1967, p.187) to observe that the antitrust laws 'exempt those who possess the market power and concentrates on those who would try to possess it.'

Thus, the American antitrust approach, which has its origins one century ago in a society trying to stem the rising tide of economic concentration and market dominance, was not only adapted by the European Community in the 1950s, but is also now being more or less adapted by institutions in Central and East Europe. But the problem of industrial structure confronting Central and East Europe in the 1990s is not at all analogous to that in the United States at the end of the last century or in Western Europe during the early post-war years. Rather, as discussed above, the essential problem is not firms trying to create market dominance but rather firms and political coalitions inherited from the previous political regime that already possess considerable dominance. Not only does this raise doubts about the efficacy of competition policies essentially constructed to stem a tide of rising concentration in the United States 100 years ago, but what is particularly relevant here is that these institutions are particularly vulnerable to capture by the incumbent dominant enterprises which can then wield competition policies, such as merger control and cooperative agreements, as a mechanism to impede smaller competitors and foreign rivals from entering the market and posing a threat.

More generally, the case of institutions mandated to formulate and implement competition policies serves as an example where institutions that are appropriate in the European Union may be subject to a greater degree of capture in the CEECs.

7.4.3 Privatization

There are a number of controversial issues associated with the privatization programmes which have a direct impact on the ability of the economies of the CEECs to become restructured. At the heart of the restructuring debate is whether the formerly state-owned enterprises should be restructured prior to being privatized or subsequent to privatization. As Carlin and Mayer (1992) point out, this issue is being dealt with differently in different countries. For example, the proposals for mass privatization in Poland have generally involved first restructuring the enterprises and then privatizing them. By contrast, the use of vouchers in Czechoslovakia has resulted in the enterprises generally being privatized before they are restructured. Still other large-scale enterprises will be privatized by the Privatization Ministry after approving a business plan. But it is not clear whether a business plan which proposes privatizing only certain factories or even parts of factories will be approved by the Privatization Ministry. It has been reported by the Privatization Ministry that a clear tendency exists for foreign investors to propose a cream-skimming business plan, which results in a joint venture between the foreign partner and the most efficient plants and establishments of a previously state-owned enterprise. The Privatization Ministry expressed a clear scepticism towards such cream skimming behaviour. How could the remainder of the enterprise be successfully privatized, if the most efficient plants and parts of establishments had already been sold off?

It is also unclear to what extent a privatized enterprise must adhere to the business plan approved by the founding Ministry and the relevant Privatization Ministry. That is, will a newly privatized enterprise be held liable for pursuing the goals and conditions stated in the proposed business plan? If not, then there is little incentive for revealing the true operating plan anticipated for a privatized firm. Indeed, there would exist a clear incentive for applicants to state the preferences of the Founding Ministry and the Privatization Ministry. This would create a considerable agency problem. Given the traditionally close ties between the Founding Ministries and the enterprises to be privatized, the problem of regulatory capture discussed in section 7.4.2 becomes particularly relevant. To what extent will the interests of the former managers, employees and communities be represented, and to what extent will those of the new owners be represented?

The transformation of state-owned enterprises into private entities has generally proceeded quite slowly in the CEECs. Carlin and Mayer (1992, p.3) are certainly not alone in concluding that the 'deficiency of East European privatization is an institutional one'. While their analysis focuses on an inadequacy of managerial and financial resources involved in the privatization process in both the private and public sectors, the tendency for the regulatory agencies, that is the privatization agencies, to be captured by the enterprises they are charged with privatizing has also contributed to the problem. As Carlin and Mayer (1992, p. 55) conclude, the privatization process in the CEECs has been 'undermined by the poor finances of the public sector, and inefficient and corrupt bureaucracies.'

The German approach to privatizing the former East German *Kombinate*, or Combines, may, in fact, provide a useful model to the CEECs. Regulatory capture has been avoided to a large extent in the case of German privatization because the inevitably bureaucratic nature of the privatization process has been moderated by the creation of a privatization agency – the *Treuhandanstalt* – which is independent of the state government. The *Treuhand* has been responsible for implementing four essential functions:

1. The creation of supervisory boards and the monitoring of management.
2. The evaluation of the potential viability of enterprises and the adjustment of balance sheets, in terms of writing off old debt.
3. The reorganization of enterprises and their closure in appropriate cases.
4. The search for, and evaluation of, potential purchasers, along with the imposition of conditions such as employment and investment targets.

No other bureaucratic agency mandated with privatization has operated as effectively as the *Treuhandanstalt*. One of its most distinguishing features has been to delegate certain restructuring tasks to other institutions and agents. By creating relatively independent supervisory boards charged with overseeing the privatization process of specific enterprises, the *Treuhand* ensured that the development of restructuring plans would be shared by a number of institutions. This enabled experienced West German experts to become involved in the privatization process by participating on supervisory boards. The reliance upon high quality and distinguished individuals with an international reputation to sit upon the supervisory boards has served as a buffer against concentrated private interests in what otherwise would have resulted in regulatory capture in a number of cases. In addition, Carlin and Mayer (1992, p. 55) point out that the 'carefully balancing of interests of the state-local authorities, finance, industry and workers in the composition of the *Treuhandanstalt's* board' has tended to dissipate the political power held by individual special interest groups.

What the nations of East and Central Europe can perhaps learn from the experience of the *Treuhandanstalt* in the privatization process being completed in East Germany is that the role of outsiders is important, but at that the same time their role has been kept to one of providing advice. The institution of the Supervisory Board has served well in drawing in a larger community of external institutions and firms. In addition, scarce administrative and managerial resources should be concentrated first on the board of the privatization agency, second in the administration of the privatization agency, third on the boards of banks, and fourth in the administration of banks. While the privatization process in East Germany had the expertise of West Germany upon which to rely, in the CEECs such expertise needs to be solicited from Western countries. Perhaps such an exchange of personnel could be financed by the European Union.

Even in the privatization process of East Germany, however, the *Treuhandanstalt* has been completely unable to pre-empt rent-seeking activities. In particular, Western firms have engaged in asset-stripping and (skilled) labour-stripping. In addition, the political power of incumbent management in the *Kombinante* has, in fact, prevailed in shaping the privatization process to the detriment of the needed restructuring and defaults, in certain cases needless, have occurred. Given the mixed results of the German process of privatization, even with a strong and independent bureaucratic agency like the *Treuhandanstalt*, it is hard to imagine that the privatization process in the CEECs can avoid regulatory capture in the absence of such an independent bureaucratic administration.

7.4.4 Avoiding Regulatory Capture

There are a number of precautions which can be built into the institutions of industrial policy to help impede the process of regulatory capture. Such procedures generally fall under the heading of accountability, independence and transparency. According to the principle of *accountability*, government regulatory agencies are held accountable to the general public through the general public. This suggests that a greater degree of political scrutiny is required to help compensate for the inevitable imbalance between the concentration of producer interests on the one hand, and the relatively dispersed interests of the general public on the other. What this has amounted to in more practical terms is a greater degree of oversight of regulatory agencies by legislative committees. One example of such regulatory oversight is the House of Commons Select Committees in the United Kingdom. Another is to increase public funding for government agencies mandated with consumer safety or with the environment. Accountability can be viewed either as a shortening of the hierarchical chain of responsibility from the public to the civil service, or alternatively, as an increase in the influence of previously under-represented interests in the regulatory process.

To some extent the second principle to mitigate regulatory capture is the antithesis of the first. According to the principle of independence, weakening the link between the control of administrative agencies by elected officials may also reduce the likelihood and extent of capture. This is based on the theory that, in fact, it is elected politicians that often serve as the mechanism by which the regulatory agencies are captured. There are actually two distinct theoretical foundations underlying the principle of *agency independence.* The first is the belief that regulation faces a problem of time inconsistency. Regulators would like the industries they regulate to invest optimally, but politicians will be more tempted than independent regulators to seek to expropriate any rents accruing to such investments after they have been made. The second refers to the unequal influence concerning day-to-day policies distributed across various interest groups. The point is that policy-makers who are independent are in a better position to make decisions more closely related to the public interest rather than being captured by the interests of highly concentrated groups of special interests.

The third principle for institutions implementing industrial policy to follow in order to mitigate the adverse influence of regulatory capture is that of *transparency*. This principle of *transparency* generally suggests that institutions implementing industrial policies should be charged with revealing to the public the maximum amount of information and reasoning upon which policies are based. While *ex ante* transparency may prove to be problematic, *ex post* transparency is generally considered to be a sufficient condition. Making such information and decision-making processes transparent reduces the cost to the public of monitoring the institution. In addition, *transparency* tends to promote the internal consistency of policies, since exceptions are more exposed to public scrutiny. Perhaps the greatest benefit accruing from transparency is a reduction in information costs to those interest groups, and in particular the general public, which would otherwise have to incur non-trivial transaction costs to obtain that information.

In conclusion, to avoid ,or at least to minimize, regulatory capture, industrial policy has to be relatively inexpensive and simple to administer. In the design of specific industrial policies, market-enhancing aspects should emphasized, and the following principles should be followed:

- *Transparency* in choice and delivery;
- *Decentralized* where possible (i.e. third party delivery)
- A corollary need to strengthen intermediary bodies (i.e. trade associations)
- *Accountable, Assessable* and *Evaluable*;
- Sunset clauses.

7.5 Conclusions

In evaluating the prospects for reform in Czechoslovakia two years subsequent to the November 1989 revolution, Begg (1991, p.258) concluded that 'Commitment to the market does not absolve the government from the need for a view about the economy. Establishing the market economy is the priority, but market failures are still first-order effects. Market prices are not instantly at world levels; domestic monopoly is present; and the market economy is not yet assembled.' Begg (1991, p.264) warned that 'Current discussions of industrial, regional and state owned enterprises policy are *ad hoc*, mutually inconsistent, and vulnerable to lobbying for special cases'. Some three years later this assessment by Begg is still as valid as ever.

The purpose of this chapter has been to suggest how institutions charged with devising and implementing industrial policy can be created and modified in the emerging market economies. By following a fairly straightforward set of administrative rules, the capture of regulatory agencies by political coalitions can be mitigated, if not avoided.

Notes

1. The *Europe Agreements* are not without problems, particularly with respect to conflicts and implementation. According to L. Alan Winters (CEPR, 1992, p.1), 'The agreements are disappointing in the degree of support and encouragement they guarantee to CHP (Czechoslovakia, Hungary and Poland)... Indeed, they sometimes appear to be designed as much to minimize the adjustment that the revolutions of 1989 cause in the EC than to maximize the benefits that accrue to CHP.'
2. These changes in customs duties and quantitative restrictions do not apply to the sensitive sectors of textiles, clothing, iron and steel, or agricultural products. For these products special rules are applicable (Mayhew, 1992).
3. Laura D'Andrea Tyson, who is the current Chairman of the Council of Economic Advisors under President Bill Clinton, and John Zysman (1983) pointed out that the distinction between industrial policy and government policies that apply across all sectors of the economy is perhaps the most decisive criterion for what constitutes an industrial policy. While policies focusing on economic phenomena, such as macroeconomic growth, unemployment, inflation, environmental quality and welfare programmes, generally touch all sectors of the economy, *bona fide* industrial policies are restricted to specific sectors or industries.
4. Cited from 'Think Small: Midsize Companies Give Germany's Export Powerhouse its Punch,' *Business Week*, 7 October 1991.
5. The European Union definitions of high technology, medium technology, and low technology are adopted here.
6. For an excellent discussion of the political economy of trade policy, see Baldwin (1985).
7. For a mathematical derivation of these propositions, see Audretsch and Woolf (1987).
8. Article 85 of the Treaty of Rome explicitly forbids certain restrictive practices and has constituted the kernel of a Europe-wide competition policy.
9. For a detailed distinction between European competition policies and American antitrust, see Audretsch (1989).
10. In fact, Section 2 of the Sherman Act states that, 'Every person who *shall* monopolize or *attempt* to monopolize...'.

References

Acs, Z. J. and Audretsch, D. B. (eds) (1993), *Small Firms and Entrepreneurship: An East–West Perspective*, Cambridge University Press, Cambridge.

Audretsch, D. B. (1989), *The Market and the State: Government Policies towards Business in Europe, Japan and the U.S.*, New York University Press, New York.

Audretsch, D. B. (1993), 'Industrial policy and international competitiveness: the case of East Europe,' in K. Hughes (ed.), *European Competitiveness*, Cambridge University Press, Cambridge, pp.259–90.

Audretsch, D. B. (1995), *Innovation and Industry Evolution*, MIT Press, Cambridge, MA.

Audretsch, D. B. and Woolf, A. G. (1987), 'Regulatory reform in the 1980s: an anti rent-seeking movement?' *European Journal of Political Economy*, **3**(3), 335–49.

Balcerowicz, L. (1989), 'Polish economic reform, 1981–88: an overview,' *Economic Reforms in the European Centrally Planned Economies*, United Nations and the Economic Commission for Europe, New York.

Baldwin, R. E. (1985), *The Political Economy of U.S. Import Policy*, MIT Press, Cambridge, MA.

Bannasch, H.-G. (1993), 'The evolution of small firms in East Germany,' in Z. J. Acs and D. B. Audretsch (eds), *Small Firms and Entrepreneurship: An East–West Perspective*, Cambridge University Press, Cambridge, pp.182–90.

Begg, D. (1991), 'Economic reform in Czechoslovakia: should we believe in Santa Klaus?' *Economic Policy*, **13**, 243–86.

Benacek, V. and Zemplinerova, A. (1995), 'Problems of and assistance to small business in the Czech Republic,' *Small Business Economics*, forthcoming

Bundesminister für Forschung und Technologie (1985), *Statistische Informationen*, Bonn.

Bundesminister für Wirtschaft (1987), *Bericht des Bundeskartellamtes über sein Tätigkeit in den Jahren 1985/1986 sowie über die Lage und Entwicklung auf seinem Aufgabengebiet (§50 GWB)*, Bundestagsdrucksache, Bonn.

Carlin, W. and Mayer C. (1992), 'Restructuring enterprises in East Europe,' CEPR Discussion Paper No. 700

CEPR (1992), 'The association process: making it work: Central Europe and the European Community,' CEPR Occasional Paper No. 11.

Estrin, S. and Petrin, T. (1991), 'Entry and exit in Yugoslavian manufacturing,' in P. Geroski and J. Schwalbach (eds), *Entry and Market Contestability: An International Comparison*, Basil Blackwell, Oxford.

Feinberg, R. M. and Hirsch, B. T. (1989), 'Industry rent seeking and the filing of 'unfair trade' complaints,' *International Journal of Industrial Organization*, **7**, 325–40.

Finger, J. M. (1981), 'The industry-country incidence of less than fair value cases in the U.S. import trade,' *Quarterly Review of Economics and Business*, **21**, 260–79.

Finger, J. M., Hall, H. K. and Nelson, D. R. (1982), 'The political economy of administered protection,' *American Economic Review*, **72**, 452–66.

Galbraith, J. K. (1967), *The New Industrial State*, Houghton Mifflin, Boston, MA.

Granick, D. (1987), *Job Rights in the Soviet Union: Their Consequences*, Cambridge University Press, Cambridge.

Hughes, K. (1991), 'Trade performance in the main EC economies relative to the USA and Japan in the 1991 sensitive sectors,' Wissenschaftszentrum Berlin für Sozialforschung Discussion Paper FS IV 91-4.

Johnson, S. and Loveman, G. (1993), 'The implications of the Polish economic reform for small business: evidence from Gdansk,' in Z. J. Acs and D. B. Audretsch (eds), *Small Firms and Entrepreneurship: An East–West Perspective*, Cambridge University

Press, Cambridge, pp.190–207.
Kornai, J (1980), *Economics of Shortage*, North-Holland, Amsterdam.
Krueger, A. O. (1974), 'The political economy of the rent-seeking society,' *American Economic Review*, **64**(3), 291–303.
Laffont, J.-J. and Tirole, J. (1993), *A Theory of Incentives in Procurement and Regulation*, MIT Press, Cambridge, MA.
Lipton, D. and Sachs J. (1990), 'Creating a market economy in East Europe: the case of Poland,' *Brookings Papers on Economic Activity*, pp.75–133.
Mayhew, A. (1992), 'Fact sheet on the Association (Europe) Agreements between the Czech and Slovak Federal Republic, Hungary, Poland and the European Community,' in CEPR (ed.), *The Association Process: Making it Work: Central Europe and the European Community*,' London, CEPR Occasional Paper No. 11, pp.13–6.
McDermott, G. A. and Mejstrik, M. (1992), 'Plan neglect, reform challenges, and transformation potential: the role of small firms in Czechoslovak manufacturing', *Small Business Economics*, **4**(3), 179–200.
McDermott, G. A. and Mejstrik M. (1993), 'The role of small firms in Czechoslovak manufacturing', in Z. J. Acs and D. B. Audretsch (eds), *Small Firms and Entrepreneurship: An East–West Perspective*, Cambridge University Press, Cambridge pp.155–81.
Murrell, P. (1990), *The Nature of Socialist Economies: Lessons from Eastern Europe*, Princeton University Press, Princeton, NJ.
Neven, D., Nuttall, R. and Seabright, P. (1993), *Merger in Daylight: The Economics and Politics of European Merger Control*, CEPR, London.
Noll, R. G. (1989), 'Economic perspectives on the politics of regulation,' in R. Schmalensee and R. Willig (eds), *Handbook of Industrial Economics*, vol 2, North-Holland, Amsterdam, pp.1253–87.
Puchev, P. (1990), 'A note on government policy and the new entrepreneurship in Bulgaria', *Small Business Economics*, **2**(1), 73–6.
Reich, R. B. (1990), 'Who is us?', *Harvard Business Review*, January/February, 53–64.
Sorge, A. (1985), *Informationstechnik und Arbeit im sozialen Prozess - Arbeitsorganisation, Qualifikation und Produktivkraftentwicklung*, Campus Verlag, Berlin.
Stigler, G. J. (1971), 'The theory of economic regulation,' *Bell Journal of Economics and Management Science*, **2**(1), 3–21.
Streeck, W. (1991), 'On the institutional conditions of diversified quality production', in E. Matzner and W. Streeck (eds), *Beyond Keynesianism*, Edward Elgar, Aldershot, pp. 21–61.
Tullock, G. (1967), 'The welfare costs of tariffs, monopolies, and theft,' *Western Economic Journal*, **5**, 224–32.
Tyson, L. D'A. and Zysman J. (1983), 'American industry in international competition,' in J. Zysman and L. D'A. Tyson (eds), *American Industry in International Competition: Government Policies and Corporate Strategies*, Cornell University Press, Ithaca, NY.
Tyson, L. D'A., Petrin, T. and Rogers, H. (1994), 'Promoting entrepreneurship in Eastern Europe,' *Small Business Economics*, **6**(3), 165–84.
Winters, L. A. (1992), 'The Europe Agreements: with a little help from our friends,' in: CEPR (ed.), *The Association Process: Making it Work: Central Europe and the European Community*, CEPR, Occasional Paper No. 11, pp.17–30.

8

Trade Law and Environmental Issues in Central and East European Countries*

Michael Rauscher

8.1 Introduction

For a long time, international trade and environmental problems have been viewed as being separate issues. This has changed recently. Concern about the interdependencies of trade and the environment is growing. Environmentalists argue that trade damages the environment and should, therefore, be restricted.[1] Industry lobbies fear that the international competitiveness of the domestic economy or some of its sectors may suffer from tight environmental standards. Often the harmonization of environmental standards across different countries is viewed as a solution to these problems. Trade liberals, in contrast, think that harmonization diminishes the gains from trade and is, therefore, undesirable. Moreover, environmental policies may be captured by protectionist interests and environmental protection may be turned into environmental protectionism very easily. The NAFTA negotiations and a number of international disputes (e.g. the US–Mexican tuna dispute and the Danish bottle case) have shown that this fear is justified.

Central and East European countries (CEECs), having overcome socialism, central planning and the ideal of economic autarky of the Eastern Bloc, are now being integrated into international markets. This is an opportunity to rethink the basic economic institutions that govern market economies in general and international economic relationships in particular. This chapter deals with institutions related to foreign trade and the emphasis will be placed on environmental issues. What are the principles on which the trade laws of a country

* I am indebted to Petros Mavroidis, Richard Portes and Alan Winters for helpful comments on an earlier version of this chapter. The usual disclaimer applies.

should be based when environmental issues matter? Which institutions should be developed? How can international disputes be dissolved? Institutions dealing with these issues have existed in market economies for a long time and they evolve by being adapted to new problems. Should these institutions be copied by the CEECs or should new approaches be sought? The former centrally planned economies are different from Western countries in many respects, e.g. in their environmentally intensive production, and one is led to ask whether this should be reflected in a different institutional framework. An additional motivation for finding new ways of designing trade law and institutions may be to avoid the mistakes that have been made elsewhere in the past.

The central issues in the context of international trade and the environment are the following ones:

- Empirical studies cast some doubt on the relevance of the relationship between trade and the environment. This fact raises the question whether trade law should deal with environmental issues at all.
- Environmental regulations often have protectionist consequences. In many cases it is difficult to distinguish environmental protection from environmental protectionism. Trade law should be designed in such a way that it contains mechanisms that prevent green policies from being captured by protectionist interests.
- Some international environmental agreements like the Montreal Protocol on Substances that Deplete the Ozone Layer (hereafter: Montreal Protocol) provide for trade restrictions to achieve global environmental objectives. The CEECs may be affected by this in two ways. They may be subject to sanctions themselves if they do not comply with these agreements, or they may be asked to participate in sanctions. Should trade institutions take account of these possibilities?
- Production in the CEECs is still relatively pollution intensive and there are economic reasons as to why will this will continue over the medium term. CEECs may be accused of environmental dumping and countervailing duties may be imposed on them. Mechanisms for conflict resolution are to be developed in the framework of international trade agreements.

Three layers of institutions may be distinguished. Firstly, each of the CEECs has to decide on its own trade law. Secondly, the CEECs will be integrated into the European Economic Space and the Europe Agreements between the European Union on the one hand and Poland, Hungary and the former Czechoslovakia on the other, and the Association Agreements involving Bulgaria and Romania, develop a timetable for the abolition of the barriers to trade. Presumably, the CEECs will be asked to adopt some of the EU regulations that affect the trade in environmentally sensitive goods. Finally, there is the global scale on which the GATT and the World Trade Organization are the most important institutions. The

CEECs will have to adjust to some of the GATT's principles. Moreover, there are strong forces arguing that the next GATT round should be a green round and one may ask which position in these negotiations the CEECs should take.

The chapter is organized as follows. The next section will review the theoretical literature on international trade and the environment and survey the empirical studies on this subject. This section will establish the theoretical links between foreign trade, environmental quality and environmental regulation and discuss their practical relevance. Section 8.3 will address environmental disruption and environmental policies in the CEECs as far as they are relevant for their foreign trade. Section 8.4 will review the basic principles that have to be taken into account in trade law and international trade agreements when environmental regulation and pollution matter. Next, existing multilateral agreements that deal with international trade and the environment will be addressed. Section 8.6 derives conclusions for the consideration of environmental issues in the trade law of the CEECs and multilateral trade agreements involving the CEECs. Some final remarks will conclude the chapter.

8.2 Foreign Trade and the Environment: Theoretical Considerations and Empirical Evidence

In an integrated world, foreign trade and environmental issues are closely related – at least in theory. Environmental regulation affects production costs and, therefore, has an impact on the international allocation of the factors of production. The question is then whether the relocation of the factors of production due to regulatory differences is beneficial or not. If not, this may justify trade restrictions. In a next step, one may ask in which way environmental taxes and standards can be used to achieve trade-policy objectives. If environmental policy measures have an impact on the international division of labour, they may be used to influence the terms of trade, to achieve strategic trade-policy objectives or to give some support to domestic producers who compete in international markets. If more than one country uses its environmental law in this way, there will be an international competition of national environmental legislations and this may be detrimental to environmental quality. If this is a problem in the real world, the necessity arises of accompanying international trade agreements by international environmental agreements in order to avoid the undesirable consequences of jurisdictional competition. Moreover, not only the production of commodities is affected by environmental regulation, there are also regulatory measures that are targeted at consumption activities. Often they take the shape of product standards, which may easily be used as protectionist devices. Additional issues that are important in the context of CEEC integration into the world economy are international trade in hazardous waste and the relationship between foreign debt and environmental disruption.

There is now a substantial literature on theoretical aspects of the interdependencies of foreign trade and the environment. Examples are Baumol (1971), Markusen (1975), Siebert (1977, 1979), Siebert *et al.* (1980), Merrifield (1988), Krutilla (1991), Rauscher (1991, 1994a, b) and Snape (1992). In this literature, trade is based on comparative advantage, and comparative advantage is explained by differences in endowments. A country is well endowed with environmental resources if the damage caused by emissions is small, i.e. if the assimilative capacity of nature is large, if the country is not densely populated, or if its citizens do not care much about environmental quality. A benevolent government would choose an environmental policy which takes account of these variables and correctly reflects the scarcity of environmental resources. Thus, it is natural that countries differ in their environmental regulations. As long as there are no transfrontier pollution spillovers, the harmonization of environmental policies is neither necessary nor desirable. Differences in environmental regulation between jurisdictions are not a reason to complain about environmental dumping.[2] Within federations, the subsidiarity principle should be applied and each jurisdiction should be given sovereignty in the decisions on its environmental policy. See Hansson (1990) and Siebert (1991).

There are basically two channels through which environmental regulation has an impact on the allocation of the factors of production and on the international division of labour. On the one hand, some factors of production, in particular capital, are internationally mobile. Everything else being equal, environmentally intensive industries tend to move to countries where the regulation is relatively lax, i.e. where pollution-abatement requirements can be met easily and production costs are low. On the other hand, there are specialization effects. If factors of production are mobile across sectors within an economy rather than across national borders, the relocation will take place inside the economy. A country with lax environmental regulation has a comparative advantage in the production of environmentally intensive goods and the corresponding industries will attract factors of production from the other sectors of the economy. In theory, this is beneficial to all countries involved in the international division of labour. Problems may, however, arise if a country specializing in the production of environmentally intensive goods has employed an environmental policy which is too lax. Then the marginal damage due to increased emissions may well dominate the gains from trade and the country may be worse off. This may be a realistic scenario for some of the CEECs. Trade restrictions can be used to achieve welfare gains. But they are only second-best instruments. The first-best policy is an improvement in environmental policy. Moreover, it should be noted that the standard models of international trade and the environment, on which the above considerations are based, look merely at the static effects of trade liberalization. If dynamic effects are also considered, the costs of restricting trade are fortified such that a case for restricting trade can hardly be made (Romer, 1994).

Matters are different if transboundary pollution spillovers are considered. A country specializing in the production of clean goods may experience an increase in transfrontier pollution which offsets the gains from trade. Closely related to this is the carbon-leakage problem. A country tightening its environmental policy standards induces international factor movements and specialization effects that lead to increased emissions in the rest of the world.

How relevant is this in practice? Is there considerable evidence that environmental regulation has indeed had an impact on capital movements and foreign trade? Is environmental quality significantly affected by factor relocation? Empirical studies on trade, factor movements and the environment have been surveyed by Ugelow (1982) and Dean (1992) and the following paragraphs will give a short overview of this literature and more recent publications. One of the big problems in the empirical assessment of the relationship between international trade and the environment is the quantification of the environmental variables and the variables that have been used in the empirical studies are in most cases only crude proxies.

The first empirical studies (e.g. Walter, 1973) looked at the pollution content of exports and imports but did not relate it to environmental policy variables. Robison (1988) uses the same approach but introduces the dimension of time. The results indicate a shift in US imports from goods with low abatement requirements towards goods subject to stricter regulation during a time period in which US environmental policies have been tightened. Since changes in the environmental policies of the trading partners of the United States are not taken into account, however, this result does not prove that differences in environmental policies have an impact on international trade.

More recent studies have used international data sets on environmental regulation. Tobey (1989, 1990), for instance, uses a set of factor endowment variables that includes an index measuring the stringency of pollution control measures for various countries. In none of the five industries under consideration has the environmental policy variable a significant impact on net exports. An omitted-variables test (the omitted variable being environmental regulation) reveals the same result. Murrell and Ryterman (1991) also use an omitted-variables test in a similar model framework and come to the same result. These studies, therefore, cast some doubt on the empirical relevance of the standard model of environmental regulation and international trade.[3]

The other way in which trade influences the international allocation of capital is foreign direct investment. If the theory is correct, pollution-intensive production processes should move to countries with lax environmental standards, where abatement costs are relatively low. Several studies have tested this hypothesis. Walter (1982), Leonard (1988) and Bartik (1988) do not find substantial support for it in the data. Rowland and Feiock (1991), in contrast, come to the conclusion that environmental regulation affects locational decisions of investors. They use data on the chemical industry and consider the allocation of new capital across federal states of the United States. Other studies that use indirect methods to identify the impact of environmental regulation on international capital movements, for instance Hettige *et al.* (1992), Lucas *et al.* (1992), and Low and Yeats (1992) arrive at similar conclusions. Since these studies do not look at the delocation effects directly, however, but only infer them from some other observations, they are not true tests of the theoretical considerations.

The effects of free trade on the environment have been analysed by van Bergeijk (1991) for OECD countries and Birdsall and Wheeler (1992) for Latin American countries. Both studies find that increased openness and trade lead to lower pollution. van Bergeijk's results may be explained by specialization effects or by changes in environmental policy as a consequence of the income gains from increased openness.[4] Birdsall and Wheeler explain their results by the fact that open economies have better access to new technologies, which are generally less pollution intensive. See also Wheeler and Martin (1992), who show that adaptation lags for the introduction of new, clean technologies are significantly higher in inward-oriented than in open economies. The diffusion of technological knowledge, which is not taken into account in standard models of foreign trade, may play a major role in the cleaning-up of the CEECs.

Simulation models of the impact of trade on the environment have been used by Anderson (1992a, b) and Burniaux *et al.* (1992). Anderson looks at the market for agricultural products and shows that there is a high correlation between domestic prices of agricultural products and the utilization of fertiliser and pesticides. If barriers to trade were removed, agricultural production would be shifted from highly protected industrialized countries with intensive use of chemicals to less developed countries that produce with a lower input of chemicals. This would be beneficial for environmental quality. Burniaux *et al.* (1992) use the OECD general-equilibrium model to show that the removal of existing distortions in energy markets, whose purpose is predominantly protectionist, would result in a drastic reduction of CO_2 emissions on a global scale. Thus free trade in energy resources tends to mitigate the greenhouse effect.

Although trade liberalization in markets like energy and agricultural products may reduce environmental problems, there are other markets in which the converse is true. In the cases of tropical deforestation and endangered species, trade contributes to the environmental problems and trade restrictions may be welfare improving. However, they are rarely the best instruments. See Amelung and Diehl (1992) for a study on tropical deforestation and Barbier (1991) for a case study dealing with the ebony trade.

Calibrated models have been used to address the carbon leakage effect empirically. Will unilateral greenhouse policies by one country or a group of countries cause substantial increases in emissions in the rest of the world? Oliveira-Martins *et al.* (1992) use the OECD computable general-equilibrium model and find carbon leakage effects of up to 16%. Their model is based on the assumption of perfect competition and international factor immobility. Ulph (1994) relaxes both these assumptions and, depending on the parameter constellations, he finds carbon leakage effects of much larger magnitude, in some cases even more than 100%.

Summarizing the results of the empirical studies, one may conclude that the evidence concerning the relationship between trade and international capital movements on the one hand and environmental regulation and environmental quality on the other is rather mixed. There are particular markets in which there is a strong relationship between environmental regulation and foreign trade or factor movements. On the aggregate level, the relationship postulated by the theoretical models cannot be supported. This is also the conclusion drawn by Cropper and Oates (1992) in their recent survey on environmental economics. If it is true that there is not much evidence of an impact of environmental regulation on international trade, then environmental economists should not care too much about international competitiveness and trade economists should not care too much about environmental issues. The policy recommendation would be to have a regime of free trade and tough environmental policies. International environmental problems, e.g. the emission of greenhouse gases and CFCs, should be solved in a cooperative fashion.

International environmental agreements are difficult to achieve, however, and this raises the question whether second-best considerations should be applied.[5] Moreover, notwithstanding the fact that the link between trade and environment is not significant on the average level, there may be a strong relationship in some sectors of the economy. This may suggest the use of trade policy instruments to achieve environmental policy goals. None the less, trade restrictions are to be expected to do more harm than good in such a situation.

A case for trade interventions emerges in the context of the carbon leakage problem. If unilateral policies to solve environmental problems have undesirable consequences, in that the pollution-intensive industries move to less regulated countries, tariffs and other barriers to trade and factor mobility may be beneficial. They raise the domestic production of environmentally harmful goods, which is subject to tight standards, and reduce the production in less regulated areas. Of course, barriers to trade are only second best compared to a cooperative situation in which international agreements solve global environmental problems and trade is unrestricted. The other motivation for trade barriers is to use them as a disciplinary device to stabilize international environmental agreements. If potential deviants face the risk of losing access to international markets, compliance will be increased. This threat is credible if the punishing countries profit from restricting trade, e.g. by the reduction of leakage problems. An example is the Montreal Protocol. According to this agreement, signatory parties have the option to restrict imports of goods containing CFCs or produced by means of CFCs. Similar restrictions may be thought of as a means to stabilize an international greenhouse-gas agreement.

Not only can trade restrictions be used to achieve environmental objectives; it is also possible that environmental policy instruments are used to achieve trade-related policy goals. This option becomes attractive if the traditional instruments of trade policy, tariffs and quotas, are not available, e.g. if a country has signed free trade agreements that prohibit the use of these instruments. Environmental policies may be used to improve the terms of trade or to support particular sectors of the economy. I do not think that the terms-of-trade argument is particularly relevant in practical policy-making and I will, therefore, concentrate on the other motives. Lax environmental standards can be used to support infant or ailing industries, to shift rents from abroad into the home country in a strategic-trade-policy setting (see Barrett (1994a) and Conrad (1993)) or to support trade lobbies that fear a loss of competitiveness. In all these cases, lax environmental standards are used as a means to give hidden subsidies to particular sectors of the economy. If other countries retaliate, this may result in a jurisdictional competition which leads to under-regulation everywhere and to disastrous effects on environmental quality. Markusen *et al.* (1992) and Rauscher (1994b) develop conditions for such a scenario. If there is the danger that the utilization of environmental policies for trade-related purposes leads to undesirably low levels of regulation, an institutional framework which establishes general rules for the jurisdictional competition may be useful. None the less, in many Western countries there exist green counter-lobbies which may be sufficiently strong to help avoid this kind of legislational competition.

Up to now, pollution problems arising from production activities have been discussed. But the consumption of final goods causes environmental problems as well. In the theoretical literature on trade and the environment much less emphasis has been placed on this issue. In the comparative-advantage framework, environmental policies will affect international trade and the patterns of specialization. *Ceteris paribus*, commodities that are subject to tight environmental standards or high emission tax rates will be demanded in lower quantities. The reduction of demand will lead to a reduction of the pre-tax price. Producers of this good will be harmed. Since consumption taxes affect domestic and foreign producers in the same fashion, they are unlikely to be used as a protectionist device. None the less, domestic and foreign goods are rarely homogeneous in reality and environmental regulation seldom takes the shape of green taxes. Product standards are much more common and these can be used as protectionist instruments very easily. Many standards are (intentionally or unintentionally) designed such that it is easier for domestic than for foreign producers to fulfil them. This kind of regulatory capture has been discussed widely in the theory of regulation. See Stigler (1971) and Laffont and Tirole (1991), for example. If environmental and protectionist interests overlap, it becomes difficult to define the borderline between environmental protection and environmental protectionism.

An additional issue which is of major importance in the context of the economic integration of CEECs into world markets is the trade in toxic waste. Due to regulatory deficiencies, some of these countries have become cheap dumping sites for all kinds of hazardous substances from industrial countries. In a controversial paper, parts of which have been published in *The Economist* (1992), the then chief economist of the World Bank, Lawrence Summers, has argued that this is optimal. Theoretical considerations show, however, that this is not always true – Rauscher (1994a, ch.4). If there are regulatory or enforcement deficits, the compensation payment made to the waste-importing country tends to be too low to compensate for the resulting environmental damage. If the regulatory deficit cannot be removed, it can be useful to restrict international trade in hazardous waste. This may be beneficial also to the waste-exporting countries if there are transfrontier pollution problems, e.g. if exporting and importing countries share ground water systems.

Moreover, all international trade involves transportation. Transportation, however, requires energy and energy use generates pollution. Of course, this can be taken into account by national regulations, as long as transport does not take place in extraterritorial areas. One can show that, with increased openness, the share of long-range transport is increased and so is pollution. One may, therefore, ask whether it would be desirable to attach international transport agreements to international trade agreements.

A final issue that one may wish to take into account is the relationship between environmental disruption and foreign debt. Not all trade is direct exchange of commodities at one point of time. There is also intertemporal trade and it has led to high levels of indebtedness in many countries, among them most of the CEECs. It has been argued by Adams (1991), Morris (1991), George (1992) and others that foreign debt aggravates environmental problems. In theoretical analyses (Rauscher 1989, 1990), it has been shown that this is due to capital market imperfections. In the case of imperfect capital markets, the marginal cost of being indebted is an increasing function of the debt, and this implies that the relative cost of environmental disruption is small in highly indebted countries. An empirical study by Diwan and Shafik (1992) contends that CO_2 emissions are an increasing function of foreign debt. If this is not a spurious correlation but a causal relationship, one is led to the conclusion that an unconditioned debt relief may have a positive effect on environmental variables. In some countries, including Poland, debt-for-nature swaps have been used to simultaneously address problems of foreign debt and environmental disruption. See Zylicz (1993a) and Manser (1993, pp.122–3).

The following conclusions may be drawn from this survey of empirical and theoretical literature:

- Although economic theory predicts that environmental regulation has an impact on international factor movements and trade, this is not supported by empirical studies on the aggregate level. In specific sectors of the economy,

which are characterized by environmentally intensive production, however, delocation can be observed. On the whole, one is, however, led to the conclusion that the current debate over-emphasizes the importance of the interdependencies of trade and environmental issues.
- In cases where transfrontier pollution is not a major problem, environmental standards should not be harmonized.
- Environmental product standards are exposed to the danger of being used as a vehicle of protectionist interests.
- Environmental process standards may be used as a means of giving indirect subsidies to producers.
- This may lead to an undesirable competition among jurisdictions which leads to too-low levels of environmental quality.
- Trade interventions may be used as second-best instruments of environmental policy or as sanctions to stabilize international environmental agreements.
- Since trade interventions also (and in many cases predominantly) serve protectionist objectives, there it is difficult to disentangle environmental protection and environmental protectionism.

8.3 Environmental Policies and Comparative Advantage in Eastern Europe

Environmental policy may have an impact on the patterns of specialization and foreign trade of the emerging market economies in Central and East Europe. Before an attempt will be made to assess the issue of comparative advantage, the current position will be described.

The CEECs are characterized by large pollution problems inherited from the past. Surprisingly, some of these countries had ambient standards that were among the most restrictive in the world (see Hughes (1991), Budnikowski (1992) and Danchev (1994), for instance). Often, these standards were chosen on the basis of an 'administrative–biological approach' (Danchev, 1994) that did not care about the trade-off between environmental degradation and the level of economic activities. Thus, many standards were simply unrealistic and could not be achieved at an appropriate cost. This may also explain why over a long period of time there were no entities that were actually responsible for attaining the standards (Zylicz, 1993b). Thus, a situation was created in which 'everybody should do his or her best to meet the relevant ambient standards', but they were never seriously enforced. These standards were, *de facto*, non-binding constraints.

There are several reasons for the long-lasting neglect of environmental issues in the CEECs and for the inefficiency of the policy instruments adopted later on. First, there are ideological reasons. Marxist economic theory, based on the classical labour theory of value, does not assign an intrinsic value to unproduced goods like environmental quality. This may explain why it took so long in many

CEECs for environmental policy measures to be introduced. Another ideological factor is the emphasis which was placed on the development of heavy industries after the Second World War. Moreover, the socialist system of national accounting did not view services as a part of national income. Therefore, services, which are relatively clean in their production, had only a small share in the economy.

Although the ideological factor may have played a role in the past, the main reason for the enormous pollution problems is the highly distorted price system in socialist countries. In particular, the energy prices were much too low and did not correctly reflect the opportunity cost of energy generation. Unlike Western countries which had to adjust to a tenfold increase in energy prices after the oil crises of the 1970s, there was no structural change towards less energy-intensive production in the CEECs. The result was a waste of energy in production, but also in consumption. An additional problem is the mix of primary fuels in the CEECs which differs substantially from that in the West. The predominant source of primary energy is coal, which is the dirtiest of the fossil fuels. In 1988, Bulgaria, Poland and Czechoslovakia used between three and four times as much coal per capita as the EC average, at much lower per capita income levels (Hughes 1993, p.65).

The other problems which contributed to environmental disruption in the CEECs were the softness or non-existence of budget constraints of state-owned firms and the lack of competition. Without competition, there have been only small incentives for process innovations in production which could have led to energy saving. On the contrary, in many cases it was optimal to waste resources. In a planned economy the factors of production are allocated to the individual firms on the basis of their factor requirements (instead of their willingness to pay). Therefore, it is better to maximize than to minimize the inputs needed per unit of output, particularly in situations where future shortages are expected. Moreover, the predominant objective for the socialist firm was to fulfil the plan, i.e. to produce a certain output, but not to economize on costs. Such output-oriented behaviour was sustainable since budget constraints were not binding for state-owned enterprises. The softness of the budget constraints may also explain why emission fees did not have the desired consequences. Poland, for instance, had introduced such fees in the 1970s (See Zylicz, 1993a). Initially these fees were too small to have significant effects. But even after substantial increases they did not have the desired effects on the use of environmental resources. Socialist firms simply expanded their budgets and, therefore, did not have to adjust to the price signals.

These factors resulted in levels of emissions and pollution that were much higher than in Western Europe. Table 8.1 presents some figures for sulphur dioxide emissions.

Thus, at the beginning of the period of transition, the CEECs were characterized by a highly distorted price system and an allocation of factors of production which corresponded to this price system. This resulted in a waste of

Table 8.1. Sulphur Dioxide Emissions in 1988

	Emissions (kg/capita/year)	Emissions (g/US$ of GDP)
Poland	110	60
Hungary	115	47
CSFR	179	52
Bulgaria	114	49
Romania	78	45
United Kingdom	64	5
FR Germany	21	1
France	22	1
USA	83	4

Source: Hörhager (1992), p.36

energy and the over-utilization of environmental resources. In the meantime, there have been drastic changes in relative prices and they will lead to a long-run restructuring process of the economy. In Poland, for instance, there have already been substantial increases in energy prices. At the end of 1991, Polish households paid more than ten times as much (in US dollar terms) for natural gas, electricity and hot water than in early 1990, and the energy prices paid by industry rose by more than 200% during this period (Pasierb, 1992). This has already led to a decline in the energy intensity of GDP and a reduction of emissions. The developments in the Czech and Slovak Republics point in the same direction (Cerna, 1993). The CEECs are currently repeating the experience that the market economies of the West had in the 1970s in response to the oil price shocks. The structural adjustment to world energy prices will reduce the demand for energy and lead to a reduction of some environmental problems. Hughes (1991), for instance, argues that this structural change will accelerate the process of cleaning up Eastern Europe substantially. None the less, one has to look at the future patterns of specialization and it may well be the case that an environmentally unfavourable specialization erodes some of the gains from reduced energy consumption (Ábel *et al.* 1993, 1994).

Concerning the comparative advantage of CEECs and their future position in the international division of labour, the following considerations are relevant.

Due to the drastic changes in the price system, the capital stock has been devalued. Just as the oil price increases of the 1970s have depressed the prices of large cars in the used-car markets in the Western world, the value of the CEECs' capital stock has been reduced drastically since it is not designed to use energy in a cost-efficient way. This means that *ceteris paribus* the CEECs are capital-poor countries. According to standard trade theory, they should, therefore, become net importers of capital-intensive goods and/or they should attract foreign direct investments. The profitability of such investments, however, is at the moment still restricted by the bad state of the infrastructure. Moreover, environmental regulation may turn out to be decisive for investment decisions. This particularly concerns the way in which inherited environmental damages are dealt with. If the liability for existing contamination is attributed to the new investor, the speed of the privatization process will be reduced and foreign investors may be repelled.[6] The experience with privatization in East Germany has shown that this is indeed a relevant problem area.

The second factor of production which is decisive for comparative advantage and the patterns of trade, is labour. The generally accepted view is that the CEECs are well endowed with cheap qualified labour. Products that are human-capital intensive but do not require high-tech physical capital are likely to be the area for future comparative advantage of the CEECs. In the longer run, the capital constraint may become less binding as foreign firms, wishing to utilize the potential of the labour force, start to invest in these countries.

As far as environmental resources are concerned, the forecast is more difficult. There are some arguments in favour of the hypothesis that the CEECs will in the long run be exporters of environmentally intensive goods and some arguments against this hypothesis. Compared to West European countries, the CEECs are relatively poor. If environmental quality is a normal good, its demand should be an increasing function of national income, i.e. environmental regulation should be stricter in high-income that in low-income countries. The empirical evidence suggests that this is indeed the case (Grossman and Krueger, 1991: Holtz-Eakin and Selden, 1993). However, large parts of Eastern Europe are already heavily polluted. Given the fact that some pollutants like heavy metals are stock pollutants that have been accumulated over time and decay merely at small rates, the marginal environmental cost of additional pollution can be very high. This is an argument in favour of strict environmental standards.

Environmental regulations have been tightened already in East European countries. Polish emission fees, for instance, have been raised drastically in the early 1990s and now compare to OECD levels (Zylicz, 1993a). Poland's medium- and long-term environmental policy objectives are directed at the adjustment towards West European standards (Pasierb, 1993). One may, however, expect that over the next few years some of the pollution-intensive industries will continue to produce and some of the measures necessary to clean up Eastern Europe will be taken only with delay. This is mainly for two reasons. First, there are regulatory and enforcement deficits. Many environmental regulations do not yet exist and it will take some time until they are implemented. For example, Poland is now discussing the introduction of tradable-permit schemes for particular pollutants (Zylicz, 1993a, b). But even if environmental regulations exist, they are not always enforced. The move from an authoritarian regime to a pluralistic society has been accompanied by an erosion of the power of the state and its institutions. Thus, it has become more difficult to enforce environmental standards. Moreover, in many cases government authorities seem to lack the know-how and the technical equipment necessary to monitor emissions and to identify polluters.[7] Of course, this is a problem in Western countries as well but it may turn out to be of much greater relevance in the CEECs.

Besides these regulatory deficiencies, the political economy of transition poses a limit to the implementation of strict environmental policies. The collapse of socialism and the drastic changes in the pricing system have brought massive unemployment to the CEECs. Economic inequality has increased substantially. In such a situation, a government which additionally destroys jobs by closing dirty industries or by raising environmental taxes and energy prices will not survive a very long time, even if these measures can be justified on grounds of cost–benefit considerations. These arguments suggest that environmental regulations will remain laxer in the CEECs than in Western Europe for the rest of the 1990s.

Lax environmental standards may cause problems for the CEECs in their integration into European markets. They run the risk of being accused of environmental dumping, i.e. of supporting their export industries by means of lax environmental standards and low pollution-abatement requirements. Anti-dumping measures may be taken and the question arises of how these disputes can be resolved.

In the longer term, however, this may change. A large part of the capital stock in the CEECs is merely scrap and has to be replaced by new physical capital. Much of it will be imported from the West. These capital goods are, however, designed to comply to Western environmental norms and in many cases it does not pay to redesign them for their use in less regulated countries. Thus, it is likely that an increasing part of output will be produced by means of modern and clean equipment. Moreover, after the adjustment shock has taken place, one may expect (or hope) that the CEECs will grow at high rates , comparable to those of East Asia. With increased income, it will be possible to clean up the environmental damages inherited from the past and to convince lobbies and voters that a strict environmental law can be a good thing.

Thus, in a long-run perspective, East European countries can be expected to adjust to West European environmental standards and, therefore, the CEECs will face similar problems as the West, i.e. 'environmental dumping' by less regulated countries, problems of carbon leakage and the use of environmental regulations as protectionist devices.

Since the position of the CEECs in the international division of labour will presumably change substantially over the next decade, the general trade laws and institutions should be designed such that they can be applicable both during the period of adjustment as well as in the long run. But not only trade laws and institutions have to be discussed. In addition, the environmental policy and its institutions have to be taken into account. Since environmental policy measures can be used as barriers to trade, environmental policy is to some extent trade policy.

8.4 Basic Principles for the Design of Foreign Trade and Environmental Policy Institutions

Existing environmental and trade agreements are based on a number of basic principles and it may be useful to review them in order to see how they are related to the theoretical considerations reviewed in section 8.2 and to actual international trade and environmental agreements.

The *subsidiarity principle* is generally accepted in the theory of federalism and in practical policy-making. For a discussion of subsidiarity in a European context see European Commission (1992) and Begg *et al.* (1993). According to this principle, political decisions should be made at the level closest to the citizen. For example, local environmental problems should be dealt with by local authorities and national environmental problems by national authorities. Only in the case of substantial transfrontier pollution spillovers or other international externalities should the environmental policy be made by supranational authorities, e.g. on the community level in Europe. Decentralized decision-making is expected to reduce administrative costs and to raise the quality of the decisions: people are different and decentralization is a way to take account of these differences. None the less, the subsidiarity principle has been eroded in many cases both on the national and on the international levels. An example is the harmonization of European drinking-water standards (Begg *et al.*, 1993). Applied to the CEECs and their integration into the European Economic Space, the subsidiarity principle implies that the CEECs should be sovereign in their decisions on environmental policy measures. *Harmonization* of national environmental regulations should be limited to cases in which substantial international environmental externalities are involved. Unnecessary harmonization reduces diversity and erodes the basis of the international division of labour and the gains from trade.

The *origin principle,* which has been applied in several cases by the European Court, is to some extent in conflict with the subsidiarity principle. According to this principle, goods that are in agreement with national regulations in one country must also be tradable in other countries. This restricts national sovereignty but it is a vehicle to impede non-tariff barriers to trade. The most famous case is the Cassis de Dijon ruling and there have been follow-up cases in which the European Court stated that national regulations like the German law on the purity of beer or Italian regulations on the ingredients of pasta are barriers to trade. There are, however, limits to the application of the principle. If applied consequently, it may lead to an *ex post* harmonization of national environmental regulations, which may be undesirable. The European Court has acknowledged the limits of the origin principle in the Danish bottle case. Denmark has been allowed to restrict the use of non-refillable bottles and cans for environmental reasons although importers of beverages argued that this policy raised their costs by much more than that of domestic producers and was, therefore, discriminatory.

The *non-discrimination principle* may be viewed as a compromise. It states that individual countries are sovereign in their decisions on national regulations but these regulations have to be designed such that they do not discriminate against foreigners. Sometimes, an equal treatment of domestic and foreign goods is not sufficient for the non-discrimination principle to be satisfied. This has been revealed, for instance, in the discussions about the introduction of catalytic converters for cars in Europe. If catalytic converters become compulsory, this is discriminatory if the producers of catalytic converters are concentrated in one country. Moreover, the introduction of catalytic converters raises the price of small cars by a larger percentage than that of large cars and, therefore, discriminates against countries that have specialized in the production of smaller cars. However, there are many cases in which discrimination is desirable for environmental reasons. Many international trade agreements, therefore, use the notion that environmental policy measures should be applied in the least distortionary way.

Extraterritorialism is another principle which is important in the framework of international trade agreements when environmental issues are of concern. Some environmentalists, particularly West Europeans, argue that highly regulated countries should be able to enforce their environmental standards outside their jurisdictions if foreign standards are too lax (whatever that may mean). It has been shown in the theoretical parts of this chapter that this may make sense if issues of global pollution are concerned, where the environmental damage is independent of the source of emission. But in all other cases, extraterritorialism aims at unnecessary and undesirable harmonization of environmental laws. Third world representatives are correct in calling this 'green imperialism'. There remains the case of global pollution problems and some international environmental agreements. The Montreal Protocol contains the possibility of trade sanctions against non-compliants. These trade sanctions encompass embargoes not only of goods that contain CFCs but also goods that have been produced in production processes involving CFCs. Most trade agreements do not contain provisions for this kind of trade restriction.

The *polluter pays principle* is generally regarded as a good and unquestionable foundation of environmental policies. At a first glance, the application of this principle in environmental policy-making seems to have nothing to do with international trade issues. This impression is, however, wrong. The choice of the polluter pays principle as the basic principle of environmental policy is based on a value judgement, rather than on efficiency considerations. According to Coase (1960), the application of the *pollutee pays principle* – under certain assumptions – leads to the same allocation of environmental resources and it may in some cases be superior in solving environmental problems. In the case of transfrontier pollution, the polluter pays principle can, in general, not be enforced since the polluter is located in a different sovereign state. In such a situation there may remain no alternatives but to acknowledge the property rights of polluters and compensate them for lost profits if they reduce the emissions. A prominent example is the debt-for-nature swap. It can be shown that international environmental agreements that involve compensation payments usually lead to results superior to environmentally motivated barriers to trade.

Sustainability is a term that has been coined in the Brundtland report. Loosely speaking, it means that current economic development and growth should not restrict the opportunities of future generations. While economic theorists still discuss what sustainability exactly means, it has already been used in multilateral agreements. In most cases the preamble of an agreement is used to express the will of the contracting parties, to recognize the necessity of sustainable development and their will to avoid unsustainable policies. Since these declarations are so general that they do not lead to concrete obligations for the contracting parties, they do not affect foreign trade. From the point of view of an economist, the value of such a preamble is mainly a cosmetic one.

8.5 Existing Trade Agreements and Environmental Issues

8.5.1 The GATT[8]

The General Agreement on Tariffs and Trade was formulated at a time when environmental issues were not yet a major concern. Therefore, the environment or environmental issues are not mentioned explicitly. Article XX, however, may be interpreted as covering environmental issues. It states that

> Subject to the requirement that such measures are not applied in a manner which would constitute a means of arbitrary or unjustifiable discrimination between countries where the same conditions prevail, or a disguised restriction on international trade, nothing in this Agreement shall be construed to prevent the adoption or enforcement by any contracting party of measures:
>
> (b) necessary to protect human, animal or plant life or health;....
>
> (g) relating to the conservation of exhaustible natural resources if such measures are made effective in conjunction with restrictions on domestic production or consumption;

This article is rather vague and it offers a broad scope for interpretation. For instance, it does not specify the location of individuals, animals or plants to be protected and of the resources to be conserved. The open question, therefore, is whether or not national authorities may enforce measures to protect resources that are outside their own jurisdiction. It is also far from clear under which circumstances discrimination becomes arbitrary or unjustifiable.

Some GATT Panels may offer some insights on how the relationship of free trade and environmental protection is being viewed by the GATT. The tuna dispute between Mexico and the United States is the most prominent case.[9] The GATT Panel decided that a ban on Mexican tuna imports by the United States was incompatible with GATT rules. The US Marine Mammals Protection Act limits dolphin kills and the ban on Mexican tuna was launched since the Mexican fishing fleet used less dolphin-safe fishing methods. The United States argued that this measure was in accordance with Article III (which states that imported goods should be treated in the same way as like or competing domestic goods) and with Article XX. The GATT decided that Article III referred to products but not to methods of production and that the ban, therefore, was not in accordance with Article III. The GATT Panel's main arguments concerning Article XX were that the measure was discriminatory, that it was a disguised barrier to trade, and that less distorting measures of environmental policy would have been possible in this case.[10] Moreover, the Panel argued that Article XX does not permit a country to take measures to enforce its own environmental standards outside its jurisdiction. This is, however, only one of the feasible interpretations of this article, which does not explicitly prohibit the extraterritorial use of environmental policy measures.

Ambiguities like the ones discussed here suggest an amendment to the GATT with the objective to clarify the relationship between environmental policies and free trade. The recently established World Trade Organization has the goal of striving for sustainable development in its preamble and environmental issues are on its agenda.

8.5.2 The Europe Agreements between the EU and the CEECs

The Europe Agreements between the EU on the one hand and the CEECs, develop a timetable for the removal of barriers to trade between the signatory parties and provide a legal framework for foreign trade and the resolution of disputes. As far as environmental issues are concerned, the Europe Agreements are identical. The following remarks refer to the Polish Europe Agreement.

Article 26(1) is based on GATT Article III. It states that none of the signatory parties shall use measures of internal taxation that discriminate products of one signatory party against another party's products of the same kind. This is closely related to the origin principle. The article, however, does not specify what is meant by products of the same kind. If a narrow definition of the term 'product' is used, then the way in which a product is produced is one of its characteristics. Products that are physically identical may, nevertheless, be viewed as being different if different processes have been used for their production. The Montreal Protocol makes such a distinction. It provides the possibility of barriers to trade against commodities that have been produced in production processes that involve CFCs even if the goods themselves do not contain these substances. In this context, it is unclear how the Europe Agreements and international environmental agreements are related to each other.

Article 35 is based on GATT Article XX. It states that the Agreement does not prevent a signatory party from introducing barriers to trade that are justified for the protection of human, animal or plant life and health. These measures may, however, not constitute a means of arbitrary discrimination or of disguised restriction on international trade. This Article is more explicit than GATT Article XX in one respect. It deals with barriers to trade, whereas the GATT Article refers to 'measures'. In other respects, this Article involves the same ambiguities as GATT Article XX. It is neither explicit on the location of the resources to be protected nor on the meaning of arbitrary discrimination and disguised barriers to trade.

Article 63 states that distortionary subsidies that favour certain firms or industries in one country are incompatible with the agreement. It is unclear whether this Article can be used to deal with hidden subsidies that take the shape of low emission taxes or pollution abatement requirements. If this were true, it could be a vehicle to enforce tight environmental standards on countries with low levels of regulation.

Finally, Article 80 specifies the areas of collaboration in the field of environmental protection. One area of cooperation is the harmonization of environmental regulations. It is not clear which kinds of environmental regulation will be covered by this Article and how this is related to the subsidiarity principle stated in Article 35. There exists the danger that the CEECs will be forced to adopt EU standards in cases where this is neither necessary or desirable.

8.5.3 The European Energy Charter

In December 1991, the European Energy Charter was adopted by the member states of the European Community, the EFTA countries, the CEECs, the former republics of the USSR and a number of other countries including the United States, Canada, and Japan. It may be viewed as the basis of a green Marshall plan for Eastern Europe. Its main concern is the collaboration of the signatory parties on energy issues, the creation of undistorted energy markets, and the dissemination of new, clean technologies of energy generation and utilization. Its basic ingredients are:

- the consideration of the problems of transition in the CEECs and in the former republics of the USSR and the recognition of the desirability of joint efforts in resolving these problems;
- the recognition of the sovereignty of the signatory states in designing their own energy and environmental policies;
- the will to create an open and competitive market for energy in Europe and to remove barriers to trade;

- the promotion of foreign direct investment;
- the necessity of taking into account social costs in the pricing of energy; and
- the acknowledgement of the possibility of adaptation lags during the transition period in the former socialist countries.

The European Energy Charter describes the future design of European energy markets in rather general terms. As far as trade issues are concerned, the recognition of sovereignty (subsidiarity) and the creation of open and competitive markets are important. The Charter may be viewed as a prelude or general framework for future agreements that contain more detailed rules and mechanisms of conflict resolution.

8.5.4 The North American Free Trade Agreement

The North American Free Trade Agreement (NAFTA) which was signed by Canada, Mexico and the United States in 1993 may serve as a prototype for future agreements involving former socialist countries. First, the signatory parties of the NAFTA are two highly developed countries (Canada and the United States) and an industrializing country (Mexico) and there are large income disparities between them. Similar disparities prevail in the case of Western Europe and the CEECs. Second, the NAFTA is the first trade agreement whose negotiations have been influenced to a large extent by environmental concerns (Esty, 1994). US environmentalists expect that NAFTA will lead to major delocation of industries to Mexico, where environmental regulations are relatively lax, and that this will cause substantial environmental problems. This point was taken up by unions and industry lobbies that fear delocation as well – however, for different reasons. The problem for the negotiating parties has been to distinguish between justified environmental concern and protectionist interests that would have undermined the spirit of NAFTA. Similar problems may arise in the process of the integration of the CEECs into the European Economic Space and it is, therefore, worthwhile to have a closer look at the NAFTA. For a more detailed discussion of NAFTA's environmental rules and their meaning, see Wilkinson (1994) and Esty (1994).

In the preamble of the NAFTA, the signatory parties state their willingness to perform the process of economic integration in a manner consistent with environmental protection and conservation and to promote sustainable development. This preamble acknowledges that account should be taken of the environmental aspects of the free trade agreement. The text of the agreement then specifies the obligations and the rights of the signatory parties in the process of achieving this objective.

Article 104 states that international environmental agreements such as the Montreal Protocol, the Convention of Trade in Endangered Species of Wild

Flora and Fauna (CITES), and the Basle Convention on the Control of Transboundary Movements of Hazardous Waste and Its Disposal (hereafter: Basle Convention), that propose restrictions of international trade, are given precedence over the NAFTA in the case of inconsistencies. Thus, one signatory party of NAFTA may ban imports from another party if the goods under consideration have been produced in processes using CFCs, for example. This Article represents a major change in the view on the relationship between foreign trade and the environment. The GATT and other trade agreements have not been explicit on this issue. One may be led to the impression that in the past priority has been given to free trade over environmental issues, in particular by the GATT Panel decision on the US–Mexican tuna dispute. NAFTA Article 104 in contrast gives priority to the environment.

There is an additional difference between GATT and NAFTA. GATT Article XX does not mention the environment explicitly. NAFTA Article 904 fills this gap:

> Each Party may in accordance with this Agreement, adopt, maintain or apply any standards-related measure, including any such measure relating to safety, the protection of human, animal or plant life or health, the environment or consumers, and any measure to ensure its enforcement or implementation. Such measures include those to prohibit the importation of a good of another Party ... that fails to comply with the applicable requirement of those measures ...

Another difference between this Article and GATT Article XX is the explicit mention of the fact that these measures may involve trade restrictions. As in the GATT, the application of these measures is restricted: they should not result in arbitrary or unjustifiable discrimination of imported goods or constitute disguised barriers to trade (NAFTA Article 907(2)).

Article 1114 refers to environmental measures that affect foreign direct investments. Besides acknowledging national sovereignty in environmental policy issues:

> The Parties recognize that it is inappropriate to encourage investment by relaxing domestic health, safety or environmental measures. ... If a Party considers that another party has offered such an encouragement, it may request consultations with the other Party and the two Parties shall consult with a view of avoiding such an encouragement.

This Article is meant to prevent the downward competition of national environmental regulations. None the less, it remains to be seen whether this remains a mere declaration of will or becomes an enforceable agreement.

NAFTA contains a number of provisions for conflict resolution (Chapter 20). A Trilateral Trade Commission is created which regularly reviews the performance of trade relations within NAFTA. To resolve trade disputes, it may establish multilateral panels of trade experts. In the case of conflicts concerning environmental and health issues, a party may call on scientific and environmental experts to support its point (Articles 2007 and 2015) Esty (1994) argues that environmental experts will gain a larger weight in the dispute settlement process at the expense of environmental lawyers.

Moreover, there exists an Environmental Side Agreement to the NAFTA, which establishes a Commission for Environmental Cooperation. See Esty (1994) for details.

NAFTA is a prototype of a trade agreement which (1) involves highly developed and industrializing countries and (2) takes account of environmental issues in a way hitherto unknown. Therefore, it may serve as an example of a legal framework for free trade agreements involving the emerging market economies of Eastern Europe.

8.6 Trade Laws and Institutions for Eastern Europe

As has been argued earlier, there are different layers of trade law that are of concern. First of all, the CEECs have to design their own trade laws and institutions. In this context, environmental policy is also very important because it can be (ab)used for protectionist purposes and, therefore, is – to some extent – also trade policy. In a second step, one may wish to address bilateral or multilateral agreements that regulate the trade relations of the CEECs and their trading partners by defining a set of rights and obligations. This is important for the economic integration of the CEECs into the European Economic Space. Finally, the position of the CEECs with respect to the GATT and the World Trade Organization may be addressed. The last issue, however, will not be discussed in much detail since the problems arising in this context are not CEEC specific.

National trade laws and institutions should be based on the acknowledgement that free trade enhances welfare and that trade restrictions should in general be avoided. This refers to the use of tariffs and quotas but also environmental standards that discriminate against foreigners. Not only free trade in final goods is important, however, but also free factor movements. The capital stock of the CEECs is composed to a large extent of outdated capital which has been designed for low energy prices and non-binding environmental standards. Thus there is a need for foreign direct investment and one should try to design national institutions such that the country is attractive to foreign investors.

8.6.1 'Green' Barriers to Trade

In section 8.2, it was shown that, from an economic theory viewpoint, there exist situations where trade barriers may be used to improve environmental quality and to raise welfare. In the case of regulatory and enforcement deficits, trade restrictions may be useful as second-best instruments, particularly in the case of hazardous-waste imports. If the country under consideration does not have the means to monitor the storage or processing of toxic waste in a satisfactory way, trade restrictions may be justified for reasons of environmental protection. The national trade law should, therefore, provide for the possibility of restrictions on the imports of hazardous substances. Since this is in accordance with the spirit of the Basle Convention, it will probably not cause international disputes or retaliation measures by other countries.

A case where trade restrictions should be avoided, although they can in theory be beneficial, is that of deficits in the regulation of production processes. A low-regulation country tends to specialize in environmentally intensive goods and under particular circumstances the welfare loss due to increased pollution may be larger than the gains from trade. The unfavourable specialization effect can be mitigated by restricting exports. But this solves only part of the problem and may, in the longer run, cause substantial welfare losses since dynamic gains from trade are diminished. It is better to regulate the polluting industries appropriately and participate in the international division of labour by allowing for unrestricted exports and imports.

A second motive for trade restrictions is extraterritorialism, i.e. the desire to enforce tight national environmental standards on other countries. This may not be a problem now since the CEECs themselves still use dirty technologies and do not have much reason to complain about lax environmental policies elsewhere. Some of the CEECs have suffered from such tremendous pollution problems, however, that citizens may be willing to sacrifice some economic growth and improvements in material living standards for a better environment. These countries may, therefore, be driven to apply environmental standards that are much tighter than those prevailing in other countries with similar states of development. Those countries will be more competitive in markets for 'dirty' goods and one may be tempted to impose countervailing duties in order to stop this 'environmental dumping'. The results derived from standard trade theory, however, are unambiguous in this case. Extraterritorialism reduces welfare and 'green countervailing duties' should not be at the disposal of the policy-maker.

There remains, however, one scenario in which trade barriers can be justified on environmental grounds. If there are substantial transfrontier pollution problems, tariffs, quotas and embargoes may be useful to reduce the carbon leakage effects caused by capital delocation and to stabilize multilateral environmental agreements. The problem with these policy measures, however, is that they also protect domestic industries. Thus, how can one avoid legitimate environmental concerns being captured by protectionist interests? A possible solution is to make the implementation of green barriers to trade conditional on the joint decision of the signatory parties of a multilateral environmental agreement like the Montreal Protocol. NAFTA Article 104 is an example of such a rule. In the case of multilateral sanctions, the governments of numerous countries have to agree on a common policy. Therefore, the outcome of the negotiation process is less likely to be dominated by national protectionist lobbies than in the case of measures taken unilaterally by a single government. The larger diversity of interests, perhaps including counter-lobbies in other countries, restricts the power of domestic protectionist lobbies to influence environmental policy-making process. This increases the probability that the trade-restricting measure is really implemented for environmental reasons. Moreover, multilateral trade restrictions used as sanctions are more likely to be credible and, therefore, tend to be more effective than unilateral measures. Credible threats have the advantage that they need not be implemented because the mere threat of a sanction disciplines potential non-compliants. Thus, it may be possible to have both: gains from free trade and the enforcement of international environmental agreements.

8.6.2 Protectionist Interests and Environmental Policies

The case for environmentally motivated trade restrictions is not very strong and these instruments have not often been used in the past. The capture of environmental policy instruments for protectionist purposes, however, appears to be omnipresent and may be a major source of dispute in international trade negotiations. Regulatory capture may take the shape of environmental and other health or safety standards that discriminate against foreigners. Another case is the use of lax environmental standards as a means of indirect subsidization to support exporting or import-competing industries. Regulatory capture leads to welfare losses for two reasons. On the one hand, inefficient policy measures will be taken and, on the other hand, productive resources tend to be wasted by their being allocated to unproductive rent-seeking activities. Notwithstanding that attempts to influence government decisions are inherent in pluralistic and democratically organized societies, one should aim at keeping the impact of idiosyncratic interests on the policy-making process small. This can be achieved by appropriate design of the institutions dealing with environmental policies but also by the choice of the policy instruments.

According to Olsen (1965), small interest groups with specific interests gain influence over government decision-making because (1) they can appropriate large rents whereas the costs of providing these rents are widely dispersed and (2) these groups are relatively homogeneous and, therefore, are able to solve their internal free-rider problem more easily. This explains why producers' lobbies are more influential than groups that lobby for the interests of the consumers of commodities and ambient quality.[11] If one aims at keeping the influence of these groups small, one should, therefore, attempt to organize the policy-making process such that the groups affected by these policies are large and heterogeneous. If they are large, the potential costs of providing rents to them are large and this may raise the resistance of those who have to pay. Moreover, large and heterogeneous groups face higher transaction costs and internal free-rider problems. Of course, the objective of reducing the probability of regulatory capture may be in conflict with other policy goals. In the field of environmental policy, however, this is unlikely to be the case.

According to the standard result of environmental economics, polluters should be signalled the environmental costs of their activities. For instance, they should pay an emission tax which equals the marginal environmental damage. This Pigouvian tax does not depend on the kind of activity which causes the damage and is, therefore, also independent of who the polluters are. Thus, environmental policy should be directed primarily at pollutants but not at polluters. The regulatory approach predominantly used in West European countries often does the converse. Sector- or plant-specific process standards are used rather than environmental taxes or tradable-permit schemes that could be applied on a broader basis. Specific standards, however, tend to be more subject to interest group influence than more general policies that affect various sectors of the economy at the same time. A group of producers who are active in different sectors of the economy is rather heterogeneous and will therefore face larger transaction costs and free-rider problems if it wishes to organize lobbying activities than a group of producers whose production activities are very similar. The probability of regulatory capture is smaller if environmental policy instruments that are not industry or plant specific are used. For this reason, environmental policies that are directed at pollutants and use emission taxes or tradable-permit schemes should be given priority over the command-and-control approach where this is possible.

Another aspect of the choice of policy instruments is that the regulatory approach to environmental policy as applied in many Western countries often uses grandfather clauses and thus favours incumbent firms over new entrants.[12] This serves to stabilize non-competitive market structures. It not only leads to inefficiencies but it also raises the power of the incumbents with respect to the government. Market-oriented environmental policy instruments, in contrast, would result in a more dynamic structure of the industry and fluctuations in the composition of an industry would make it more difficult to organize protectionist lobbying activities.

Similar considerations to those in the case of process standards can be applied to product standards. These standards can easily be used to discriminate against foreigners and, thus, it makes sense to replace them by environmental consumption taxes where possible. Since these taxes are directed at the pollution contents of the goods, they discriminate against those who should be discriminated against: the users of environmentally unfriendly goods. Groups interested in influencing the outcome of the political process will face more difficulties coordinating their activities if the environmental policy measure addresses the pollution contents of a large variety of different goods than if environmental policies use specific standards for goods that are produced by particular industries.

It is not only the choice of policy instruments that has an impact on regulatory capture; the organizational framework in which environmental policy is taking place is also important. Socialist administration was usually organized such that specific ministries were responsible for the regulation of particular industries. With such an organizational structure, the regulated firms have strong incentives to collaborate and to influence the regulation process. Additionally, close relationships between the representatives of the administration and of the regulated groups develop over time. Therefore, the regulation process is likely to be captured by the people to be regulated. One may, therefore, wish to – loosely speaking – maximize the distance between environmental policy institutions and protectionist interest groups. Thus, alternative organizational structures would not be based on an industry-specific division of the regulating administration but would use a broader concept. In the case of environmental policy, the responsibility for environmental regulation would lie with the ministry of the environment and its affiliated institutions but not with, e.g., the ministries of agriculture, energy or specific industries.

None the less, although market-oriented environmental policies possess many advantages over the command-and-control approach, it will neither be possible nor desirable to abolish environmental product and process standards completely. In many situations, administration and monitoring costs may be much lower than in the case of taxes and tradable permits. Moreover, even environmental taxes and tradable-permit schemes are not necessarily free from protectionist influence. Since no one exactly knows the true social cost of environmental disruption, environmental policy inherently involves a high degree of discretion and the regulatees will attempt to influence the information-gathering process. Thus, environmental taxes may also be captured by protectionist interests. Domestic producers can be protected from foreign competition by low emission taxes and environmental consumption taxes can be used to discriminate against foreigners.[13] For these reasons, it is desirable that the public be informed about the protectionist content of environmental regulation. Usually, the majority of voters are (often rationally) uninformed about existing protectionist measures and about the true costs of protection and this is a necessary condition for regulatory capture to take place. It is, therefore, advisable to create institutions that have the task of making hidden protection public and thereby act as the advocates of the consumer. Such an institution should review environmental regulations (but also other kinds of regulation) with respect to their protectionist contents and report its findings on a regular basis. It would be desirable to have the committee consist of independent experts such as natural scientists and economists, but also of representatives of the groups that are disadvantaged in the process of regulatory capture, i.e. consumers and perhaps foreign producers.

Finally, it may be useful to introduce elements of direct democracy into the process of environmental policy-making. The underlying rationale is that representative democracy creates the discretionary space that the policy-maker can use to distribute rents. Direct democracy tends to reduce the discretionary space and, therefore, on average will lead to a policy outcome in which pressure groups with idiosyncratic interests are less over-represented.[14] This may turn out to be useful to prevent non-tariff barriers to trade and the indirect subsidization of some producers by means of lax environmental standards.

8.6.3 Environmental Regulation and Foreign Direct Investment

The CEECs are capital-poor countries and rely on foreign direct investment for their future development. This problem area is connected to environmental issues in two ways. On the one hand, technical equipment produced in industrialized countries outside the former Soviet Bloc is adjusted to high energy prices and tight environmental standards. Thus, new capital will accelerate the process of cleaning up the environment in Eastern Europe. On the other hand, environmental regulation may to some extent affect the locational choices of foreign investors. Although the empirical evidence concerning such a relationship is not particularly strong, policy-makers could attempt to use environmental policies strategically in order to attract foreign direct investment.

Since an influx of foreign capital is beneficial to the CEECs not only with respect to economic development and growth but also with respect to environmental quality, there should be no unnecessary restrictions to free capital mobility. Foreigners should be allowed to repatriate their profits and corporate taxes should be internationally competitive. This can be achieved rather easily. What is more difficult to solve is the problem area where the major obstacles to foreign direct investment into the CEECs lie, i.e. the bad state of the infrastructure and the institutional framework. As far as environmental issues are concerned, the treatment of inherited environmental damage is important. Environmental damage inherited from more than 40 years of socialist management of the economy and the natural environment is omnipresent and the question arises as to who pays for the decontamination of soil, water and buildings. The polluter-pays principle suggests that the government should pay, but it is also possible to pass the burden through to the new owner of an enterprise who may be a foreigner. There is a clear trade-off for the government. Either the pressure on the budget is increased or disincentives for foreign investors are created. Since foreign direct investment also has long-run welfare effects, a strategy assigning the costs of cleaning up inherited environmental damage to foreign direct investors is myopic. In any case, the mere uncertainty surrounding these liability issues may prevent foreign capital owners from investing in the CEECs. In order to reduce uncertainty, existing loopholes in the legislation should be eliminated as soon as possible and the government should credibly declare its willingness to pay.

The impact of the environmental regulation of production processes on the international allocation of capital has probably been over-emphasized in the discussion of the past few years. None the less, there are some aspects that may be of importance for the CEECs. A first issue is the choice of policy instruments. In the context of foreign direct investment, environmental taxes or tradable discharge permits are superior to the command-and-control approach. Regulatory solutions that generate rents to incumbent firms may lead to an outflow of money. If large shares of the regulated enterprises are owned by foreigners (a scenario which is realistic for the CEECs in the medium term), then they will appropriate these rents and repatriate them. Domestic income is reduced. This can be avoided if firms have to pay for the right to pollute.

Finally, there is the issue of downward competition of environmental regulations. Although the theoretical literature has established only a few scenarios in which this is possible and there is no empirical evidence on under-regulation due to competition for mobile capital, this possibility cannot be excluded. A first step to avoid under-regulation can be taken unilaterally by a single country: treat new foreign investors and incumbent firms equally. Exemptions from existing environmental rules should not be possible. Again environmental policies should be targeted at the internalization of the cost of environmental disruption, independently of who causes the damage. Moreover, multilateral agreements can provide a framework in which non-cooperative behaviour leading to the downward competition of environmental standards can be avoided. This will be discussed in the next section.

8.6.4 International Trade Agreements

Free trade agreements are a means to reduce the impact of protectionist lobbies. The policy-makers tie their hands by signing such agreements and reduce their discretionary power in the field of trade policy. If the standard instruments of trade policy are no longer available, however, interest groups may seek protection via alternative policy instruments like environmental taxes and standards. Thus, free trade agreements, although meant to be mutually beneficial for the signatory parties, bear significant new potentials of conflict.

Sovereignty and the subsidiarity principle require that each country be free to choose its own environmental policy. This is acknowledged by all the agreements that have been reviewed in section 8.4. Since countries are different with respect to their endowment with environmental resources, environmental standards and emission taxes should be country specific. This subsidiarity principle has been eroded in the EU in some areas of environmental regulation. On the one hand, national sovereignty has been restricted by application of the origin principle. On the other hand, regulations have been harmonized in policy areas where harmonization is unnecessary.

The application of the origin principle is not problematic. Its acknowledgement will help the CEECs to remove some of their existing barriers to trade. If applied in the opposite direction, EU member countries would have to acknowledge that goods that are traded in CEECs be also tradable inside the EU. This is implicitly contained in the Europe Agreements. Articles 26 and 35 of the Europe Agreements exempt measures that constitute means of arbitrary discrimination and disguised trade restrictions from the set of environmental policy instruments of the signatory parties.

Harmonization of environmental policies, however, may be a problem area in the future. There may be pressure on the CEECs to adjust some of their environmental standards to West European levels. As long as no substantial transfrontier externalities occur, however, such an upward harmonization is neither necessary nor desirable and the CEECs should in general define their national environmental norms in accordance with domestic criteria. This is not only in their own interest but is also beneficial to their trading partners.

Matters may be different in the case of transfrontier pollution. Cooperative solutions to environmental problems have to be sought, but this rarely requires the harmonization of environmental policies. Siebert (1991), for instance, has suggested the use of transfrontier pollution norms which define an ambient-quality standard of the environmental medium (e.g. a river) at the border and determine compensation payments depending on the difference between the actual state of the environment and the standard. In theory, the only case in which the same emission fees or standards should be used in all countries is the global environmental problem where the damage is independent of the source of the pollutant. There may be some other kinds of international externalities where an upward harmonization is desirable. An example is nuclear-reactor safety. The adjustment towards West European safety norms, however, will presumably require technical and financial aid and, thus, the pollutees will have to pay for the reduction of the environmental risk.

This pollutee-pays principle may be applicable in other policy areas as well. In border regions between EU member states and the CEECs, in particular, it may be the most cost-efficient way to deal with environmental problems. Improvements in pollution-abatement technologies that are used in the West are often very expensive but yield only small progress in environmental quality since existing technologies achieve already high rates of abatement (e.g. more than 90% in the case of sulphur dioxide). It would be cheaper and have a greater environmental effect to subsidize the introduction or improvement of abatement in the East. One ECU spent on abatement in the East will in many cases have larger environmental effects in a border region than ten ECUs spent on the improvement on abatement in the West. Another instrument of the pollutee-pays approach is the debt-for-nature swap, which is used to address simultaneously environmental and foreign debt problems. Although this instrument is being discussed in some of the CEECs, it is unlikely that it will be applied on a scale which leads to substantial improvements in either the environmental or the debt situation of the CEECs. Nevertheless, like other instruments where the pollutee pays, it is an example of how stricter environmental standards can be introduced in a mutually beneficial way.

In most other cases, however, the subsidiarity principle should be applied and the CEECs should be sovereign in their environmental policy decisions, at least as far as the regulation of environmentally intensive production is concerned. Notwithstanding that the case for the harmonization of environmental regulations is a limited one, the CEECs will probably not be able to avoid adjusting some of their standards towards EU levels. The costs of doing this, however, may well be outweighed by the positive trade-creation effects of integration.

One of the problems of the integration of the CEECs into the European Economic Space is the Common Agricultural Policy of the EU. Due to the massive subsidization of agricultural products in Western Europe, the CEECs will be unable to utilize their comparative advantages in this sector.[15] Agriculture is less environmentally intensive than many other sectors of the economy and specialization on these goods may contribute to the cleaning-up of Eastern Europe. Given the experience of the Uruguay Round, however, where countries like the United States with substantial negotiating power did not succeed in convincing the EU to change its agricultural policy significantly, it is highly unlikely this will be achieved by the CEECs. Nevertheless, the CEECs should try to exert some pressure on the EU in this respect. Similar arguments apply to the textile industry.

The issue of legislational competition may be an issue to be addressed by international trade agreements. Although the incentives to undercut the environmental taxes or standards in other countries are probably smaller than environmentalists fear, there is still the danger of an unfavourable downward competition in the field of environmental norms. The CEECs are highly dependent on foreign direct investment for their future development and in this situation strategic considerations may lead to a prisoners' dilemma. International agreements help to avoid this problem and NAFTA Article 1114 is an example of what such an agreement can look like. However, this Article is still rather vague and it should be possible to find rules that offer less space for interpretation of what is meant by 'relaxing environmental standards to encourage investment'. For instance, one could agree on minimum environmental standards for certain sectors that are particularly sensitive. Such an agreement would involve the CEECs themselves but not necessarily West European countries. West European voters are unlikely to accept downward adjustments in environmental regulation that turn their countries into pollution havens. Therefore, the minimum standards that would be appropriate for some the CEECs would presumably be non-binding constraints to West European countries. In contrast, the inclusion of West European countries into the agreement might drive up the minimum standards to levels which may not be compatible with the interests of emerging market economies.

The relationship between trade agreements and existing multilateral environmental agreements still has to be defined. The GATT and the Europe Agreements are not explicit on this issue and it is not clear whether, for example, a ban on goods that have been produced in production processes involving CFCs but that do not themselves contain these substances is in accordance with these agreements. NAFTA is explicit on the issue and in Article 104 gives precedece to environmental agreements in the case of inconsistencies. One may argue that this is the right way to proceed. If environmental agreements are to work, their sanction mechanisms have to be credible and should not be undermined by free trade agreements. From the point of view of the CEECs, however, the question arises whether they should really support the inclusion of provisions like NAFTA Article 104 into the agreements to which they are signatory parties. As long as they continue to use pollution-intensive production processes in many sectors, they may be subject to such measures. Therefore, it may be better to leave international trade agreements ambiguous in this respect. This argument, however, neglects some of the positive effects the acknowledgement of the sanction mechanisms of international environmental agreements may have. Subjecting oneself to an international sanction mechanism may serve as a useful self-binding device for the policy-makers. The more a country exposes itself to external pressure in the case of lax environmental policies, the smaller the influence of domestic 'pro-competitive' anti-environmental lobbies will be.

Conflict resolution mechanisms are of particular importance in a policy area where environmental protection and environmental protectionism are difficult to disentangle. The best method to avoid disputes is to ensure that some issues are not negotiable. This would, however, require a degree of specificity and unambiguity that has deliberately been avoided in the formulation of international trade agreements. But there may be other ways to reduce the scope for disputes to arise. Some of them may be avoided merely by monitoring the protectionist contents of national environmental regulation. Since many protectionist practices survive only because they are hidden, the first (and sometimes also sufficient) step towards their removal is to make them public. Like a commission which monitors trade and environmental policy on the national level, an international monitoring institution should involve independent experts and representatives of consumer interests. Its main focus should be on the use of environmental regulation for protectionist purposes, on the indirect subsidization of certain industries by means of lax environmental standards and, additionally, on transfrontier pollution issues.

If disputes arise, dispute settlement mechanisms are necessary. In my view, the design of these mechanisms does not have to be changed because of environmental issues. An exception is perhaps the involvement of experts from the natural sciences in consultations concerning environmental disputes. In other respects, the considerations relevant for other kinds of trade disputes apply. The Draft Understanding on Rules and Procedures Governing the Settlement of Disputes which emerged from the Uruguay Round negotiations contains significant refinements of the former GATT dispute settlement mechanism and can serve as an example of an elaborated instrument for the resolution of disputes. See Kohona (1994) for an overview. Basic ingredients are the introduction of strict timescales in the dispute settlement procedures, automatic processes that can only be stopped by a consensus agreement of the parties involved, and a more detailed specification of the procedures to be adopted and of the criteria for the nomination of Panel members. The use of automatic processes and strict timescales in particular will enhance the efficiency of dispute settlement processes and should be adopted in any international agreement on trade and/or the environment.

The Understanding also provides the possibility for a member with substantial interest in a matter of dispute between two other members to participate in the consultations. There are some good arguments in favour of the idea to make the participation of third parties in the dispute settlement process mandatory, i.e. always to use multilateral forums to resolve bilateral disputes.[16] Multilateral forums may be useful because (1) bilateral disputes sometimes concern issues that are of more general interest and touch upon the basics of the multilateral agreement, (2) non-involved parties may serve as mediators, (3) sometimes multilateral negotiations lead to more cooperation than a set of bilateral negotiations,[17] and (4) third parties can introduce additional issues into the negotiation process and the nesting of issues may enhance the potential for cooperation.[18] Multilateral negotiations, however, do not always enhance cooperation among the disputing parties and, moreover, their transaction costs are often higher than those of bilateral negotiations.

A final instrument in the process of dispute settlement is the use of independent referees. GATT Panels are one example; their decisions are, however, not enforceable. None the less, a country ignoring a GATT Panel decision will lose international standing, and thus there will be an opportunity cost. The creation of the World Trade Organization may be seen as a step to increase the power of the GATT and to raise the opportunity costs of non-compliance. On the European level, the European Court of Justice has been successful in removing several non-tariff barriers to trade and it can be expected that this will continue in the future if these barriers take the shape of environmental regulations. For the CEECs, it makes some sense to give up some national sovereignty and to submit themselves to the jurisdiction of an independent supranational court. A decision on this issue is, however, a highly political issue and it is questionable whether, after more than 40 years of Soviet hegemony, the CEECs are willing to give up part of their sovereignty in important policy fields like international trade and environmental policy.

8.7 Conclusions

The environmental situation of the CEECs and their integration into the world economy raise the question as to which institutional framework should be chosen to achieve the objectives of economic integration and environmental improvement. Although empirical studies reveal that the link between trade and the environment is rather weak, there are still good reasons for considering environmental issues in the framework of national trade law and international trade agreements. They include the avoidance of regulatory capture, the problem of green barriers to trade, the question of whether or not to harmonize environmental standards, the problem of jurisdictional competition towards low levels of environmental regulation, and the ambiguity of existing agreements concerning the relationship of trade and environmental policy.

The basic conclusions drawn in this study are the following ones. The appropriate design of environmental policy and of the organizational structure in which it takes place will help to tame lobbies with idiosyncratic interests and to mitigate regulatory capture. Industry-specific policies and command-and-control solutions should be avoided where possible. This recommendation harmonizes to a large extent with the policy suggestions of environmental economics that have been made on pure efficiency grounds. Green barriers to trade should, by and large, be avoided. Their use should be made conditional on the joint decision of the signatory parties of an international environmental agreement. Harmful legislational competition – if this is a problem in the real world – can be addressed in the framework of international agreements that perhaps include minimum environmental standards.

The NAFTA appears to be suitable as a prototype of how the integration between countries of different development levels and different environmental regulations into a free trade zone can be achieved under the acknowledgement of the importance of environmental issues. Moreover, the NAFTA avoids some of the ambiguities that are contained in the GATT and in the Europe Agreements. None the less, it remains to be seen whether the NAFTA's emphasis of environmental issues will open a Pandora's box of a new kind of protectionism which merely pretends to be green.

Towards the end, one may once again raise the question of whether the CEECs are different. Is it necessary to design individual trade rules that are fitted to the special needs and problems of the CEECs? I doubt that this is the case. Although these countries are now in their very difficult period of transition, the relationship between trade and environmental issues is not much different from that prevailing elsewhere. Thus, the objectives underlying the design of trade law and institutions can be based on some very general principles, and this has been the approach in this chapter.

The special historical situation of the CEECs offers new and promising possibilities for them, albeit the current situation looks anything else but rosy in many respects. After the collapse of socialism and the planned economy, there has been an institutional vacuum. Although part of it has been filled already, there still remains an opportunity to develop new institutions that in their design incorporate the experience of the mistakes that have been made in the West. One example is the adoption of market-oriented instruments of environmental policy instead of the command-and-control philosophy. However, there remains the question of whether this road will be taken. The decision on the design of a regulatory framework, on law and institutions, is itself subject to forces concerned with the protection and appropriation of rents (Hillman, 1994). The former ruling class still holds key positions in politics and in administration. These people are hurt by the introduction of institutional changes that weaken the state bureaucracy and therefore tend to resist such measures. An example is the replacement of command-and-control solutions of environmental problems by a system of emission taxes, which requires a smaller bureaucracy and provides less opportunities to appropriate rents. But it is not only the former ruling class which will resist institutional changes like those suggested in this chapter. After the enormous adjustment problems of the first years of transition, the general enthusiasm about the market economy has faded and the people living in the CEECs are more sceptical about the price mechanism. The success of the former communists in the recent Hungarian elections vividly demonstrates this change in perceptions. None the less, it is to be hoped that the majority of the citizens can still be convinced that a revival of centralism and of the command-and-control philosophy in economic and environmental policy would cause inefficiencies and increase regulatory capture. Alternative approaches are feasible that are less bureaucratic and provide incentives to use scarce resources in the most productive way rather than to waste them on rent-seeking activities. Given their endowment with labour, land and human capital, the CEECs have the potential to achieve West European levels of material living standards and environmental quality in the long run. The speed of catching up, however, will be affected by the laws and institutions that govern international trade and the use of environmental resources.

Notes

1. There are a number of articles in recent issues of *The Ecologist* that entertain this view. The title of a paper by Morris (1991), 'Free Trade: The Great Distroyer" is a good example. See also Cobb and Daly (1989), Ekins (1989), Shrybman (1991, 1991/92), and Arden-Clarke (1992), for instance.
2. Rauscher (1994c) argues that a definition of environmental dumping on the basis of an international comparison of the tightness of environmental standards is not particularly useful. It would be preferable to use domestic criteria for the definition of this subject. They include the degree of internalization of social costs or differences in environmental regulation between different sectors of the economy. The underlying idea is that governments tend to choose too-lax environmental policies in sectors that are affected by international competition.

3. A deficiency of most of the empirical studies is the neglect of adjustment lags. The standard model of international trade is based in the assumption of intersectoral factor mobility. And factor relocation across sectors takes time, sometimes decades. Thus, one may be led to argue that the changes in environmental regulation are reflected by the patterns of trade only with a substantial lag. But this possibility has been considered by Tobey by regressing changes in net exports on the stringency of environmental policy and he did not find significant evidence for the validity of the standard trade model.
4. This argument is based on the assumption that environmental quality is a normal good, the demand for which has a positive income elasticity. Similar arguments are used by Grossman and Krueger (1991) in their attempt to assess the environmental effects of the North American Free Trade Association. For medium-income industrializing countries they find a strong negative correlation of pollution and income. Similar results are reported by Holtz-Eakin and Selden (1992).
5. Theoretical models like those of Barrett (1994b) and Black *et al.* (1993) suggest that this problem is inherent in international environmental policy coordination processes.
6. For the management of environmental liability issues in Poland see Bell and Kolaja (1993).
7. An example of the regulatory and enforcement deficits is given by the hundreds of tons of German toxic waste that have been detected recently by Greenpeace environmentalists in Romania and Albania. Neither country has any facilities to store or process these substances. Manser (1993) argues that Poland also has attracted foreign hazardous wastes due to lax regulation and enforcement deficits.
8. For a comprehensive survey of the GATT and environmental issues, see Rege (1994).
9. For a more detailed discussion, see the original GATT Panel, Charnovitz (1993) and Pearce (1993).
10. A similar decision was made in the case of Thailand's import ban on foreign cigarettes which had been launched under the pretext of national health reasons.
11. According to Vaubel (1994), only 7 out of more than 500 European pressure group organizations represent consumers or environmentalists. The rest lobby for industry, commerce, professions and other services.
12. This is one of the reasons why incumbent firms usually prefer command-and-control solutions of environmental problems to market-oriented approaches like emission taxes or tradable pollution permits. See Hoekman and Leidy (1992).
13. As an example, consider a government that wishes to protect the domestic automobile industry and has at its disposal a tax on fuel. Everything else being equal, the tax rate will be high if the industry produces a large share of small cars and low if the share of large cars is large.
14. This does not mean that direct democracy will always be 'unbiased' or oriented towards free trade. Deviations from free trade policy are due to the fact that in direct democracy the median voter, but not the mean voter, decides on the policy to be adopted. See Mayer (1984) for a theoretical model which demonstrates the underlying rationale.
15. The Europe Agreements acknowledge the sensitivity of agricultural production and contain special provisions on trade in agricultural goods.
16. I owe this idea to Richard Portes.
17. See Pahre (1993) for a game-theoretic model which shows this result.
18. See Folmer *et al.* (1993) for a game-theoretic model in which it is shown that the separation of an interconnected game (in which, for instance, trade and environmental issues are treated simultaneously) into two isolated games (a trade game and an environmental policy game) will, under certain circumstances, reduce cooperation.

References

Ábel, I., Csermely, Á. and Kaderják, P. (1993), 'Environmental implications of economic restructuring: the case of Hungary', Karl Marx University of Economics Working Paper 3/94, Budapest.

Ábel, I., Csermely, Á. and Kaderják, P. (1994), 'Some environmental implications of economic restructuring: the case of Hungary', mimeo, Budapest.

Adams, P. (1991), *Odious Debts: Loose Lending, Corruption, and the Third World's Environmental Legacy*, Earthscan, London.

Amelung, T. and Diehl, M. (1992), *Deforestation of Tropical Rain Forests: Economic Causes and Impact on Development*, Mohr, Tübingen.

Anderson, K. (1992a), 'Effects on the environment and welfare of liberalizing world trade: the cases of coal and food', in K. Anderson and R. Blackhurst (eds), *The Greening of World Trade Issues*, Harvester Wheatsheaf, Hemel Hempstead, pp.145–72.

Anderson, K. (1992b), 'Agricultural trade liberalization and the environment: a global perspective', *The World Economy*, **15**, 153–71.

Arden-Clarke, C. (1992), 'South–North terms of trade – environmental protection and sustainable development', *International Environmental Affairs*, **4**, 122–38.

Barbier, E. B. (1991), 'Managing trade and the environment: the demand for raw ivory in Japan and Hong Kong', *World Economy*, **14**, 407–30.

Barrett, S. (1994a), 'Strategic environmental policy and international trade', *Journal of Public Economics*, 54, 325–38.

Barrett, S. (1994b), 'Self-enforcing international environmental agreements', *Oxford Economic Papers*, **46**, 878–94.

Bartik, T. J. (1988), 'The effects of environmental regulation on business location in the United States', *Growth and Change*, **19**, 22–44.

Baumol, W. J. (1971), *Environmental Protection, International Spillovers, and Trade*, Almkvist and Wicksell, Stockholm.

Begg, D., *et al.* (1993), *Making Sense of Subsidiarity: How Much Centralization for Europe?*, CEPR, London.

Bell, R. G. and Kolaja, T. A. (1993), 'Capital privatization and the management of environmental liability issues in Poland', *Business Lawyer*, **48**, 943–61.

Birdsall, N. and Wheeler, D. (1992), 'Trade policy and industrial pollution in Latin America: where are the pollution havens?', in P. Low (ed.), *International Trade and the Environment*, World Bank Discussion Paper No. 159, New York, pp.159–67.

Black, J., Levi, M. D. and de Meza, D. (1993), 'Creating a good atmosphere: minimum participation for tackling the greenhouse effect', *Economica*, **60**, 281–93.

Budnikowski, A. (1992),'Foreign participation in environmental protection in Eastern Europe: the case of Poland', *Technological Forecasting and Social Change*, **41**, 147–60.

Burniaux, J. M., Martin, J. P. and Oliveira-Martins, J. (1992), 'The effect of existing distorsions in the energy markets on the cost of policies to reduce CO_2 emissions', *OECD Economic Studies*, **19**, 141–65.

Cerna, A. (1993), 'Environment and economy in the former CSFR', *Quarterly Journal of Economic Theory and Policy*, **2**, 69–79.

Charnovitz, S. (1993), 'Environmentalism confronts GATT rules: recent developments and new opportunities', *Journal of World Trade*, **27**, 37–53.

Coase, R. H. (1960), 'The problem of social cost', *Journal of Law and Economics*, **3**, 1–44.

Cobb, J. B. Jr. and Daly, H. E. (1989) *For the Common Good: Redirecting the Economy toward Community, the Environment, and a Sustainable Future*, Beacon Press, Boston.

Conrad, K. (1993), 'Taxes and subsidies for pollution-intensive industries', *Journal of Environmental Economics and Management*, **25**, 121–35.

Cropper, L. and Oates, W. C. (1992), 'Environmental economics: a survey', *Journal of Economic Literature*, **30**, 675–740.

Danchev, A. (1994), 'Adjustment in Eastern Europe to EU environmental requirements', *Intereconomics*, **29**, 43–8.

Dean, J. M. (1992), 'Trade and the environment: a survey of the literature', in P. Low (ed.), *International Trade and the Environment*, World Bank Discussion Paper No. 159, New York, pp.15–28.

Diwan, I. and Shafik, N. (1992), 'Investment, technology and the global environment: towards international agreement in a world of disparities', in P. Low (ed.), *International Trade and the Environment*, World Bank Discussion Paper No. 159, New York, pp.263–85.

The Economist (1992), 'Let them eat pollution', *The Economist*, 8 February, p.66.

Ekins, P. (1989), 'Trade and self-reliance', *The Ecologist*, **19**, 186–90.

Esty, D. C. (1994), 'Making trade and environmental policies work together: lessons from NAFTA', *Aussenwirtschaft*, **49**, 59–79.

European Commission (1992), 'Position of the European Commission on defining and implementing the principle of subsidiatity', Europe Documents No. 1804/05, Agence International d'Information pour la Presse, Luxembourg.

Folmer, H., v. Mouche, P. and Ragland, S. (1993), 'Interconnected games and international environmental problems', *Environmental and Resource Economics*, **3**, 313–35.

George, S. (1992), *The Debt Boomerang: How Third World Debt Harms Us All*, Pluto, London.

Grossman, G. M. and Krueger, A. B. (1991), 'Environmental impacts of a North American free trade agreement', NBER Working Paper No. 3914, Cambridge, MA.

Hansson, G. (1990), *Harmonization and International Trade*, Routledge, London.

Hettige, H., Lucas, R. E. B. and Wheeler, D. (1992), 'The toxic intensity of industrial production: global patterns, trends, and trade policy', *American Economic Review (Papers and Proceedings)*, **82**, 478–81.

Hillman, A. L. (1994), 'The transition from socialism: an overview from a political economy perspective', *European Journal of Political Economy*, **10**, 191–225.

Hoekman, B. and Leidy, M. (1992), 'Environmental policy formation in a trading economy: a public choice perspective', in K. Anderson and R. Blackhurst (eds), *The Greening of World Trade Issues*, Harvester Wheatsheaf, Hemel Hempstead, pp.221–46.

Holtz-Eakin, D. and Selden, T. M. (1992), 'Stoking the fires? CO_2 emissions and economic growth', NBER Discussion Paper 4248, Cambridge, MA.

Hörhager, A. (1992), 'An environmental perspective for Eastern Europe', *European Investment Bank Papers*, **18**, 35–57.

Hughes, G. (1991), 'Are the costs of cleaning up Eastern Europe exaggerated?', *Oxford Review of Economic Policy*, **7**(4), 106–35.

Hughes, G, (1993), 'Clean air but no jobs: environmental priorities and policies during the transition in Central and Eastern Europe', in: *Proceedings of the Conference on Energy and Environment in European Economies in Transition*, Paris: IEA and OECD, pp.61–75.

Kohona, P. T. B. (1994), 'Dispute resolution under the World Trade Organization', *Journal of World Trade*, **28**(2), 23–47.

Krutilla, K. (1991), 'Environmental regulation in an open economy', *Journal of Environmental Economics and Management*, **10**, 127–42.

Laffont, J.-J. and Tirole, J. (1991), 'The politics of government decision making: a theory of regulatory capture', *Quarterly Journal of Economics*, **106**, 1089–127.

Leonard, H. J. (1988), *Pollution and the Struggle for the World Product: Multinational Corporations, Environment and International Comparative Advantage*, Cambridge University Press, Cambridge.

Low, P. and Yeats, A. (1992), 'Do "dirty" industries migrate?', in P. Low (ed.),

International Trade and the Environment, World Bank Discussion Paper No. 159, New York, pp.89–103.
Lucas, R. E. B., Wheeler, D. and Hettige, H. (1992), 'Economic development, environmental regulation, and the international migration of toxic industrial pollution: 1960-1988', in P. Low (ed.), *International Trade and the Environment*, World Bank Discussion Paper No. 159, New York, pp.159–67.
Manser, R. (1993), *The Squandered Dividend: The Free Market and the Environment in Eastern Europe*, Earthscan, London.
Markusen, J. R. (1975), 'International externalities and optimal tax structures', *Journal of International Economics*, **5**, 15–29.
Markusen, J. R., Morey, E. R. and Olewiler, N. (1992), 'Noncooperative equilibria in regional environmental policies when plant locations are endogenous', NBER Working Paper No. 4051, Cambridge, MA.
Mayer, W. (1984), 'Endogenous tariff formation', *American Economic Review*, **74**, 970–85.
Merrifield, (1988), 'The impact of abatement strategies on transnational pollution, the terms of trade, and factor rewards: a general equilibrium approach', *Journal of Environmental Economics and Management*, **15**, 259–84.
Morris, D. (1991), 'Free trade: the great destroyer', *The Ecologist*, **20**, 190–5.
Murrell, P. and Ryterman, R. (1991), 'A methodology for testing comparative economic theories: theory and application to East–West environmental problems', *Journal of Comparative Economics*, **15**, 582–01.
Oliveira-Martins, J., Burniaux, J.-M. and Martin, J. P. (1992), 'Trade and the effectiveness of unilateral CO_2 abatement policies: evidence from GREEN', *OECD Economic Studies*, **19**, 123–40.
Olson, M. (1965), *The Logic of Collective Action*, Harvard University Press, Cambridge, MA.
Pahre, R. (1993), 'A model of Marshall and multilateralism: multilateral cooperation when equivalent bilateral agreements fail', University of Michigan Research Forum on International Economics, Discussion Paper 328, Ann Arbor.
Pasierb, S. M. (1993), 'A review of energy and environmental policies in Poland', in *Proceedings of the Conference on Energy and Environment in European Economies in Transition*, IEA and OECD, Paris, pp.137–53.
Pearce, D. W. (1993), 'The greening of the GATT: some theoretical considerations', mimeo, Norwich.
Rauscher, M. (1989), 'Foreign debt and renewable resources'. *Metroeconomica*, **40**, 57–66.
Rauscher, M. (1990), 'The optimal use of environmental resources by an indebted country', *Journal of Institutional and Theoretical Economics*, **146**, 500–17.
Rauscher, M. (1991), 'Foreign trade and the environment' in H. Siebert (ed.), *Environmental Scarcity: The International Dimension*, Mohr, Tübingen, pp.17–31.
Rauscher, M. (1994a), 'International trade, factor movements, and the environment', mimeo, Kiel.
Rauscher, M. (1994b), 'Environmental legislation as a tool of trade policy', in G. Boero and Z. A. Silberston (eds), *Proceedings of the 1993 CEEA Confereence on Environmental Economics*, Macmillan, Oxford, forthcoming.
Rauscher, M. (1994c), 'On ecological dumping', *Oxford Economic Papers*, **46**, 822–40
Rege, V. (1994), 'GATT law and environment-related issues affecting the trade of developing countries', *Journal of World Trade*, **10**(3), 95–169.
Robison, H. D. (1988), 'Industrial pollution abatement: the impact on the balance of trade', *Canadian Journal of Economics*, **30**, 187–99.
Romer, P. (1994), 'New goods, old theory, and the welfare costs of trade restrictions',

Journal of Development Economics, **43**, 5–38.

Rowland, C. K. and Feiock, R. (1991), 'Environmental regulation and economic development: the movement of chemical production among states', in M. J. Dubnick and A. R. Gitelson (eds), *Public Policy and Economic Institutions*, JAI Press, Greenwich, CT, pp.205–18.

Shrybman, S. (1991), 'International trade and the environment: an environmental assessment of the General Agreement on Tariffs and Trade', *Ecologist*, **20**, 30–4.

Shrybman, S. (1991/92), 'Trading away the environment', *World Policy Journal*, **9**, 93–110.

Siebert, H. (1977), 'Environmental quality and the gains from trade', *Kyklos*, **30**, 657–73.

Siebert, H. (1979), 'Environmental policy in the two-country case', *Zeitschrift für Nationalökonomie*, **39**, 259–74.

Siebert, H. (1991), 'Environmental policy and European integration', in H. Siebert (ed.), *Environmental Scarcity: The International Dimension*, Mohr, Tübingen, pp.57–70.

Siebert, H., Eichberger, J., Gronych, R. and Pethig, R. (1980), *Trade and the Environment: A Theoretical Enquiry*, North-Holland, Amsterdam.

Snape, R. H. (1992), 'The environment, international trade and competitiveness', in K. Anderson and R. Blackhurst (eds), *The Greening of World Trade Issues*, Harvester Wheatsheaf, Hemel Hempstead, pp.73–92.

Stigler, G. (1971), 'The economic theory of regulation', *Bell Journal of Economics*, **2**, 3–21.

Tobey, J. A. (1989), 'The impact of domestic environmental policies on international trade' PhD Dissertation, Department of Economics, University of Maryland, College Park.

Tobey, J. A. (1990), 'The effects of domestic environmental policies on patterns of world trade: an empirical test', *Kyklos*, **43**, 191–209.

Ugelow, J. L. (1982), 'A survey on recent studies on costs of pollution control and the effects on trade', in S. J. Rubin and T. R. Graham (eds), *Environment and Trade: The Relation of International Trade and Environmental Policy*, Allanheld and Osmun, Totowa, NJ, pp.167–90.

Ulph, A. (1994), 'Environmental policy, plant location and government protection', in C. Carraro, (ed.), *Trade, Innovation, Environment*, Kluwer, Rotterdam, pp.123–63.

van Bergeijk, P. A. G. (1991), 'International trade and the environmental challenge', *Journal of World Trade*, **25**(6), 105–15.

Vaubel, R. (1994), 'The public choice analysis of European economic integration: a survey', *European Journal of Political Economy*, **10**, 227–49.

Walter, I. (1973), 'The pollution content of American trade', *Western Economic Journal*, **11**, 61–70.

Walter, I. (1982), 'Environmentally induced industrial relocation to Developing countries', in: S. J. Rubin and T. R. Graham (eds), *Environment and Trade: The Relation of International Trade and Environmental Policy*, Allanheld and Osmun, Totowa, NJ, pp.67–101.

Wheeler, D. and Martin, P. (1992), 'Prices, policies, and the international diffusion of clean technology: the case of wood pulp production', in P. Low (ed.), *International Trade and the Environment*, World Bank Discussion Paper No. 159, New York, pp.197-224.

Wilkinson, D. G. (1994), 'NAFTA and the environment: some lessons for the next round of GATT negotiations', *The World Economy*, **17**, 395-412.

Zylicz, T. (1993a), 'Pollution and natural resource taxes in Poland', Economics Department, Warsaw University Discussion Paper.

Zylicz, T. (1993b), 'National environmental policy: outline of economic instruments after 3 years', mimeo, Ecological Economics Center, Warsaw University.

Legal Materials

Europa-Abkommen zur Gründung einer Assoziation zwischen den Europäischen Gemeinschaften und ihren Mitgliedstaaten einerseits und der Republik Polen andererseits, *Amtsblatt der Europäischen Gemeinschaften*, L348/1.

European Energy Charter, Europe Documents, No. 1754 (1991).

North American Free Trade Agreement, *International Legal Materials*, **32** (1993), pp.289–456 and pp.605-99.

United States – Restrictions on Tuna. Report of the Panel, DS 21/R, *GATT Basic Instruments and Selected Documents Supplement* **39** (1993), pp.155–205.

Index